The Blows
of Yesteryear:

An American Saga

John Le Bourgeois and Ashton Le Bourgeois

ISBN-10: 1480024090
ISBN-13: 978-1480024090

Where are the snows of yesteryear?

From *Ballade of Dead Ladies*
(Translation by Dante Gabriel Rossetti, 1870)

Mais où sont les neiges d'antan?

de *Ballade des dames du temps jadis*
(par Francois Villon, ca. 1461)

CONTENTS

PREFACE

Francis Villon in his grand poem of the 15th century celebrated mythic but half-remembered ladies of antiquity. In our book we recall a family of real but largely forgotten women in American history. All were descendants of Elizabeth Taylor and Peter Blow. Their lives were full, far-flung and unscripted, emblematic of the nation's course over five generations.

Our story begins on the eastern shore of Virginia in 1800 and ends on the Pacific coast of California in 1970. It radiates from St. Louis down the Mississippi River to Belmont Plantation near New Orleans. It curls back east to the Genesee Valley in upstate New York and to Dupont Circle in Washington, D.C. It takes us across the Atlantic Ocean to London, Paris, and down to Johannesburg in South Africa, and to Sofia, St. Petersburg and Moscow in eastern Europe.

Our women are mostly fortunate in love, and marry good men. They are motivated. One creates a home for indigent women, another starts the first successful public kindergarten in America, another builds a school to train nurses in the care of infants, another commands a field hospital on the Eastern Front during World War One, and another helps organize a preservation society.

They all experience prosperity and suffer financial adversity. They battle with disease: cholera, tuberculosis, typhoid, yellow and scarlet fevers. They know death, even murder; and they live with slavery and its aftermath. They meet, help, and are encouraged by many people – some remembered, some not: Dred Scott, Lizzie Keckley, Aunt Rachel, Henry Adams, Henry James, Isadora Duncan, Little Martha, Joseph Chamberlain, Paul Kruger, Baroness Uxkull, the Tsarina Alexandra of Russia, Douglas MacArthur, Mark Twain and Diego Rivera.

Our story is as broad as Walt Whitman and as intense as Emily Dickinson.

RELATIONSHIPS
OF THE
PRIMARY WOMEN IN
THESE STORIES

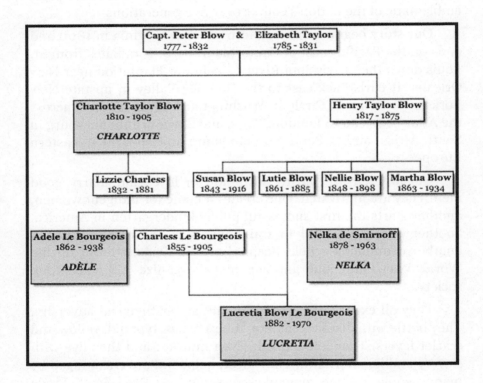

Capt. Peter Blow & Elizabeth Taylor
1777 - 1832 / 1785 - 1831

Charlotte Taylor Blow
1810 - 1905
CHARLOTTE

Henry Taylor Blow
1817 - 1875

Lizzie Charless
1832 - 1881

Susan Blow
1843 - 1916

Lutie Blow
1861 - 1885

Nellie Blow
1848 - 1898

Martha Blow
1863 - 1934

Adele Le Bourgeois
1862 - 1938
ADÈLE

Charless Le Bourgeois
1855 - 1905

Nelka de Smirnoff
1878 - 1963
NELKA

Lucretia Blow Le Bourgeois
1882 - 1970
LUCRETIA

CHARLOTTE'S STORY

Charlotte Taylor Blow Charless

1810-1905

(All quotations in Charlotte's Story, except where noted, come from Charlotte Charless' *Biographical Sketch* (see *Sources*).)

1

1

Charlotte Blow searched the ballroom. The elite of St. Louis society were dancing aboard the steamer *Atlantic* at the invitation of Captain Ryan. Charlotte's mother had advised her daughters to wear their best street dresses, but as newcomers they mustn't dance. So Charlotte was watching the women in their sumptuous gowns when she spotted a young man who riveted her attention.

She was struck by the "calm serenity overspreading his handsome features, which wore a joyousness of expression that was irresistible." Transfixed she sized him up: he was about five feet nine inches tall and well proportioned with a fair complexion, dark hair and eyes of gray. She looked on as he danced with a Miss Selby, the belle of the evening. He seemed in good spirits, evincing "a gentleness, a suavity, and a modest grace of deportment." She asked a friend of her father who he was, but he didn't know.

Charlotte had arrived in St. Louis earlier that day on the *Atlantic*, the 8th of May 1830. Her mother and father, two sisters, four brothers and she had travelled from Florence, Alabama to start a new life in Missouri. Her father planned to open a hotel in the city whose population was rapidly expanding.

The levee along the river was chock-a-block with steamboats, which were arriving at a rate of a hundred a day, bringing passengers and cargo from as far away as Cincinnati and New Orleans. The port was bustling, raucous and dusty (or muddy when it rained). The scene was very different from the day thirteen years earlier when the first steamboat reached what was still a mere settlement. The contrast between one steamer in 1817 and one hundred in 1830 reflected the huge transformation the nation experienced with President Jefferson's purchase of the Louisiana Territory from the Emperor Napoleon.

Captain Ryan boasted that his was the best boat ever to reach the shores of Missouri. To drum up business he invited the finest of St. Louis to celebrate at his ball, and since he had found the Blows excellent company during the voyage, he asked them to attend as well. He was sure that the fresh beauty and fine manners of the young Blow women – Elizabeth Rebecca age twenty-four, Charlotte twenty, and Martha Ella eighteen – would charm his visitors.

The attractive man who had danced with Miss Selby had noticed Charlotte as well. A few weeks later he called to introduce himself and soon Joseph Charless was a regular visitor. He and Charlotte discovered that they both liked horseback riding and sleighing when winter came. Suggesting his intentions, Joseph gave her Mrs. William Parkes' *Domestic Duties; or, Instructions to Young Married Ladies on the Management of Their Households, and the Regulation of Their Conduct in the Various Relations and Duties of Married Life*. When it first appeared a reviewer at *The Critic* noted that this book "ought to occupy a place in every lady's library, and cannot be too frequently perused." He also gave her a small leather bound journal embossed "Miss C. T. Blow," in gold, in which he wrote "a slight testimony of friendship" dated 2 February 1831.

Joseph, who was smooth and even eloquent in ordinary conversation, had a hard time actually saying that he loved her. Shortly after presenting his bookish gifts, he wrote her a letter:

> That I love you is but a faint expression of my feelings, and should I be so happy as to have that feeling reciprocated by *you*, I pledge you the best efforts of my life to promote your happiness. Nature, I fear, has wrought me in her rougher mold, and unfitted me to appear to advantage in an undertaking like this, in which so much delicacy of sentiment seems to be required in these, our days of refinement. Such as I am – and I have endeavored to appear without any false coloring – I

offer myself a candidate for your affections, for your *love*. You have known me long enough to find out my faults – for none are without them – and to discover what virtues I may have (if any), and, from these, to form a just estimate of my character.

I feel that my future happiness, in a great measure, depends on your answer. But suspense to me is the greatest source of unhappiness. Naturally impatient and sanguine, I cannot rest until the result is known. May I hope that my offer will be favorably received, and that hereafter I may subscribe myself, as now, Your devoted

Jos. Charless, Jr

Charlotte found Joseph irresistible. She accepted his offer and never doubted her choice. In November 1831, exactly eighteen months after her arrival in St. Louis, the two were married. Yet, the fact that Charlotte and Joseph met at all was fortuitous, the result of parental decisions made long before.

Charlotte's mother and father, Elizabeth Taylor and Peter Blow, had grown up in Virginia and seemed unlikely candidates for uprooting themselves from their native soil. Their ancestors had arrived from England back in the 17th century and settled in Southampton County in the southeastern corner of the colony. Both families adhered to the Anglican faith and were proud members of the local gentry. As a younger son, Peter brought no land to the marriage but some wealth and considerable energy. Elizabeth, orphaned as a child, inherited from her father, Etheldred Taylor, numerous possessions and several slaves, and from her uncle, Henry Taylor, a well-improved plantation about three miles north of the town of Capron and a mile from the Blow plantation where Peter grew up. Elizabeth was fifteen years old when she and Peter married in 1800. He was twenty-three.

Although without formal schooling, Elizabeth was literate and intelligent. She took the raising and education of her children

4

seriously, for they were "her jewels." Proud of her ancestry, she hated cant and dishonesty, and possessed, Charlotte wrote, "an uncontrollable aversion to whatever was mean or cowardly." Peter was active, friendly, honorable, high-toned, and devoid of pretension. The couple was well matched and devoted to each other. Children came in quick succession. Charlotte, the sixth child, was born on 9 May 1810, though she was the third oldest by the time they left Virginia.

Elizabeth Taylor Blow   *Peter Blow*

Over the years, Peter added several hundred acres to his wife's family's plantation. By the time Charlotte was a young girl, the Blows had a new house that stood in the center of a large, fenced-in area on the plantation grounds. The back door of the house opened onto a charming garden containing flowers, vegetables and beehives. Beyond the garden lay an apple orchard and a cider mill. An enormous oak tree commanded the front yard. Charlotte used to play house with her dolls and bits of broken china among the tree's gnarled roots. Her favorite doll was John Bull, a jolly figure dressed in red trousers and a blue coat. By pulling a wire, Charlotte could open his mouth and give him a bit of bread to eat.

One winter John Bull disappeared in the snow. When he emerged in the spring, his colors had faded, but Charlotte loved him better than ever.

Charlotte recalled that her family lived comfortably "with nothing to interrupt the quiet and ease of their existence" except for a brief period in 1814 when her father was commissioned a captain in the war against the British. Writing nearly fifty years later, Charlotte may have idealized her childhood, for plantation life was often difficult. Her three oldest brothers died young, one before she was born and the others when she was two and three years old. The years 1814 and 1815 moreover were particularly bad for farming in Southampton County, made worse by several generations of intensive planting. To make ends meet, Peter got a license in 1810 to use their house as an inn to take in travelers and even orphans.

Whether they lived in easy comfort or not, Peter and Elizabeth succumbed to Western Fever – a burst of mania that drove men and women to flee their homes and head for the West. The great gold rush to California is the classic case, but this earlier fit of enthusiasm hit the mid Atlantic states around 1815. After his victory over the British at New Orleans at the end of the War of 1812, General Andrew Jackson led the fight against the Indian tribes of the Southeast. The outbreak of Western Fever occurred after the Creek, Cherokee, Chickasaw and Seminole Indians were compelled to give up their native lands, which speculators, including General Jackson, bought in 1818 and began to re-sell to newcomers who came rushing in. The population of Alabama suddenly jumped in just a few years from under 10,000 to over 125,000 by 1820. When the price of cotton hit new highs in 1818, the fever of excitement reached a crescendo. Most people believed the virgin lands would make a man his fortune.

Peter and Elizabeth sold their 860-acre estate in October 1818 for $5500, packed their belongings, gathered their children and slaves, and trekked seven hundred miles to the new town of Huntsville, Alabama. They needed several large wagons to carry provisions, household goods, and twenty persons. There were eight family members: father and mother; four girls ages sixteen, twelve, eight and six; two boys ages four and one; and a number of slaves, including one named Dred Scott. The entourage, along with thousands of other fortune seekers, journeyed across southern Virginia and down the Appalachian Trail into northern Alabama along poorly marked roads. After several months of travel, they were decidedly tired and dirty when they arrived at their destination.

The eldest daughter, Mary Ann, left an ardent suitor behind in Virginia. Like his cousin Francis Scott Key who had recently written the fiery words of the "Star Spangled Banner," John Key was a romantic. He promised her that he would be at the Huntsville annual ball the next year to claim the first dance. True to his word, he rode horseback from Capron to Huntsville and won her heart. The two were married and had one son before Mary Ann contracted a painful illness and died a few years later. In her agony she found final comfort among the Methodists. Impressed by her daughter's patience and piety, Elizabeth switched her religion as well. Charlotte thought of her as "a pioneer who went before to show us the 'straight and narrow path' through the rugged scenes of this sinful world." She felt keenly the loss of her favorite sister.

Charlotte was not impressed with the new frontier. "Alabama was then the El Dorado of the far West," she wrote long after, "and I well remember the disappointment I felt, upon our arrival there, at not seeing 'money growing upon trees,' and 'good old apple brandy flowing from their trunks!'" Her negative view did not improve as time passed.

Peter bought several hundred acres to make a cotton plantation ten miles north of the Tennessee River. Farming went well at first. In 1821 he shipped nearly ten thousand pounds of cotton to New Orleans for sale, but his crop fetched only 12 cents a pound, far below the 34 cents he might have earned three years before. Over-production in Alabama and elsewhere had flattened prices and ruined expectations. The price of cotton stayed low for the rest of the decade. Discouraged, Peter gave up farming after five years and sold the plantation. Today the site is the home of

Oakwood University, a historically black Seventh-day Adventist institution.

Peter then moved his family seventy miles west to Florence, Alabama. There he operated and later owned the Peter Blow Inn at the intersection of Pine and Tennessee Streets. He also entangled himself in a major speculation. In 1827 the General Assembly of the new state of Alabama authorized nine men, including Peter, to organize a lottery to raise up to $8000 to build and furnish a lodge for the Florence chapter of the Ancient Freemasons. There is no record that the lottery materialized, but the legislation held the organizers responsible for paying awards whether or not they had raised enough money to cover their cost. The fact that Peter moved again suggests that neither lottery nor inn had worked out as he had expected. Elizabeth meanwhile had delivered two more sons. Past fifty, Peter now had three daughters reaching a marriageable age and four boys fifteen years and younger. His third attempt to make a living had failed and his self-confidence was shot. With greater responsibilities and fewer resources, he decided to operate a hotel in St. Louis, Missouri.

Looking back, Charlotte saw the move from Virginia to Alabama as the beginning of a downward spiral in her family's fortunes. She loved and admired her father, but saw his deficiencies. He was honest and confiding, but also somewhat naïve. He believed "every man a *gentleman* who seemed to be one" and "in transactions with them, considered their '*word* as good as their bond.'" In Virginia where he was known and knew others, he could rely on trust between men. But, "as soon as the old and well-tried associations of his native State were dissolved, he suffered many pecuniary losses." Exactly what happened on the rough and tumble western frontier is unclear, but her father paid an emotional as well as a financial price. Charlotte described Peter as generally cheerful and animated, but subject to periodic mood swings when he became acutely depressed.

2

While Joseph courted Charlotte, Peter's latest business venture collapsed. He had come to St. Louis to run the Jefferson Hotel at the corner of Main and Pine Streets, but six months into the effort an advertisement appeared in the *Missouri Republican* announcing that all of Mr. Blow's hotel furniture was up for sale. The auctioneers, Savage and Bostwick, printed a complete list of the inventory, which started with 36 beds, 21 chamber tables, 12 wash stands, 8 dozen chairs, 5 stoves, much assorted china, tableware, various kitchen items, and ended with bells and spit boxes and a "Negro Girl, about 16 years old," described as "likely," that is, healthy enough to be a good breeder.

When Peter arrived in 1830, St. Louis was on the verge of a population explosion. A small outpost on the Mississippi River at the beginning of the century, the town had grown slowly at first. But after the Louisiana Purchase and Lewis and Clark's magical exploration of America's new territories, it picked up momentum. By 1820 the city had become a magnet attracting a new wave of fortune-seekers. Between 1830 and 1835, the size of St. Louis doubled, and then nearly doubled again in the last five years of the decade, creating a serious shortage of housing. The failure of Peter Blow as a hotel manager was not owing to a lack of opportunity.

The family's plight worsened when Elizabeth Blow's health began to break down. The surge in population that brought immense prosperity to St. Louis also overwhelmed the city's ability to cope with its sewerage. Without proper drainage and disposal, human waste seeped into the ground, spawning a stew of cholera bacteria. Fast growing cities like St. Louis and Chicago built on flat, poorly drained terrain were particularly susceptible. Inevitably many people were infected once the deadly bacteria leached into the city's water supply. Chicago solved its problem in part by dredging silt from the Chicago River to raise the level of the ground in order to create an artificial flow away from the population center. St. Louis discovered no such solution. Exhausted by years of hard travel and giving birth to eleven children, Elizabeth was unable to withstand the disease. Eight months after the hotel auction, she died of cholera, an early victim of an epidemic that ravaged the city a year later.

The emotional and financial woes of the family, however, did nothing to diminish Joseph's ardor. He had discovered that Charlotte was a bright, congenial, upright and handsome young woman, in short, the love of his life. Although she brought no wealth to the marriage, she had an intangible asset that he, as a second-generation Irishman, did not have: an aura of Virginia aristocracy. Shortly after Elizabeth's death, they married.

The wedding was a small, quiet affair. Charlotte remembered how, "Evergreens, provided by my little brothers, and festooned with flowers by my sisters, set off to great advantage the transparent white curtains, and gave a look of freshness and gaiety to our neat, but plain parlor." The company included the Blow and Charless families and a few friends. Charlotte wore a plain white dress of Italian Mantua silk that she made herself, trimmed about the waist and sleeves with black silk in memory of her mother. In her hair she entwined a simple wreath of white flowers but wore no veil or jewelry except a string of pearls that Joseph had given her as an engagement gift. After the wedding they spent a few days alone before going to his parents' house to live. The evening they arrived Sarah and Joseph Charless Sr. put on a grand reception to introduce Charlotte to their friends.

Joseph Sr. was a printer by trade. A staunch Irish republican, he had emigrated at the end of the 18th century to escape arrest for printing articles hostile to the British crown. He spent his first years in Philadelphia where he worked with the printer Mathew Carey and added an extra "s" to his last name in the hope that Americans might pronounce it correctly. In Ireland the name Charles was pronounced with two syllables, as "Chorlus." Few Americans, however, ever pronounced the name correctly with the extra "s" or without it. In Philadelphia, he met and married a young widow, Sarah Jordan McCloud. Experiencing a touch of Western Fever himself, he soon moved to Kentucky, first to Lexington and then to Louisville. In the meantime, President Jefferson had purchased Louisiana from France and engaged Meriwether Lewis and William Clark to explore and map the vast lands west of the Mississippi River. After their expedition, Jefferson appointed Lewis the governor of the territory. Understanding he needed a press to print official proclamations and to convey general information, Lewis urged Joseph Charless Sr. to move his printing business to St. Louis. The *Missouri Gazette, and Louisiana Advertiser; by Joseph Charless* became the first newspaper west of the Mississippi in 1808. The relationship between the two men, however, was short-lived. In the following year Lewis died from a gunshot wound to the head, most likely self-inflicted.

Joseph Charless, Sr.

Aside from providing the news, printing documents and running ads, Joseph Charless Sr. expressed his opinions in his newspaper. Some of these were pretty unpopular. He criticized the military leadership of the territory for its knee-jerk reactions to Indian grievances, lambasted lawyers for their lack of professional training and demeanor, and condemned dueling as uncivilized. He attracted a lot of enemies, but adhered to his paper's motto, "Truth Without Fear." Opponents abused him verbally and attacked him with fists, daggers and cudgels. One even shot at him near his house, but missed. Although he owned several household servants, he despised slavery. When Congress passed the Compromise of 1820 that made Missouri a slave state – a piece of legislation that he vigorously opposed – Joseph Sr. was thoroughly disgusted. He sold his printing business, and started an even more successful drug and paint company. Within a year or two, he made Joseph Jr. his partner in what became known as J. Charless & Son. Between 1808 when Joseph Sr. arrived and 1831 when his son married Charlotte, St. Louis had transformed itself from a small French settlement into the major entryway to the newest western frontier, making Joseph and Sarah Charless rich, widely known and well connected, if not universally liked.

On their first morning home, the newlyweds overslept and were late to breakfast. They were a little embarrassed, but Joseph's mother and his sister Anne greeted them warmly. A black servant appeared bringing hot battercakes to the dining table. Everything seemed fine, until Sarah told Charlotte "to pour out the coffee." After breakfast when Joseph left for work, Charlotte returned to their room to find it just as they had left it. No servant had come to tidy up. Anne popped in, smiled and offered to help her make the bed. Realizing that she was now her own chambermaid, she asked for a broom. For a long time she rested her chin on the broom handle, feeling a little sorry for herself. After a while, Joseph returned and sheepishly asked: "Has mother put you to work already?" Charlotte soon understood that Sarah had not intended to put her down, but was simply more direct than gracious.

Sarah Jordan McCloud Charless

Charlotte, however, faced a serious problem. Her father's health was failing fast and the doctors didn't expect him to live much longer. She began to worry about what would become of her sisters and brothers. With cash running short and debts mounting, Peter made such provision for them as he could. He found places for his two oldest sons as shop-boys, Peter Jr. in a dry goods store and Henry in the drug store under the wing of his new brother-in-law. He appointed Joseph his executor and declared that the balance of his estate should go to supporting "my two daughters Elizabeth and Patsy [Martha Ella] and my two youngest sons Taylor and William." There was little left, however, after he died. Peter owed various creditors a total of $1685.36, including eighteen months of unpaid rent, a large bank loan, and overdue accounts with sundry merchants, including J. Charless & Son for medicines. To satisfy his father-in-law's debts, Joseph sold much of the family's furniture, silverware and household items at auction. Peter had owned six slaves before he died. He had already sold one, Dred Scott, to Colonel Emerson. Joseph sold another, named Sam, for $500. One named Solomon, an old servant, died shortly after his master. (Solomon's coffin cost the estate $5; his master's $22.) There remained three – Hannah, William and Luke – who could be hired out to provide revenue for Peter's four children.

When her father died on 23 June 1832, Charlotte felt depressed and miserable, compounded by the fact that she was four months pregnant. At the time of their engagement and into the early months of their marriage, Joseph had warned Charlotte that there was little that he could do to help her siblings. Dismayed, she tried her best to muffle her feelings, but couldn't. "Tears, scalding tears, nightly chafed my cheeks, and it was only when emotions were too strong to be suppressed," Charlotte wrote, "that I would sob out in my agony sufficiently loud to awake my husband from sound repose." Joseph sympathized but couldn't bring himself to act, afraid of taking a step that his parents might not approve. However, seeing her wracked with worry and remembering that he had promised to cherish and comfort her, he re-considered. Folding her into his arms one evening, he finally said: "Charlotte, *your* sisters and *your* brothers are *mine*." As it turned out, Joseph and Sarah made no objections, and probably approved.

Charlotte and Joseph found a small two-storied house to rent and moved in. Downstairs a pocket door separated the two best rooms – the parlor and dining room. They were neatly furnished with nice carpets, cane-bottom chairs, an extension dining table, and very pretty, straw-colored venetian blinds, trimmed with dark blue cords and tassels. Their best piece of furniture, which Joseph had ordered from the East Coast, was a mahogany desk that stood in the parlor. Charlotte was satisfied that no one's home, not even the richest, looked so charming as hers. After her unsettled years moving from Virginia through Alabama to Missouri, she was extremely happy to have her own place to live, crowded as it was. In addition to Joseph and Charlotte, her two sisters and four brothers, there were two young men from the store living in the house "from motives of economy."

3

On 8 November 1832, exactly one year after her marriage, Charlotte gave birth to her first and only child. She named the baby Elizabeth Ann in honor of her mother, but from the beginning she was always called Lizzie. It was not however a happy time.

Lizzie's birth came three days after all of the Blow family possessions were sold at auction and on the eve of the city's first major epidemic. A week after Lizzie was born, Joseph's sister Anne died of cholera at the age of twenty-six. A few weeks later Charlotte came down with the disease and was extremely ill with a high fever that lasted more than a month. Then, in the following May, Joseph's other sister Eliza died at the age of twenty-four. In all, about four hundred people died of cholera from the end of 1832 through the spring of 1833, killing roughly one of every fifteen people living in St. Louis. Fortunately, Charlotte's sisters stayed well and took turns nursing her and Lizzie. But it was Joseph who provided the best care, tending Charlotte's pains and walking the baby at night to lull her to sleep.

Charlotte improved enough to be out of danger, but needed constant care for another six months. Swollen badly with toxins, her arms and legs required daily wrapping with hot lotions and flannels, and only Joseph could do it right. "In the morning, immediately after returning from market," Charlotte wrote, "he would go through the tedious process of bandaging – meanwhile keeping up a cheerful conversation, which is so reviving to the invalid; and, after breakfast, he would return to my room, to bid me an affectionate adieu, before leaving for the store."

As she regained strength, Charlotte realized that she had experienced a spiritual change, much like the one her sister Mary Ann had gone through eight years earlier. Unable to care for her own baby, frightened of dying, and driven nearly wild with raging fever, Charlotte had soothed herself by pleading for God's help. In the depths of her sickness she promised that if He spared her life she would "upon my recovery, turn my attention to the consideration of Divine Truth." She pledged to study the Bible and govern her life accordingly. Once she got better, however, she couldn't keep her promise. The Bible proved too difficult to read, and she gave up. Feeling guilty, she confessed to Joseph, who bought her a copy of "Scott's Commentary" to explain what she couldn't understand. Thomas Scott, an Anglican churchman, originally published his *Commentary on the Whole Bible* as a series of newspaper articles in England before it came out as a book. An American edition appeared just as Lewis and Clark left on their expedition to explore the West. As a comprehensible guide, the book was extremely popular throughout the United States during the 19th century.

Charlotte began with the New Testament. Before she had finished Scott's discussion of the book of Matthew, she was convinced that she was on the right track. When Joseph saw that she was committed, he began to read with her. Soon they were praying together in the evening. Until then, the two rarely had participated in any religious exercises, but in October 1834 they decided to join the First Presbyterian Church.

Salmon Giddings founded the church in 1817, the year that the first steamboat arrived in St. Louis. He had just come from Connecticut the year before riding all the way on horseback. He received, however, a rather cool reception. The *Missouri Gazette*, Joseph Charless Sr.'s newspaper, had recently warned against preachers coming to the city to mix religion and politics in the pulpit. Ignorant of or simply ignoring the advice, Giddings advocated social justice, including the abolition of slavery. Impressed by his preaching, Joseph and Sarah Charless, became early members of his church and were instrumental in its development.

A quiet and well-mannered man, Giddings also thought big. Whenever the congregation reached two hundred in number, he would start another church. The First Presbyterian, perhaps as a consequence of this expansionist policy, remains the oldest continuously operating church west of the Mississippi. Unfortunately, Giddings died in 1828 after falling from his horse, so by the time Joseph and Charlotte became regular worshippers, William S. Potts, Doctor of Divinity, had succeeded as Pastor. Joseph and Charlotte became fast friends with the Reverend Potts, the two new members relying on the Reverend for spiritual guidance and he relying on Joseph for business advice.

Charlotte also drew her brothers and sisters to the church. Dr. Potts married her sister Martha Ella to Charles Drake, her brother Henry to Minerva Grimsley, and her brother Taylor to Joseph's niece Elizabeth Ann Wahrendorff. When Dr. Potts left the church to become president of Marion College, his successor the Reverend Samuel McPheeters married her brother William Blow to Julia Webster.

Joseph's father, who outlived five of his seven children, died in July 1834 at the age of sixty-two, just before Charlotte and Joseph joined the First Presbyterian congregation. His death made his son the sole proprietor of J. Charless & Son, which Joseph Jr. renamed J. Charless & Co. The firm was the main distributor of medicines and paint supplies in Missouri and southern Illinois, and regularly ran a large, front-page ad in the *Missouri Republican* to market its extensive inventory. Before the early 20th century when the Pure Food and Drug Act was passed, pharmaceuticals were unregulated and sold without prescription. J. Charless & Co. purveyed some powerful drugs: Peruvian bark and Turkish opium and their refined products quinine and morphine. They also sold belladonna, calomel and strychnine and a wide variety of salts and herbal medicines. The paint department stocked large supplies of white lead-based paints and a rainbow of dyestuffs and coloring agents, like Venetian red, Spanish brown, Chrome yellow and green. Both parts of the business required frequent travel to buy inventory and to sell wholesale.

In early September after his father died, Joseph suggested that Charlotte and the baby go with him on a business trip into Illinois. Lizzie was twenty-two months old and quite delicate. They agreed that a fortnight's journey in the open air of the countryside would be healthy and wonderful. They hitched up their barouche, a small four-wheeled covered carriage with two bench-seats facing each other, and set out from the slave state of Missouri to the free state of Illinois. Three adults, which included Lizzie's nurse, the baby, a small trunk, a carpetbag, and a little basket of things for Lizzie filled the carriage. The nurse was most likely a young black woman and a slave. Little did they think that their going into Illinois could trigger her freedom.

Joseph mapped out a 300-mile itinerary that included visits to four towns – Jacksonville, Lewiston, Calhoun and Canton. All four were new towns – no more than eleven years old – and named for a prominent person or place. Jacksonville was named for General Jackson, who had become President in 1828; Lewiston for Meriwether Lewis; Calhoun for John C. Calhoun, a forceful politician who became Vice President during Jackson's administration; and Canton for Canton, China, which was allegedly but incorrectly thought to lie directly under the town on the far side of the world. Two years earlier, the citizens of Calhoun, irate over their namesake's increasingly strident voice in favor of slavery, had changed the name of their town to Springfield. After Abraham Lincoln moved there, Springfield became the capital of Illinois.

Joseph expected that they would travel about ten to twelve days, at a pace of twenty-five to thirty miles a day. Most of their voyage took them across the sparsely populated plain of southern Illinois. The outward trip met all their expectations, as Charlotte made clear in her account:

> I'll tell you there is no such traveling these days of railroads and steam boats! Every body is in too great a hurry to stop and go slowly, as we did in our little barouche, trotting gently across the prairies of Illinois. How balmy and bracing the air; how quiet the scene; how beautiful the prairies! Some four, some ten, some twenty miles in width – all covered with tall grasses and a profusion of large autumn

flowers that waved in graceful undulations before the sweeping breeze. An apt representation of a gently swelling sea, upon whose dark green waves, nature had emptied her lap of richly varied blossoms.

During the heat of the day they rested a few hours before setting out again. They learned from their host of the evening where they should stop to eat and sleep the following night. Each day they started early in the morning and usually kept going until the sun went down. And, "what magnificent sunsets!" they were. They passed through many small hamlets on their way to the larger towns. They spent their one Sunday on the road in Lewiston where they worshipped in the local church.

The road back proved more trying. Joseph lost his way, and then, for the first time, clouds appeared and it began to rain. The hills became slippery and difficult for the horse to climb. It grew dark just as they left the open fields to enter a dense forest. To Charlotte, it seemed as if they had left light and hope behind, "for cloud and tempest, lightning, and loud claps of thunder quickly succeeded." They found themselves enveloped in darkness so total that they couldn't see their hands in front of their faces. Sharp flashes of lightning guided them through the black and swaying trees. About nine o'clock in the evening they discovered a light from a window in the distance and heard "the watch-dog's honest bark." The next day they arrived home filled with stories of their adventures on the open plains with all their pleasures and narrow escapes. Best of all sweet Lizzie "brought the roses of the prairie home upon her little cheeks."

4

Despite the sicknesses, deaths and uncertainties of their first few years together, Charlotte and Joseph began to enjoy a greater degree of comfort in their lives. They bought the house where his sister Anne and her husband Charles Wahrendorff had lived. It was a grand mansion "second to none" in the city, located on Market and Fifth Streets near his parents' house. It was the place where Lizzie would spend seven years of her childhood with her parents and her Blow aunts and uncles. Charlotte recalled how father and daughter romped together, and "how she would watch for him at the alley-gate, with hands full of snow-balls to pelt him with." He would pick her up in his arms, kiss her cheeks and dip her face gently into the snow bank; and then let her pelt him again.

About the same time, Joseph, who relished gardening, also bought a small plot near the edge of the city. Often when he stopped by on his way home to inspect his fruits, flowers and vegetables, he would throw off his jacket, roll up his sleeves, grab a hoe or spade, and set to work. It didn't occur to him that he shouldn't work side by side with a black man, a slave, who seemed to enjoy the work as much as he. He was particularly attentive to the smallest detail. A tiny wild flower along side of the road could catch his attention. He would stoop down to examine it closely.

On the other hand, he had a temper that could flare when provoked. In their new house they had a domestic servant, a slave named Anthony, who was unwise enough to treat Charlotte with impertinence, often sneaking off without warning or permission. His excuses were so implausible that Charlotte sometimes couldn't help but laugh, though afterwards she would be annoyed with herself for failing to be forceful. When finally she lost patience with him, he responded with "the most unheard-of impudence." As soon as Joseph came home, Charlotte explained what had taken place. "In an instant, as Anthony was passing the dining-room door, my husband sprang at him – caught him by the collar, shook and twirled him around into the gallery, and pounded him with his bare fists to his heart's content." To allay any suspicion that he only expressed his anger against black servants, Charlotte recounted how he forcibly removed from the house a "saucy" white servant and how on various occasions Joseph escorted from his store customers who were unwise enough to bad mouth a friend.

Punishment – just or not – may have accounted for another incident in the Charless household. In October 1838 the *Daily Commercial Bulletin* reported that Hannah, a black woman owned by neighbor Silas Drake, persuaded one of Joseph and Charlotte's domestic slaves named Emily to poison the Charless family. Susan, who also worked for the Charless family, overheard the conversation, which took place over the fence that separated the respective houses. Susan reported the conversation, which led to Hannah's arrest and commitment.

Joseph also had a passion for fires. Whenever a fire broke out, he would rush to the rescue, and sometimes climb to the rooftop to protect property and save lives. He stayed until the flames were under control and went home exhausted. Charlotte dreaded the cry of "Fire!" Fortunately, the first official fire brigade in St. Louis, the Central Fire Company No. 1, was organized the year Lizzie was born, giving her some peace of mind.

Charlotte admired her husband's open, bold and generous nature, up to a point. When he presented Charlotte the string of pearls that she wore as a bride, he actually had shown her two sets to select from, uncertain as to which was finer. After Charlotte chose the one she preferred, Joseph offered the rejected set to her sister Elizabeth Rebecca. When Joseph first called on the Blows, conventional etiquette required him to pay his initial attention to the oldest unmarried daughter. Though she never married, Elizabeth was attractive and bright, but obviously didn't spark Joseph's interest. He may have assuaged any sense of guilt he felt by offering the second set of pearls to her. In any event, Charlotte was a little miffed. "While I was pleased to see my sweet sister with a set of pearls, like mine," she confessed, "I would have been more pleased with his *attention* if it had been directed to me *only*." Later, Charlotte realized that she had been quite selfish to let Joseph's generosity towards her sister diminish her own sense of joy in his gift to her.

Although they usually thought alike, sometimes they disagreed. One winter morning Joseph bought some things at market from "a plain, honest-looking youth" who accompanied him home, carrying the goods with him. They went into the kitchen to warm up. When the family breakfast was ready in the dining room, Joseph asked that a place be set for the youth. Charlotte demurred, and asked if it wouldn't be better for him to eat in the kitchen. Joseph replied, "*No*. The golden rule directs us to do unto others as we would they should do unto us." Charlotte couldn't agree. She thought that, according to the rule, the boy should eat in the kitchen because he would feel more at ease there than at the family dining table. Joseph looked at her "with that kind but reproving expression which was characteristic of him" and said, "'Charlotte, if we were to stop at the house of that young man's father, I doubt not but that he would give us the best place, and the best of everything he has.'" Unconvinced, Charlotte conceded the point. The lad ate his breakfast in the dining room. Afterwards, Joseph teased Charlotte about her "Virginia pride."

Occasionally, Charlotte won a round. It annoyed her that Joseph sometimes dressed carelessly. Once on a steamboat she met a woman who, having observed them, asked her if "that old gentleman" was her husband. Caught a little by surprise, Charlotte saw that the woman meant no offense, and replied, "Yes, he was," and added, "He suits me very well, ma'am." She could hardly wait to tell him about her conversation, "really taking pleasure in doing so." Although he was only six years older than she, she assured him that "he looked twenty years older when he neglected to dress with care, especially if he had not shaved." The next morning Joseph dressed with extra care, declaring that he intended "to create a sensation." They were delighted when the woman, on reconsideration, told Charlotte that her husband "was the handsomest young gentleman she had ever seen."

In time Charlotte learned that to influence her husband a direct approach was less effective than the "silken chords" of love and tenderness. She was amused when she saw her daughter copy her technique. One day Lizzie said on the sly, "I am going to make Papa let me do it." How are you going to do that, Charlotte asked. "The way mamma does," came the answer. Lizzie turned to her father and "with her most bewitching little smile" said, *Do please, dear papa, let me.*"

Not always the master of his house, Joseph relied on Charlotte's good nature and common sense. When he was away on business, he depended on her to keep an eye on the store as well as the house and farm nearby. In December 1835 he embarked on a seven-week trip to buy inventory. He booked passage on the steamboat *Potosi*, which paddled down the Mississippi and then turned up the Ohio River with stops at Louisville, Cincinnati and Wheeling, West Virginia. It was the first time that he and Charlotte were separated for such a long period.

Joseph wrote Charlotte twenty-one letters during his journey. Typically, he recounted what and whom he had seen, asked after family and friends, and wanted to know how the store was doing. A major portion of each letter was devoted to religious thoughts. Writing from Cincinnati on New Year's Day, he expressed a great reliance "on our divine Savior" and thought that they should devote more attention than ever to eternal realities. "I am satisfied," he wrote, "that love to God will purify our souls, and make us better fitted for the trials of this world, and will ensure eternal happiness to us hereafter."

Two years later, Joseph and Charlotte became pioneers in the creation of the Second Presbyterian Church. As the city was growing rapidly, the Reverend Dr. Potts, following Salmon Giddings's directive, persuaded a small group within the community to establish a branch several blocks away. Potts saw that Joseph would be instrumental in raising money for the new church and ordained him a Ruling Elder.

5

In their first years together Joseph and Charlotte prospered enormously. When they were married in 1831, the number of people living in St. Louis was less than 5,000. By 1840 the number had swollen to over 16,000. The influx of folks from the East propelled economic growth throughout the region and benefited every type of business, including J. Charless & Co. Joseph found himself richer but working harder, so in December of 1836 he invited Charlotte's brother Henry to become his business partner. At the time Henry, Elizabeth Rebecca, Taylor and William Blow were still living with Joseph and Charlotte.

Henry had started in the store as a clerk six years earlier at age fourteen. He was hard-working and talented, and naturally delighted with the offer. Joseph renamed the company Charless & Blow to reflect the change. Buoyed by success, the two partners decided to expand the paint side of the business. To do so, Joseph and Henry, along with Joseph's older brother Edward and Dr. Silas Reed formed the Charless, Reed & Co. in 1838. Together they bought a piece of land in the city to build and operate the St. Louis White Lead Factory to refine oil and process lead to produce their own paint supply. Joseph focused more time on the white lead works and Henry took over the store's operations. The idea was sound, but the plan was too ambitious and the timing couldn't have been worse. The astonishing growth of the 1830s had created an economic bubble in St. Louis. Lacking sufficient capital in the firm, Joseph and Henry borrowed heavily just as one of the deepest and longest business recessions hit the United States. The Panic of 1837 began with the collapse of banks in New York City and spread across the country. The ensuing recession lasted six years, the worst in American history until the Great Depression. Joseph and Henry faced a major crisis.

Joseph, who had never experienced a serious reverse in business, became unnerved. His health finally broke down that year. "I do not recollect how long his ill health lasted," Charlotte wrote, "but I well remember how his flesh went away – how pale he was – how he perspired at night, from nervous prostration, and how his skin seemed to cleave to his bones." Outwardly he seemed calm and sensible, "but" Charlotte noted that, "his elasticity, his free-hearted joyousness was gone."

She was totally mystified, because Joseph wasn't willing to say what was wrong. He was afraid that the truth would frighten her, but eventually she got him to talk. She learned that the assets of the partnership exceeded its debts, and that, in the event that the company ran out of cash to pay its bills, forcing it into liquidation, she and Joseph still would have sufficient funds to meet all their financial obligations. Once she understood the full extent of the problem, she assured him that, if the worst happened, she was prepared to "begin life afresh."

Charlotte's understanding and assurance had a positive effect. Joseph suddenly felt better. He determined that he would make a trip into the countryside for a fortnight – for his health as well as business. When he returned, he looked brighter and began to think more clearly. He and Charlotte decided to downsize. In the fall they sold their mansion and all its contents, except their silver, and enough furniture for two bedrooms. Charlotte's oldest brother Peter and his wife, who had just bought a new house, were happy to have them as boarders for a while. Joseph also rented out the second and third floors of the store. He felt immense relief, telling Charlotte "we begin now to see our way clear." In one respect they were very fortunate, for they had sold their house at a good price, even in a weak market. But the same prolonged recession that caused property values to fall by half also precipitated a severe liquidity crisis in the city. The next year Charless & Blow became temporarily insolvent.

Like many businesses at the time, the firm both borrowed and lent money, and sometimes co-signed the loans of others. When Charless & Blow were "compelled to suspend payment," it was because they had endorsed the note of someone about whom "they had no apprehensions." The unexpected call for payment came like a shock. "At first," Charlotte wrote, "my husband (pale from emotion) thought all was over!" After an anxious, sleepless night, in which Charlotte agreed to part with her tea service and all her silverware, they learned that the debt was not overwhelming. But, it had to be paid. The next day Joseph sent Charlotte a message to send the tea service to the store. With "a beating heart, (for this was a birth-day gift from him)," Charlotte wrote, "I parted with my beautiful tea-service, and have never seen it since. It was sold to pay that debt."

The recession cut a wide swathe through society. No tall reed went uncut. Peter Blow was obliged to sell his new house, forcing Joseph and Charlotte to move out. Sarah Charless, distressed by her son's setback, was pleased to have him and his family come back to her house. She was even willing to accept, at Joseph's insistence, rent for their room and board, but adamant that she receive "not a cent more" than actual cost.

6

Sarah's house was no longer new, built, according to Charlotte, "in the year *one*." The second floor was divided by several partitions that they knocked down to make one large room that extended across the entire house. Part of it became a small bedroom for Lizzie and the rest served as the parlor cum bedroom where they put the piano, pier-stand and bed. The ceiling was so low that they had to remove the feet and cornice from the bed. "I had," she said, "so constant and disagreeable an impression that often, when rising suddenly from my chair, I would dodge, from fear of bumping my head against [the ceiling]." Though a bit tight, the living arrangement was in fact so cozy that she and Joseph often preferred to receive their friends there than in Sarah's reception room.

Charlotte and Joseph evaluated their situation. Their house, Joseph's farm, Charlotte's tea service, and their fine carriage and beautiful horses all had been sold. Money "helps materially, perhaps too much, toward giving one position in society. All things considered, it is hard to lose it," Charlotte admitted. She imagined how people might talk about those who had lost their wealth as they passed along the street: "There goes poor Mrs. A., or B. She has come down in the world!" She realized that women were much more mortified by a reverse in fortune than men, but they felt it too. "My husband was humbled, and disappointed" and so was she.

They tried not to complain. "It would have been ungrateful if we had done so; for, although not by any means elegant, we were comfortable." She, Joseph and Lizzie were as happy at Sarah's as they had ever been. Charlotte was proud when Joseph discovered what an exquisite needlewoman and "jewel of a wife" she was. With a little imagination and a nice touch, she could transform one of her old garments into something perfectly new and even more charming than before. Lizzie, now nine years old, "looked just as sweet and pretty in her *bit calicos* as she had ever done in better and more expensive clothes." Touched by their recent experiences, Lizzie amused her parents by suggesting that in their old age she might support them by teaching music and French, at which she was quite proficient. Lizzie went to a small private French school where the master was less than gentle. One day she complained to her mother that he had thrown books at her head. Charlotte replied: "You should learn how to dodge, my dear" – but she withdrew Lizzie as soon as the term was over.

Unhurt by the recession, Sarah Charless still owned her house as well as a fine carriage and a strong horse, which "would have appeared very respectable, if (as the stable boy said) the calves had not 'chawed off his tail!'" Joseph liked to drive his three Charless ladies into the countryside. The rides tended to be long and rough, making the women complain that they were being jolted to death. He responded that he could find many more potholes and stumps to drive over without upsetting the carriage. His boyish playfulness prompted Sarah to entertain Charlotte and Lizzie with stories about his childhood pranks, like the time he threw a dried squash from an upstairs window at an old Indian who promptly returned fire with an arrow into the windowsill. At the end of the trip they wondered why they enjoyed it so much.

Life was now simpler and in some ways better, but others were not so lucky. Shortly after they moved to his mother's house in the fall of 1842, Joseph took a business trip up the Mississippi River. In a letter he described to Charlotte the beauty and endless variety of fall colors in the forests along the way. But in the towns and villages he found people who were destitute and infinitely worse off than he and Charlotte. They seemed cheerful, resigned to their poverty and submitting to God's will. Seeing "how little we do," Joseph suggested that he and Charlotte do more. "Let us, therefore, exhort one another," he wrote to her, "and provoke each other to well-doing, in the service of our God. Let us love each other more and more, and make Jesus the great object of our praise and prayer."

To Joseph adversity as well as prosperity came from the hand of a loving God. His financial fall did not lessen but strengthened his faith so that, instead of becoming more anxious and ambitious about accumulating wealth, he became less so. Still he felt it was his duty to work hard at his business. In a time when a six-day workweek was the norm, Joseph rejoiced when Saturday night arrived. He could lay aside the commercial world and "engage in the delightful exercises of the holy Sabbath." When Monday came, "his mind was clearer, and his hopes stronger" and everything looked bright again.

Joseph Charless, Jr.

Joseph opened the company's books for inspection by an outside committee. After a thorough review, the committee agreed that Charless & Blow remained a viable firm, and that its creditors and vendors would fare best if it continued in business rather than liquidate, provided the partners extracted only a small stipend for living expenses. Prospects brightened by the spring, but it took another two years for the company to fully recover. By then Joseph and Henry had decided to split the firm and dissolve the partnership. Joseph retained the drugs and medicine business. He eventually chose as his new partners Charlotte's youngest brothers Taylor and William, who like Henry, had begun as clerks in the store. In 1844 the three men formed "Charless, Blow & Co." Henry took over the oil and lead factory, which began to thrive. Henry would find it necessary to rebuild the entire factory after it was destroyed by fire in 1849. The new works were organized as the Collier White Lead and Oil Company with Henry in partnership with two prominent St. Louis businessmen George Collier and Alexander Lyle.

7

With his business revived and reorganized, Joseph bought the house that his brother-in-law Peter had owned and where he, Charlotte and Lizzie had lived for a while. But just as Joseph's financial situation recovered, Charlotte fell ill again. Five years of anxiety had drained her. After she consulted three doctors, none of whom could diagnose her illness, Joseph decided she needed a vacation. "With his accustomed dispatch," she wrote, he "hastened to the river, secured our passage on a boat, which was to leave in three days, and at dinner asked me if I would not like to take a trip to Havana?" Although delighted by the proposal, Charlotte objected that the timing was bad. She knew that more business was done in March and April than any other two months of the year, but Joseph brushed her worries aside: "Business is of no importance compared to health. Can you be ready by day after tomorrow?" Besides he had already paid for their tickets. Lizzie would leave school, and Charlotte's sister Elizabeth, would go with them.

They took a steamboat to New Orleans where they were told that it was too late in the season to visit Havana, so they decided to head for Pensacola in the Florida panhandle. Arriving at Mobile, Alabama, friends suggested that Pascagoula at the eastern end of the Gulf Coast of Mississippi was a better place to enjoy the sea breeze. So they changed course again, arriving at a grand and posh hotel that catered to the wealthy families of New Orleans and Mobile. The proprietors, as it turned out, were old acquaintances, Malcolm McRae and his wife Mary Ann. The McCraes had settled in Pascagoula and built their hotel in the mid 1830s. Before the great recession of 1837-43, the Gulf Coast from Mississippi to Florida experienced a real estate boom that saw property values increase ten-fold. By the time Joseph and Charlotte arrived in the area the bubble had burst. Values had recovered a bit but were still less than half of what they had been in 1837. At the hotel room and board was $2 a day or $12 for the week, excluding wine, which could run as high as $12.50 a bottle. The meals, predominantly seafood, were invariably excellent with a delicious assortment of fish, crabs and oysters. A slave would row out in the early morning, as one visitor recalled, and return with a skiff full of oysters that he raked up from the water.

Charlotte fell in love with the McRae Hotel, which had a long piazza surrounded by pillars that supported trellises of wisteria and bougainvillea. Standing on the high ground with a great lawn sweeping down to the shore, the hotel commanded a striking view of the Gulf of Mexico. "Nothing," she wrote, "was so sweet to me as the unadulterated sea air, which I delighted to drink in, every breath of which seemed to send vigor into my wasted and weakened frame."

At first she could barely make it down to the water's edge, but within a few days she could go half a mile at a stretch with Joseph's help. She liked to rest in a reclining chair at the end of the hotel's long pier while the others caught crabs and speared flounders. In her repose, she compared herself to Sir Izaak Walton, author of the first important book on fishing written in English. Walton published his book *The Compleat Angler* nearly two hundred years earlier, in 1653. Charlotte found herself as interested in fish as Walton himself, except that, where Walton ruminated and philosophized on the joys of the art of fishing, Charlotte was constantly startled by the strange creatures that Joseph and Lizzie kept pulling out of the water.

Charlotte believed that Pascagoula was the most pleasant place that she had ever been. She marveled to discover:

> Highly cultivated gardens, picturesque and tasteful cottages, and elegant mansions, contrasted, as they were, with the magnificent groves of pine and magnolia, with their rich and fragrant undergrowth of yellow jasmine, and other sweet flowers, which were indigenous to the soil of this lovely country. In these pleasant groves were many springs of soft,

clear water, which, flowing together, formed little creeks, whose gentle meanderings added freshness and increasing loveliness to the already charming scene. Some of these creeks flowed over their shining beds of sand, and some over the waving grass and lily. It tranquilizes me, even now, to recall the rustic bridge, where I have often stood (it seems to me for hours) and gazed at the gentle stream, as it murmured over the log that lay half-imbedded in the sand, and watched the never-ceasing motion of the graceful "water lilies" which arched the stream below.

One day they rowed up one of the little creeks to have a picnic on a small island so idyllic that Joseph thought for a moment of buying it as a family retreat. In Charlotte's mind, the gently murmuring bayous of Pascagoula stood in sharp contrast to the raucous noises along the big river at St. Louis and its often contaminated waters.

8

Benefiting from the change, Charlotte decided to stay in the South. For the next two years, she and Lizzie lived mostly in Mobile. A smaller version of New Orleans, Mobile had experienced a similar history. Controlled by the French and then the Spanish, the city was predominantly Roman Catholic in religion, and had inaugurated Mardi Gras parades before New Orleans seized on the idea. With Alabama's admission to the Union as the twenty-second state in 1819, Mobile expanded its natural seaport to serve planters throughout the state and parts of Mississippi. By the late 1840s when Charlotte and Lizzie arrived, Mobile was a vibrant and sophisticated cultural center.

Lizzie, who turned fourteen in 1846, enrolled in Madame De Fellon's Academy, a boarding school for young ladies of refinement. Charlotte meanwhile had re-connected with the doctor who had attended the Blows during their time in northern Alabama twenty years earlier. She boarded with him and his family about three miles outside the city. Charlotte saw Lizzie at school during the week while Lizzie visited her mother at the doctor's house on the weekends.

Joseph kept the two informed of what was happening at home while they were in Mobile. His mother Sarah admonished him to "tell Lizzie I do miss her so much." Their new dog Nimrod, he reported, has "improved wonderfully in size, beauty, manners, &c. You will be perfectly delighted with him. He is no longer a country dog, but is becoming a real city bred gentlemanly dog." He also may have told Charlotte about the status of the lawsuit that they had helped file on behalf of one of her family's former slaves.

Francis Murdoch, a local lawyer, had filed two petitions at the courthouse in St. Louis in April 1846, asking the court to allow the slave Dred Scott and his wife Harriet to sue for their freedom. The first plea argued that ten years earlier John Emerson, a colonel and doctor in the United States Army, had taken Scott from Missouri, where slavery was allowed, to Illinois and the Northwest Territory, where it was not. The second plea stated that Colonel Emerson had bought Harriet from Major Taliaferro at Fort Snelling in Wisconsin a year or two later. In his briefs Murdoch argued that both Scotts, having resided in free territory, should be released from bondage.

Although Missouri had been admitted to the Union as a slave state in 1821, there was early and ample precedent in law for granting freedom to slaves whose owners had taken them into an area where slavery was prohibited. When Murdoch took the Scotts' case he had already represented at least sixteen other slave plaintiffs in St. Louis. Joseph Charless, who had studied and practiced law for a few years before he joined his father in the family business, had represented several slaves seeking their freedom. The Scotts therefore had reason to hope that the court would act promptly in their favor and that the Blow family would help.

Born around 1805, Scott had been a member of the Blow household since childhood and was older than most of the Blow children. Among other tasks, he was eventually assigned the job of keeping an eye on the boys, who ranged from nine to seventeen years his junior. When Peter Blow sold Scott to Colonel John Emerson in order to meet his financial obligations shortly before his death in 1832, the Blow children bade farewell to a long-standing, likable and faithful servant. Fourteen years later when Scott filed suit, all six surviving children were still living in St. Louis, and in one way or another became involved in his effort to win freedom for himself and his family, which now included two daughters.

In 1840 the U.S. Army had reassigned Colonel Emerson from Fort Snelling to Florida to join the forces suppressing a rising of Seminole Indians. The Colonel, married to Irene Sanford two years earlier, deposited his wife and the Scotts, who now had a two year old baby named Eliza, at Irene's father's farm on the outskirts of St. Louis. There they stayed for three years until Emerson, whose wife seemed indifferent to having the Scotts as her servants, directed Dred and Harriet to work for Irene's sister and brother-in-law Mary and Captain Henry Bainbridge at Jefferson Barracks, the Army's base in Missouri. Shortly after Colonel Emerson, who had been in bad health for sometime, died in December 1843, the troops stationed at Jefferson Barracks were ordered south to prepare for the independence of Texas and inevitable war with Mexico. Dred accompanied Captain Bainbridge to Louisiana while Harriet returned to St. Louis and was put out to work for the Russell family. When the U.S. Army was ordered to Texas, Scott was sent back to St. Louis where he arrived in March 1846. At some point during this time, Harriet or Dred offered to buy their freedom from Mrs. Emerson. When she rejected their overture, the Scotts filed suit in April, a few weeks after Dred's return to St. Louis.

Dred and Harriet no doubt had dreamed of freedom for a long time. They knew that Missouri had a history of favorable rulings for slaves who were taken to "free" territories, but until they had a chance to spend time in the city of St. Louis as opposed to the periphery (the Sanford farm and Jefferson Barracks), there was little opportunity to act. The time came with Harriet's going to work for the Russells. Samuel Russell, a successful merchant in the city, lived three blocks from Joseph and Charlotte Charless. Harriet probably found an advantageous moment to speak with Charlotte and Joseph about petitioning the court. Joseph would have recommended Francis Murdoch, who had an established track record.

When Murdoch decided to leave St. Louis, Samuel Bay and Charles Drake, who had married Charlotte's sister Martha Ella, took over the Scott case. Drake took depositions for the Scotts while Bay prepared for trial. Henry Blow testified on Scott's behalf and Joseph Charless guaranteed the costs if the case were lost. Unfortunately the jury returned a verdict against the Scotts owing to a technicality. A re-trial three years later gave Dred and Harriet Scott their freedom, momentarily.

Little interested in the Scotts' plea, Irene Emerson looked to her brother John Sanford for direction. Sanford and his brother-in-law Pierre Chouteau were prominent figures in St. Louis and adamant proponents of slavery. They urged Irene to appeal the case to the Missouri Supreme Court as tensions in the state and throughout the country became increasingly heated. The Court, with two of its three judges pro-slavery, overruled the lower court in 1852. The case was eventually appealed to the United States Supreme Court where it established a landmark in American jurisprudence. The nation's highest court declared that slaves were property and all blacks inferior so that neither a slave nor a free black had a right to appear before the court. Once again, the Scotts were denied by a panel of predominantly pro-slavery judges. The Dred Scott decision further divided and inflamed public opinion as the nation stumbled irreversibly toward Civil War.

Throughout the slow process of the law, the Blow children, their spouses and in-laws stood by the Scotts. Taylor Blow kept in close touch with the family. Joseph Charless covered their legal costs. Peter Blow's brother-in-law Edmund La Beaume employed Scott when Mrs. Emerson began hiring him out as day labor.

Pending the outcome of the litigation, the Scotts' wages were accumulated and held in trust. Around 1850 Mrs. Emerson moved to Massachusetts where she remarried. Just after the Supreme Court rendered its decision in 1857, Calvin Chaffee, her new husband, learned to his horror that his wife owned Dred Scott. A leading abolitionist and Member of Congress, Chaffee had been unaware of the connection between himself and the Supreme Court decision and told his wife he couldn't be married to a slave owner. Under pressure from her husband and presumably placated by receiving the Scotts' escrowed wages, Mrs. Emerson released the Scotts to Taylor Blow. Taylor had been just a child when his mother and father died and Scott was sold to Colonel Emerson. It was appropriate that Taylor, as the family member who felt closest to Scott, should give him, his wife and their daughters their freedom.

Scott was in his early fifties when he became a free man and took a job as a porter at the Barnum Hotel. Had Peter Blow been successful as a hotel manager, Scott might have been working at the Jefferson Hotel as a slave rather than at the Barnum as a free man. Unfortunately, he enjoyed his release from slavery for scarcely a year, for in September 1858 he died of tuberculosis. Scott was thus spared from witnessing the consequence of his trial with the outbreak of the Civil War. Taylor Blow arranged for his burial and his brother Henry paid the expenses.

Charlotte, her siblings, their spouses and in-laws grew up accustomed to slavery. Her father had owned as many as twelve slaves, including Scott. The family, however, was not averse to freeing some. Charlotte's sister Elizabeth Rebecca emancipated her slave Luke Howard in 1850 and her brother Taylor and his wife freed Frankey Cuterfoot and Tanny Overton in 1847 and Nicene Clark in 1854. Joseph and Charlotte owned household slaves in the earlier years of their marriage, but gave them up because, as Charlotte explained to Theresa Pulszky on a steamboat to New Orleans in 1852, "they require constant watching, as they are idle, and you cannot rely on them." From the 1840s they hired Irish and later Irish and German servants, with one exception. When Joseph's mother Sarah died, she granted her maid Ophelia her freedom in her will. Ophelia married a man of color, thought to be free, but he was in fact a runaway slave. When her husband, an excellent cook named Mack, was apprehended, Ophelia ran to Charlotte and "entreated her on her knees to buy him." Charlotte did, and Mack became the Charless' cook. Mrs. Pulszky spoke with Mack, and observed: "He is constantly occupied with the children of the niece of Mrs. Charless of whom he seems eminently fond; he considers himself obviously a member of the family." (Pulszky.) Charlotte supported Dred Scott because Scott was family and it was the right thing to do. It was what her mother, whose "uncontrollable aversion to whatever was mean or cowardly," would have done.

9

In the late spring of 1847, Joseph returned to Mobile. While Lizzie remained in school, he and Charlotte went back to the MacRae Hotel in Pascagoula, which was about to become the headquarters for the disembarkation of the U.S. Army on its return from the Mexican War. A visitor recalled seeing General Zachary Taylor with his wife and daughter and a large number of his officers at the hotel.

The war with Mexico was the inevitable result of Western Fever. Like the Blows before them, Americans continued to push into territories deemed unoccupied and available. The broad area west of Louisiana belonged to the shaky nation of Mexico, which protested but could not withstand the flood of outsiders, who declared themselves the independent republic of Texas in 1836. As soon as he was elected President of the United States, James K. Polk, an ardent expansionist, orchestrated the annexation of Texas in 1845 and immediately ordered General Taylor to protect the new border along the Rio Grande River. The War with an irate Mexico thus began. Taylor (and his army) won a series of battles against much larger forces, culminating in the Battle of Buena Vista, which made him an instant hero and a ready candidate to succeed Polk as President four years later.

Missing General Taylor and his returning troops by about six months, Charlotte and Joseph enjoyed the Gulf in relative quiet. They sailed and fished with mixed results. Drenched by the spray while sailing into the wind one afternoon, the next morning they found "the fish were biting almost as fast as we could bait our lines and throw them into the water." Charlotte caught nearly two-dozen before breakfast, but, Joseph told Lizzie in a letter, "you need not come as there are no redfish or sheepshead, or trout, nothing to be caught but cats and croakers, and I know you are too fastidious in your *piscal* taste to delight in such sport."

After Lizzie passed her exams in June, they returned to St. Louis for the summer. In December Joseph accompanied them back to Mobile for the winter. He stayed a few days and then headed east to purchase stock for the coming spring, reporting his observations and encounters to Charlotte and Lizzie along the way. He stopped first in Montgomery, the capital of Alabama, and sat in the Senate chamber which he found impressive: It "was beautifully adorned with curtains, and furnished with rosewood desks and rosewood and damask velvet cushioned chairs; everything having the air of majesty – the majesty of the sovereign people." Outside the luxurious edifice, he encountered "the real democracy" traveling by coach over rough roads and eating "the roughest kind of fare."

Along the way, Joseph found himself in the company of Major General John Quitman and his family who were going to Augusta, Georgia, "to receive the congratulations of the citizens." Quitman had served under General Taylor at the battle of Monterey and under General Winfield Scott during the invasion of Mexico City where he had recently led a brigade in the assault on the castle of Chapultepec, which fell into American hands in September 1847. In his letter to Lizzie, her father confided that, "The General, accustomed to command, could not well put up with the little deference paid him by his fellow-travelers, and was much annoyed that they were not restrained until he and his family were provided for." Quitman received better treatment from the citizens of Mississippi who elected him their governor two years later.

Passing through Georgia, Joseph arrived in Charleston, South Carolina, which he found "a very beautiful and pleasant city" with wide streets and a fine market place. He saw the Citadel, "an old-fashioned fort, now used as a military school." The city appeared business-like, but also a bit stuffy. South Carolina "*is*, or claims to be," he wrote to Charlotte and Lizzie, "the most chivalrous State in the Union." Unimpressed with the chivalry, he was happy to board his ship.

Reaching New York in January, he went to see one of the great sensations of the day – Hiram Power's Greek Slave. Out of pure white marble, Powers had carved a life-sized statue of a young woman standing nude. Her hands manacled, she looks away from her viewers. She is a Christian held captive by Turkish slavers. Joseph thought it the most beautiful thing he had ever seen. He described the work to Charlotte and Lizzie: "It is a perfect model of the human form, and as you gaze at it you perceive new beauties every moment. The face, the neck, the arms, and hands, in fact every limb, and every muscle, are perfect; and the marble seems to have that softness and delicacy which we see in a young and beautiful girl." Joseph was not alone in his assessment. Except for the few who felt the statue was immodest and perhaps immoral, common opinion judged the Greek Slave a work of great art. No one seemed to have taken it as a condemnation of slavery in America.

Joseph's letters were also filled with good advice, encouraging Lizzie to remain diligent in her studies. Above all, he urged her to seriously consider her religious responsibilities:

> Do you ever think on the subject of your soul's salvation? – of its value – of the importance of giving the subject that attention its magnitude demands, in the morning of life, when the feelings and emotions of the heart are warm and generous – before the temper and disposition are soured by disappointment? It was for this reason our blessed Savior desired the young to come unto Him. My dear daughter, you cannot tell how happy your mother and I would be to know that you had consecrated yourself, heart, soul, and body, to the Lord, to serve Him faithfully in this world, that you might be permitted to enjoy Him in mansions of peace in that which is to come. This is the tenor of our morning and evening prayers, and, we trust, of yours also.

"How delighted would I be," he continued, "could I see dear daughter a bright Christian, devoting all her powers and energies

42

to the service of the blessed Savior!" He felt that it was much more important to shine in Heaven than be a star on earth.

As Charlotte noted, "the darling of our hearts was fast blooming into womanhood" and she and Joseph wanted her to be prepared for the future. Like many parents then and now, they found it difficult to strike a balance between liberality and rigidity. The problem was not unlike the one they faced regarding alcohol. They served wine at home, in moderation, even though many of their fellow Presbyterians practiced abstinence. At Madame De Fellon's academy, Lizzie had pressed to take dancing lessons. At first they resisted, worried that dancing might lead to "the theatre and the ball-room," but then relented. Madame assured them that the lessons would be offered not in the evening but in the afternoon. The girls would be supervised and confined to the right social circle. Joseph and Charlotte convinced themselves that dancing was good exercise; it was natural that Lizzie should want to do it; and continued "opposition might be attended with a still stronger desire for the forbidden thing." Even so, they wanted Lizzie to finish her education at a more serious and refined school. They enrolled her in Mrs. Gardell's at Philadelphia for the following fall. Charlotte had heard that Mrs. Gardell enjoyed "the highest reputation as an instructress of young ladies, being untiring in her efforts to cultivate their hearts, no less than their minds and manners."

In April 1848 Charlotte and Lizzie left the balmy South with their health and spirits improved. When they arrived in St. Louis, however, they discovered that another bout of cholera had broken out. Like the one in 1832-3, the epidemic of 1848-9 killed roughly one in every fifteen of the population. Without thinking too long about it, mother and daughter re-packed their bags and headed for Newport, Rhode Island. Always a sheltered seaport with a benign climate, Newport in the decades before the Civil War grew into an attractive retreat for wealthy Americans seeking an escape from summer's heat. Charlotte and Lizzie fit in easily with the vacationing crowd while Lizzie waited to begin school in Philadelphia where she intended to study until she turned seventeen in two years time. The plan, however, was cut short when cholera suddenly appeared in Philadelphia in the spring of 1849 at which point Lizzie returned home to complete her education with private tutors.

It was a bustling city when mother and daughter arrived. St. Louis in 1849 was a launching site for the biggest surge in Western Fever. The discovery of gold in California precipitated a huge migration of Americans from the eastern part of the United States to the West Coast. Several hundred thousand men, women and children boarded ships or traveled overland across the continent. Many of the land travelers passed through St. Louis and up the Missouri River to follow one of many trails that ran westward. A year later California became the nation's thirty-first state, and under the terms of the Compromise of 1850 entered the union as a free state.

10

In the fall of 1852 cholera resurfaced in St. Louis yet again and claimed the life of Aunt Rachel. Rachel was not a relative, but a poor woman whom Charlotte had met almost twenty years earlier. Like Charlotte's father-in-law, Rachel had emigrated from Ireland after her parents died in the late 18th century. She had lived for a while with her brother and his wife in Illinois, but, failing to get along with her sister-in-law, had traveled, mainly on foot, to St. Louis in search of employment and a better life. Lizzie was about one year old when Rachel appeared at Charlotte's door asking for work and a home for the winter.

Rachel had worn a dark blue cloth cloak with a hood attached and a plain straw bonnet tied under her chin. Her pale blue eyes, fair skin, gentle manner, and plaintive look melted Charlotte's heart: "I saw she had seen better days, and was indeed a lonely wanderer." Charlotte guessed that she was about sixty years old. Rachel stayed the winter and helped in the house doing various chores.

In the spring Charlotte, who really didn't need her services, recommended her to some of her friends. Rachel moved on, but she and Charlotte kept in touch with one another over the years. Eventually her health deteriorated. Without resources, she moved into the poor farm, which Charlotte described as "a charity place for the 'rabble,' black and white, drunkards and swearers, and Sabbath breakers." Occasionally, Charlotte and Joseph rode out to the farm to visit and bring her some small gift of food or clothing. The superintendent of the farm called on Charlotte one day in the early fall of 1852 to tell her that Rachel had died. Charlotte was about to leave the house to pay her respects when Joseph stopped her. He didn't want her to catch the disease that had nearly killed her twenty years before. Charlotte instead sent a shawl and cap to provide "a 'semblance' of decency to the wasted form of poor old Aunt Rachel."

On the Sunday after the funeral Charlotte talked to Joseph about establishing a home for indigent but respectable women. She had in mind asking the local bank of Page and Bacon to donate a lot near Lafayette Park to construct a building. Joseph suggested that asking for cash made a better plan. He offered to provide the first donation of $500 if she would undertake the solicitations. On Monday morning she went to the bank to present her idea to Mr. Bacon, the younger of the two partners. He rose to the occasion, pledging to give $1000 if she could match the amount with another ten subscriptions of $1000. Very quickly, Charlotte raised $20,000 for the project.

Charlotte Taylor Blow Charless
Portrait donated to the Home of the Friendless by her
great-grandson, David Charless Crockett, in 1953
(Courtesy of the Bethesda Health Group)

During her fund raising drive Charlotte learned that there was a property for sale that seemed ideal for her purposes. Located four miles south of the center of St. Louis in the suburb of Carondelet, it consisted of a handsome two-story building standing on seven acres of ground. It was originally a boarding school, but the school had failed after a year. The owners set a price of $18,500. With the help of family and friends, Charlotte successfully solicited the County Court of St. Louis to underwrite a bond issue for an additional $20,000. Within a year she had collected $40,000 to buy the property and provide operating funds.

The Home of the Friendless
(Courtesy of the Bethesda Health Group)

The General Assembly of the State of Missouri officially incorporated the home in February 1853. Its stated purpose was to "establish in the City of St. Louis a charitable institution, to be called 'The Home of the Friendless'" with the object of providing a refuge for "destitute and suffering females." The act of incorporation stated that the oversight and management of the home would reside in a Board of Trustees composed solely of women. It thus became the first retirement institution in the nation for women, staffed by women, and governed exclusively by women. Charlotte invited her sister-in-law Minerva Blow to serve as first vice president of the Home and as a board member, a position she held until her death in 1875. To honor Charlotte, the Board in 1977 changed the name to The Charless Home. The institution celebrated its 150th anniversary in 2003.

While Charlotte worked to create the Home, Dr. Potts engaged Joseph's interest in the formation of a college to prepare students to serve the Presbyterian faith. In 1834, shortly after Joseph and Charlotte joined the First church, Potts had left his pastorate to become the president of Marion College. When the college failed for lack of funds, Potts returned to St. Louis to form the Second church, but kept alive his desire to create a college for serious Presbyterian students. After much effort involving many individuals and the three synods of the Church in Missouri, Westminster College received its charter from the Missouri legislature exactly twenty days after The Home of the Friendless received its approval. For his role, Joseph was appointed one of eighteen trustees. When the college, located in Fulton about twenty miles from St. Louis, published its inaugural catalogue, Joseph's name appeared as the first trustee.

Unfortunately, Dr. Potts died just before the college received its charter. In recognition of his importance in the school's creation, the trustees of Westminster named its first professorship in his honor, the Potts Professorship. A century later, in 1946, Winston Churchill made the college famous. After leading England to victory during the Second World War, Churchill lost his position as his country's prime minister, though not his powerful voice. As a long time critic of Communism and the Soviet Union in particular, Churchill warned the world (and his audience at Westminster College) of Russian hegemony in Eastern Europe. In a graphic image, he described the descent of an impenetrable and permanent Iron Curtain separating Eastern from Western Europe.

11

A few months after Aunt Rachel and Dr. Potts died, Charlotte decided to spend another winter in the South. She, Joseph and Lizzie headed for Bailey Springs near Florence with the intention of making a circuit through Charleston, Mobile and New Orleans before returning home. When they reached the Springs, old friends from Florence suggested that they stay the winter. In the early 1840s visitors to the area had discovered that water from the Springs possessed beneficial health effects, and perhaps for this reason the family decided to accept the advice. Joseph rented several log cabins and telegraphed St. Louis for their servants, carriages and horses. Their friends provided a carpet to keep the wind from penetrating the chinks in their cabin, dog-irons to hold logs in the fireplace, a Dutch oven for cooking, and "many rare sweetmeats from their own choice kitchens." Charlotte also re-connected with her nephew, the son of her sister Mary Ann who had married her sweetheart from Virginia and died in Huntsville twenty-five years earlier. Young Mr. Key did what his grandfather Peter Blow was unable to do: he became a successful cotton planter near Florence, who once a week sent his aunt and uncle a pack horse laden with mutton, butter and other good things to eat.

Cut off from society in what she called "a wild country," Charlotte imagined that most people would find the isolation unendurable, "especially men possessing the active and stirring habits of a city life, and young ladies accustomed to a large circle of congenial friends." But Joseph and Lizzie found their circumstances invigorating. Most days, the two went hunting together while Charlotte remained at the cabins, looking forward to their return and hearing the stories of their adventures. She was rarely disappointed:

> From the appearance of both father and daughter,
> you would think they had been rambling over hill

and dale, scrambling through briars and wading creeks, without design, for the game that they sought was rarely found, or if found, lost again, before the inexperienced huntsman could level his gun. But who cared for that when they had so much pleasure and sport notwithstanding, and always such glorious anticipations for the morrow.

Sometimes they paddled along the creek in search of ducks. On one occasion when several suddenly flew overhead, Lizzie, forgetting she was in a canoe, stood up, lost her balance and fell broadside into the creek. Returning earlier than expected, Joseph told Charlotte that they had had enough *ducking* for the day.

In the evening or during the day when the weather was bad, Joseph read aloud, while Charlotte and Lizzie knitted or sewed. Sometimes Lizzie played her guitar and sang some pretty Irish airs that her father liked or some "deep-toned German song" that her mother preferred. More than once Lizzie remarked, "Mother, I did not know before that my father was such a delightful man; we really *need* no other society." They remained at Bailey Springs for three months – "happy months, never to be forgotten" – before returning to St. Louis.

As much as Lizzie enjoyed her winter in Bailey Springs alone with her parents, she had in fact visions of a different society. At some point in her travels, Lizzie met the man she would marry. They may have met in New Orleans where the family spent a few weeks during the winter, or at Belmont landing, a regular station for steamboats on the Mississippi River. Belmont was the name of a sugar plantation owned by Louis Le Bourgeois. Wherever they met, it is easy to imagine how charmed Louis was when first introduced to the pretty, lively Anglo girl from St. Louis who spoke excellent French. Louis himself was charming. He was also wealthy, educated in the classics, open-minded and exceedingly kind. Charlotte and Joseph found Louis perfectly acceptable as a son-in-law, except for one reservation. It was not a problem that Louis was a major slaveholder, even as they continued to support

Dred Scott's plea for freedom through the court system, but they were concerned that Louis was Roman Catholic.

Six months after their winter in Bailey Springs, Joseph took an extended business trip. In a letter written in the late summer 1853, he spoke his mind:

> I hope and pray that daughter will seriously bring her mind to the consideration of this most momentous subject. Oh, that she would remember how good and kind and merciful God has always been to her, and how strong is the obligation she is under to consecrate herself, with all her energies, to God's service. How happy would we be, could we be permitted to meet her at the table of our Lord, as an humble follower of the blessed Savior, to feel that her peace is made with God, and that her calling and her election is sure. Nothing which this earth offers could confer so great happiness upon her parents. And will she not now try to find the Savior, who is always found of them that seek Him earnestly and faithfully? Let us, dear wife, pray more earnestly, that our kind heavenly father would add this, our greatest mercy and blessing, to the innumerable ones that have followed us all the days of our lives.

Lizzie would reach her twenty-first birthday in November and Joseph and Charlotte wanted very much for her to be baptized. Lizzie consented, and on the first Sunday in February 1854 Joseph accompanied Lizzie to the pulpit of the Second Presbyterian Church to dedicate herself to the service of the Lord. The circumstances suggest that her accepting baptism was a precondition of her parents' consent to her marrying a Catholic. Also, perhaps to protect Lizzie's real estate holdings in Missouri that she had largely inherited from her grandfather Charless, Louis and Lizzie signed a pre-nuptial agreement separating their respective estates. Eighteen days after her baptism, Joseph walked Lizzie down the aisle of the same church to give her hand in marriage.

Elizabeth "Lizzie" Charless Le Bourgeois

12

After the wedding Lizzie and Louis traveled back down the Mississippi River to Louisiana where the Le Bourgeois family had lived since the end of the 18ᵗʰ century. Louis's grandfather Pierre had emigrated from the town of Caen in Normandy. Arriving in Philadelphia in 1772, he ignored the momentous events of American independence and moved to New Orleans in 1776. Subsequently, Pierre's son Louis married a wealthy widow, Erasie Haydel Becnel, and had two boys and a girl. After Louis died, Erasie gave each son a large sugar-producing plantation on the east bank of the river between Baton Rouge and New Orleans. Louis, the elder, received the family house and land at Belmont (the name inspired by Indian mounds on the property), while his brother Joseph became the owner of Mount Airy a few miles away. The name of neither place reflected the fact that there was no natural high ground anywhere in the area.

Charlotte and Joseph of course were sorry to have Lizzie live so far away, and made arrangements to visit as often as possible. Charlotte reckoned that, living among strangers, isolated in the countryside with major barriers in the way of social intercourse, Lizzie needed her company as much as possible. Both Joseph and Louis conceded to a pattern whereby Charlotte would spend much of the winter at Belmont and Lizzie would pass the summer months in St. Louis. The men would visit as often as their work allowed.

The arrangement bothered Joseph more than the others. In one of his letters he told Charlotte, "You ask me, in your last, how I am getting on, I must be honest and say, *bad enough*." He added that, "If I were not tied hand and foot I would cut loose from these cold regions and lonely habitations, and fly away to my 'ain wifey, and my ain bairns' in the sunny south." The most remarkable aspect of Charlotte's long visits at Belmont was her relationship with Erasie. Neither spoke the other's language. Erasie was Catholic, and Charlotte Presbyterian and almost thirty years younger. Other than the marriage of their children, they had little in common. Neither was rude to the other, but they made no real effort to communicate. Each took her morning walk around the second floor balcony that surrounded the house, one moving in one direction and the other going the opposite way. It is easy to understand why Charlotte (as well as Joseph) preferred having Lizzie in St. Louis as opposed to Belmont.

During the second summer after her marriage — two years before the Supreme Court rendered its decision against Dred Scott — Lizzie helped her dressmaker in St. Louis buy her freedom from slavery. Lizzie Keckley, like Scott, had been born in Virginia. Her owner Hugh Garland had taken her to St. Louis, where she provided the primary source of income for his family of seventeen members through her exquisite design and needlework. On several occasions, Lizzie Keckley asked Garland to allow her to buy her freedom. Garland, who was John Sanford's lawyer in the Dred Scott case, always refused. When the lawyer died in early 1855, Lizzie pressed the question with his widow who set a price of $1200. Lizzie's plan, to which Mrs. Garland agreed, was to go to New York to raise the money, provided that Lizzie obtained guarantees for her return from six reputable businessmen in St. Louis. Getting five, but failing to persuade the sixth, Lizzie fell into despair. In her memoir, she recorded what happened next:

> The first paroxysm of grief was scarcely over, when a carriage stopped in front of the house; Mrs. Le Bourgeois, one of my kind patrons, got out of it and entered the door. She seemed to bring sunshine with her handsome cheery face. She came to where I was, and in her sweet way said:

> "Lizzie, I hear that you are going to New York to beg for money to buy your freedom. I have been thinking over the matter, and told Ma [Charlotte] it would be a shame to allow you to go North to *beg*

for what we should *give* you. You have many friends in St. Louis, and I am going to raise the twelve hundred dollars required among them. I have two hundred dollars put away for a present; am indebted to you one hundred dollars; mother owes you fifty dollars, and will add another fifty to it; and as I do not want the present, I will make the money a present to you. Don't start for New York now until I see what I can do among your friends."

Like a ray of sunshine she came, and like a ray of sunshine she went away. The flowers no longer were withered, drooping. Again they seemed to bud and grow in fragrance and beauty. Mrs. Le Bourgeois, God bless her dear good heart, was more than successful. The twelve hundred dollars were raised, and at last my son and myself were free. Free, free! What a glorious ring to the word. (Keckley, 54-55.)

Lizzie Keckley

The two Lizzies had a lot to be happy about. Lizzie Le Bourgeois was about to deliver her first child, and Lizzie Keckley was about to be delivered from slavery. The baby was born in St. Louis at the end of October 1855 and the dressmaker's emancipation was certified at court three weeks later. Once free, Lizzie Keckley continued to work in St. Louis and repaid Lizzie and the other patrons the twelve hundred dollars, which she had accepted as a loan, not as a gift. She then returned to the East where she made dresses for Mrs. Jefferson Davis. When the Civil War broke out and Davis and his wife moved to Richmond, Virginia, to become the first family of the new Confederate States of America, Lizzie Keckley went to work at the White House for the First Lady, Mary Todd Lincoln. Mrs. Lincoln soon realized that her dressmaker could give good counsel as well as make fine gowns. After the President was murdered, Lizzie remained with Mrs. Lincoln, becoming her confidante and best friend.

The naming of Lizzie Le Bourgeois' first child caused a touch of discord in the family. Erasie wanted him to be called Louis to honor both her son and husband; Lizzie preferred to give him her father's name. Lizzie held her ground. The boy was christened Joseph Charless Le Bourgeois. When she gave birth to her second child in May a year and a half later, she named him Louis. Erasie was so pleased that she made up her mind to go to St. Louis to see her *petit-fils*. The night before Louis was to take his mother up river on the steamboat, Lizzie dreamed that Erasie had become agitated and died. The next day Louis sent Lizzie a telegram saying: "*Maman est morte, a trois heures, priez pour moi* [Mother died at three in the morning, pray for me.]" Later in St. Louis, when Louis told Lizzie the details of his mother's last hours, the circumstances he described accorded precisely with the images and words in Lizzie's dream. (Chapin, 7.)

A few months after the birth of his first grandchild, Joseph Charless was elected President of the Bank of Missouri. Back in 1816 when James Madison was the President of the United States, the federal government provided a charter to establish a central bank (for the second time) to operate for twenty years. When the charter came up for renewal in Congress in 1836, Andrew Jackson, in the last year of his second term in office, vetoed the bill, an action that precipitated the financial panic of 1837 and the subsequent deep recession. The abolition of the Second Bank prompted state governments to organize their own central banks, the financial strength of which depended very much on the state's oversight and the quality of each bank's managers. The Bank of Missouri proved to be one of the soundest state banks between 1836 and 1863 when they existed, issuing a stable currency that was recognized and valued throughout the Midwest and deemed by some "as good as gold."

When he was elected President of the Bank of Missouri, a newspaper account described Joseph as a man of financial ability, successful in his own business, possessing a high level of social skill, and perhaps most importantly a man who "even in moneyed panics (the worst of all panics) would probably be as calm as a summer morning." When his two-year term expired, Joseph expected to focus once again on his own business, but three new commercial banks had formed in St. Louis, and one, the Mechanics' Bank, was determined to have Joseph for its president. "He *refused positively*," Charlotte wrote, but the bank directors persisted. Joseph gave in, agreeing to allow the bank to use his image and signature on its currency but to serve for only a short period of time. Indeed, it proved to be a short period of time, but not for the reasons that anyone expected.

Mechanics Bank note signed by Joseph Charless, June 1, 1859

13

The summer months were the best part of the year for the family. Lizzie and the boys – Joseph, Louis and then Edward – would travel to St. Louis to spend the months from June to December. It was a gala time when "Grandpa would in his excess of joy forget the lonely winters."

Charlotte and Joseph accompanied Lizzie and the boys back to Louisiana where they stayed two weeks in December 1858. Charlotte decided to return to St. Louis rather than remaining at Belmont as she had been doing. When Lizzie was still a child she and Joseph had imagined "ourselves in a green old age" surrounded by "our bairn and bairn's bairns," but she saw that reality presented something different. She and Joseph now planned to spend the winters in St. Louis by themselves, apart from Lizzie.

Charlotte Blow Charless
by William F. Cogswell, 1860

Joseph Charless, Jr.
by William F. Cogswell, 1859

The spring of 1859 arrived early in St. Louis, bringing Lizzie and her boys back a little sooner than usual. Louis accompanied his family and remained in town for a few weeks. During the winter Joseph had commissioned William F. Cogswell to paint him and Charlotte so that Lizzie could hang their pictures at Belmont. Cogswell, self-taught but capable, traveled the country and happened to be in St. Louis for a time. The most famous of his many portraits are those of President Lincoln, which hangs in the White House, and President Grant, which is displayed in the United States Senate. Lizzie thought Cogswell's portrait of her father was "faultless." Seeing it for the first time, she cried.

On the morning of the first Friday in June, Joseph rose early and drove out as he often did to his garden. There he gathered some flowers to make a bouquet for Lizzie. When Charlotte came down for breakfast Joseph was sitting at the window. He had laid aside the morning paper and was watching his "sonny boys" romp in the grass outside. Charlotte saw and admired the little bouquet for Lizzie at her place at the breakfast table. He had gathered his first fuchsia of the spring for his flower arrangement.

At morning worship, their eldest grandchild, who was always known as Charless rather than Joseph, sat opposite his grandfather. Little Charless watched intently as Joseph read several passages from the Bible, including Psalm CXIII in praise of the Lord. Afterwards, with "his countenance full of his usual look of benevolence and love," Joseph asked, "What's the order of the day?" His plan was to see first whether Dr. Benjamin Palmer and his wife had arrived by boat. Palmer was the pastor of the First Presbyterian Church of New Orleans, and would a year later give a stirring sermon in favor of slavery and Louisiana's secession from the Union. The Palmers were returning from a meeting of the General Assembly of the Presbyterian Church, and Joseph and Charlotte had invited them to stay at their house before returning home to New Orleans.

About ten minutes after Joseph left to search for his guests, the doorbell rang. A young man visibly shaken stood in the front hall and in a trembling voice announced "Mr. Charless is badly hurt on Market Street." Charlotte immediately ran out of the house, hoping that he was not seriously injured. A crowd had already gathered when Charlotte arrived. There Charlotte found him in a small store that sold lace and trimmings "pale and sweet" lying on the floor. "Like an angel he looked to me. I did not lose my senses, and I was so impressed with the sanctity of the spot that it seems to me I dropped, but dropped very softly beside him." She heard a voice that seemed to come from God telling her to be still. "And I *was still*." Joseph's shirt and coat were dark with blood. It wasn't until she heard the question asked: "Who did this to you, Mr. Charless," that she realized someone had tried to kill him.

After the doctors arrived, Joseph was carried home. He knew he was dying and so did Charlotte. Joseph told Louis that now he would have to look after Charlotte as well as Lizzie and the boys. Bleeding slowly, Joseph took nearly twenty-four hours to die. Most of the time he was in intense pain, but his groans were infrequent. The Reverend Samuel McPheeters, the pastor of the Second Presbyterian Church, quietly asked, "Mr. Charless, you know something now about the sufferings of Jesus." He replied in a faint voice, "Yes, I have been thinking about that, while lying here." Facing death, Joseph looked to Jesus: "He is my all. He is very precious to my soul." He looked for salvation, felt repentance, and offered forgiveness. Colonel Thornton Grimsley, whose daughter Minerva had married Charlotte's brother Henry, was at Joseph's bedside. A forceful and respected figure who had made his fortune in the saddle-making business, Grimsley suggested lynching the bastard. Joseph looked at him and said "No, Colonel, no! I forgive my murderer; from the bottom of my heart, I forgive him."

During his final moments, he placed his hand on Lizzie's head and called her "my *precious daughter*." Over and over he looked at Charlotte and murmured, "*My poor wife*." He knew that Charlotte would be desolate without him. Towards the end, he wondered, "Will my heart strings never break?" Just before he died, he whispered to Charlotte, "I – love –– you." His last words were, "*I am satisfied*."

14

Tensions in Missouri ran high on the eve of the Civil War. The Supreme Court's recent decision in the case of *Dred Scott versus John Sandford* [sic] exacerbated the already sharp divide between free state and slave state partisans. It was no secret that Joseph Charless, one of St. Louis's most prominent and well-respected citizens, had been for a long time a quiet supporter of Dred Scott's cause. He might well have been a target for assassination. But, that was not the case.

Joseph F. Thornton had walked up to Joseph Charless on Market Street about mid morning on Friday. Thornton confronted him, and said, "You are the son of a bitch that swore against my character." He then drew a pistol from his coat and fired into Joseph's side. When he tried to get up, Thornton fired a second shot. The bullet passed through the front of his chest and out the back. "Having thus consummated his murderous purpose," according to the dispatch from St. Louis to *The New York Times*, "the assassin coolly replaced the revolver in his pocket and began deliberately to resume his morning stroll!"

Five years earlier, a thief had robbed the safe of the Boatman's Savings Institution of nearly $20,000 in cash and gold. Thornton, the bank's bookkeeper, was the prime suspect. He had access to the key to the safe where each night he deposited the bank's records; it was the same safe that held the key to the money safe. Since there was no direct evidence against him, the bank officials waited some time before deciding to encourage and accept his resignation. Thornton began to make regular deposits of between $100 and $400, which over time totaled almost $20,000, in the State Bank of Missouri during the period when Joseph was the president. In January 1857, three years after the robbery, a grand jury indicted Thornton for the crime.

When Thornton's case came to trial in May 1858, Joseph was called on to testify. He told the jury that each of Thornton's deposits contained one soiled and worn bill looking as if it had been buried in the earth. All of the deposits were accepted at the bank, but on one occasion Thornton "presented a bunch of bills very much stained, very dirty, and stuck together so that some could not be separated." When asked, Thornton told Joseph that he had gotten the bills "from a boatman who had accidentally found them under the stump of a tree" when trying to fasten a cable. Joseph called that a "very unlikely story" and declined to accept the money. He told Thornton that, if the story were true, he should advertise the discovery of what was obviously lost so that the loser could reclaim what was his.

The jury returned a verdict of not guilty. All the evidence was circumstantial and Thornton found enough witnesses to testify to his good character. Whether Thornton was in fact the bank robber or not, he allowed his anger at Joseph for his testimony to fester until it boiled over and led him to commit a capital crime. On Market Street there was a large number of witnesses to the murder; many were Joseph's friends. Several men grabbed Thornton, wrested the pistol from his coat pocket and marched him to the police station.

Very quickly a crowd gathered at the crime scene. People became extremely agitated when it became clear that someone had tried to kill one of the city's most admired citizens. Disbelief was soon followed by wrath. About eleven in the morning, a mass of men ran toward the police station intent on lynching the gunman. Policemen quickly shut the doors to the courthouse and the jail. The crowd began to chant for Thornton to be brought out. A few cooler heads asked for calm, but the crowd refused to disperse. A little after noon, Joseph's brother-in-law Charles Drake, mounted a wagon to make a plea.

Drake, a respected lawyer who had represented Dred Scott and who two months later would be elected to the Missouri House of Representatives, told his audience that he was with Joseph when he received word that there was a large number of people who wanted to take justice into their own hands and commit further violence against the law. He said that as Joseph's brother-in-law and one who had known him for a quarter of a century, he felt it was his duty to come forward "to say to you, as friends, as neighbors, that no course could be pursued more terrible to the family of Mr. Charless – more in violence to their feelings, than for you to visit upon this unfortunate criminal the merit of his crimes. I simply wish to say here, as a near family relative of our fellow-citizen Joseph Charless, that nothing could be more unpleasant, that would distress them more, than that there should be added to this other calamity the terrible consequence of Lynch law." (*New York Times*, 8 June 1859.)

Drake mollified the crowd to some extent, but Michael Cerre, the Sheriff, thought an attack on the jail highly likely. He asked Colonel Pritchard to call out the Missouri militia. At four in the afternoon a sufficient number of troops were mustered to provide Thornton protection through the night. In the morning when it was learned that Joseph had died, the mood of the city shifted from rage to melancholy as one of its great men had passed away.

On the day of the funeral the seats, galleries and vestibules of the Second Presbyterian Church were filled as people arrived to hear Dr. McPheeters' eulogy. An immense crowd also gathered on the sidewalk in front of the Charless residence and across the street. "An expression of deep solemnity pervaded the faces of all," the newspaper reported, "and we could not gaze on the scene without reading in every detail of the ceremony, as well as in the sadness of every countenance, the fact that the community had been bereaved of one of its most beloved members."

"At the time of his death," reported *The New York Times*, "he was at the head of the firm of Charless, Blow & Co., in the drug business. He was closely connected with works of general and municipal importance, had been a member of the Board of Aldermen, Director in the Public Schools, President of the Bank of the State of Missouri, President of the Mechanics' Bank, of [St. Louis], and one of the directors of the Pacific Railroad." In addition, Joseph was a Ruling Elder in the Presbyterian Church, the first patron of Charlotte's Home of the Friendless, and a vital and liberal member of the board of trustees of Westminster College.

A short time before he was shot, Joseph, while walking home from church with Lizzie, talked about the importance of the mission of Westminster College. From the beginning, he had helped to set up scholarship funds for needy students. The school also hoped to establish additional fully funded professorships. Two years earlier, while soliciting support in the South, the college president, Dr. Laws, had written to Louis about endowing a Charless Professorship. Louis responded with a check for $200, which was good but far short of the amount of money required. Acutely distressed by her father's murder and greatly affected by his devotion to the college, Lizzie immediately pledged a gift of $20,000 to fund The Charless Professorship of Physical Sciences at Westminster College. It was an enormous amount of money, but it was only slightly less than the value of the life insurance policy that her father carried.

As for Thornton, despite concerns voiced by the crowd that the governor would pardon him or a jury would free him, he was tried, found guilty of murder and condemned to death by hanging. On 12 November 1859, having shown no remorse whatsoever, he was blindfolded and brought to the scaffold where the hangman placed a stout rope around his neck. He might have fared better had he been lynched, for his death was hard:

> At three o'clock and fourteen minutes, the spring was touched, the door fell heavily against the posts supporting the scaffold, and Thornton descended five feet with a sudden plunge, which broke his neck. For nearly three minutes his body underwent convulsions and contortions horrible to look upon, in which one of his hands clutched the platform by which he seemed to raise himself up a moment and then drop. Every muscle in his body quivered with tremor, and occasionally the limbs would writhe as though stirred with the most tumultuous agitation.

These spasms occurred at intervals of thirty or forty
seconds, became less and less until twenty minutes
after three, when they ceased altogether.
(*Alexandria* (Va.) *Gazette*, 17 November 1859.)

There was no public mourning for Joseph Thornton, but his
family must have been sorely grieved. His brother John, a
reputable businessman himself, owned and operated the largest
livery stable in the city, located two blocks from the Charless
house. In 1873 his livery stable caught fire and burned to the
ground; fortunately none of the horses were killed. John Thornton
died five years later.

15

Charlotte was devastated by her husband's death. After his burial in Bellefontaine Cemetery, she returned with Lizzie and her family to Belmont. There, she began a memoir of Joseph in the form of a series of letters to their grandchildren. It distressed her to think that Lizzie's children were now and forever cut off from their wonderful grandfather. She worried deeply that, knowing little about his life, their grandchildren would remember only how he died. The violence of his death would overshadow the good work that he had done. Worse yet, the children might wonder whether he was such a good man if someone had chosen to kill him. Her memoir, written in a clear hand and plain language, was part eulogy and part history. It also served as good therapy.

She finished the first letter in January 1860, the fourteenth and penultimate letter in March 1861, and then stopped as several events intervened. When Lizzie gave birth to her fourth child and first daughter, she named the infant for her mother: Charlotte Blow Le Bourgeois, but the poor baby died seven months later in March 1861, the only one of her children who failed to reach adulthood. In April the Civil War broke out when Southern troops fired on Union soldiers at Fort Sumter in South Carolina. In May Dorothea Dix offered her services to the U. S. War Department to organize a corps of nurses to care for wounded soldiers.

An advocate for better treatment for the indigent insane, Dix had persuaded the state of North Carolina to build a mental hospital, which, when opened in Raleigh in 1856, was named in her honor. As soon as she heard that the Lincoln government had appointed Miss Dix Superintendent of Union Army Nurses, Charlotte decided to offer her services to the Confederate government in Richmond. In June 1861, the *Raleigh Register* reported that, as Miss Dix "has tendered her services to the United States," Mrs. Charless "wishes to do as much for the South."

On the eve of the Civil War the state of Missouri was deeply split in its allegiances – like the Blow family. In contrast to their brother Henry, Charlotte and her youngest brothers Taylor and William sympathized with the Confederacy. Taylor and William, who continued to own and run the Charless, Blow drug company, supplied quinine and other medicines to the Confederate forces once fighting began. It is possible that they sent some of these shipments to Belmont where Charlotte directed them to the field hospitals where they were needed. Whether Charlotte served as a conduit for medical supplies, she experienced the horrible consequences of the conflict. When she resumed writing to her grandchildren, she began the fifteenth and final letter in this way:

> It has been nearly two years since I last wrote to you, since which time, war has desolated our once prosperous and happy country, and drenched its soil with the blood of her sons. All has been excitement and turmoil. Many widows and orphans have been made – and the wail of anguish has been poured into the ear of the God of Sabbath. But I turn from the revolting facts which belong to the history of the nation – to consider the last sad hours of your revered grandfather, and to copy for your instruction and admonition his dying words.

She finished the memoir in December, dating it Christmas Eve, 1862.

By then Lizzie had given birth to another, more robust baby girl, whom she named Adèle. Subsequently she produced three more children, two boys, William and George, and another daughter, Elizabeth. Elizabeth was seventeen years younger than her eldest brother and six years younger than the next youngest. When Charlotte had her memoir of Joseph privately printed in St. Louis in 1869, she made copies for each grandchild. On the cover, which was bound in black leather, was the child's name embossed in gold, except for Elizabeth, who was born after publication.

When she returned to Belmont in the summer of 1859, Charlotte became the senior woman of the household as Erasie had died two years earlier. During the war when Union gunboats proceeded down the Mississippi River destroying Rebel property left and right, a party of soldiers disembarked at Belmont. An officer came to the house asking for Lizzie. He wanted to know where Louis was. Standing on the balcony holding baby Adèle in her arms, Lizzie told him the truth. She didn't know where he was, because Louis purposely had not told her. The officer returned to his boat, but was soon back again. "Unless Mr. Le Bourgeois gives himself up immediately," he shouted, "or you tell me where he is, we will give the women and children an hour to leave the house after which we will fire on the house." The houses on either side of Belmont had already been shelled.

Lizzie replied bravely: "I do not know where my husband is and the women and children will not leave the house – if you fire you fire into women and children." Thwarted and out of patience, the officer shouted back, "You lie." Lizzie's black nurse, Big Lucy, was shocked. Turning to Charlotte, she said, "Mrs. Charless, don't let that man speak like that to Miss Lizzie." Before Charlotte could say a word, the officer looked up at the women arrayed on the balcony, and said, "Charless – did you say Charless?" Charlotte quietly answered, "That is my name. I am the widow of Joseph Charless and this is our child." The soldier was stunned. "Great God," he exclaimed, "I owe everything to that man – he paid for my education and I shall never forget his kindness to me. Madam, this house shall be protected." (Chapin, 10.) And so it was. The name of the Union officer remains a mystery, but it is near certain that he was a Westminster man.

Although the manor house at Belmont survived, the plantation barely did. Emancipation of blacks from slavery and the general debility of commerce and agriculture in Louisiana made life at Belmont extremely difficult in the post-war years. Fortunately, Lizzie had inherited significant wealth, mainly property in St. Louis, from her grandfather Joseph Charless Sr. A steady and substantial income from Missouri underwrote the chronic losses in sugar production in Louisiana, and provided funds for travel and education.

During the postbellum years, Charlotte continued to divide her time between her Blow relatives in St. Louis and Lizzie's family at Belmont. Her life as a widow was veiled in sorrow but remarkably active. For the most part, time passed interestingly but uneventfully for her as she watched her grandchildren grow up. Toward the end of the 1870s, however, Lizzie's health began to deteriorate. She consulted the best doctors in New York, but nothing availed. Louis, Charlotte and the children accompanied her to Newport, Rhode Island, in the summer of 1881 where she died. Her death at the age of forty-eight saddened everyone.

As she had done after her husband's death, Charlotte began to write. In a book of one hundred and twelve pages she produced a poem entitled *Jesus*. In the preface she explained that, "These verses were written by a sister of the Lord who has been made to drink the cup of sorrow to the bottom." Having lost her husband at the hands of an assassin, she experienced "another blow that severed the tenderest tie that bound her still to the earth." Charlotte now found herself a childless widow "left alone with her grief, and with JESUS."

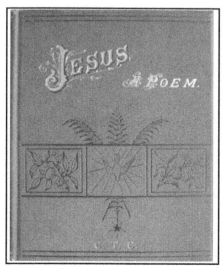

Drawing inspiration from the Song of Solomon, she chose the line "He brought me to the banqueting house, and his banner over me was love" as her theme. Dividing her poem into five parts, she testified to her love of Jesus and her faith in the Christian Church. She entitled the five sections: "Jesus, the Angel of the Covenant; The Incarnation, Life and Death of Jesus; The Resurrection and Ascension of Jesus; The Baptism of the Holy Ghost – the True Church; and The Second Coming of the Lord Jesus Christ and the Victory over Death." The book was published at Toronto and London in 1886.

Three years before Lizzie died, Charlotte had the pleasure of hosting the marriage of her grandson Charless Le Bourgeois to his cousin (and her niece) Lucretia S. Blow at her house in St. Louis. Lucretia was a daughter of Charlotte's brother Henry and his wife Minerva. Charless and Lucretia (who was known as Lutie) had four children in quick succession. Then, unexpectedly in 1885, Lutie died at the age of twenty-three, leaving behind two boys and two girls, who ranged from five to one year old. Charlotte immediately returned to Belmont to help out. At the age of seventy-five she became her great-grandchildren's mother, and stayed with them until they were old enough to go out into the world on their own. It was not a role she ever expected to play, but she performed it well. From then, she lived in Louisiana for the rest of her life.

In 1902 she attended the wedding of her great-granddaughter Elizabeth Le Bourgeois to John Richardson in New Orleans and witnessed her wear the wedding dress that Lizzie had worn when she and Louis were married forty-eight years earlier. Elizabeth also wore the pearl necklace that Joseph had given Charlotte for her wedding seventy years before.

For the fiftieth anniversary celebration of The Home of the Friendless in 1903, the Board of Trustees asked Charlotte to give an account of the institution's foundation. Writing from her home in the Garden District (on Third Street at the corner of Chestnut) she told the story of how she met and came to know and value

Aunt Rachel, the poor Irish woman who had walked from central Illinois to St. Louis.

The next year she wrote to her granddaughter Adèle to say that Saturday "will be the hundredth birthday of my beloved husband, for he was born on the 17th January 1804, which makes him six years, three months and twenty days older than his poor but loving old wife who loves him still, for he was so good, generous and kind, and withal so charming and attractive, that he made life in his family and for all around him Paradise."

Charlotte died the following year in February at the age of ninety-four, but for her Paradise had ended forty-five years before.

Charlotte Charless, ca 1900

SOCIAL LEADER BEFO' THE WAH

From the St. Louis Republic:

After ninety-five useful years Mrs. Charlotte T. Charless died Wednesday in New Orleans. She was the foremost woman of St. Louis in her day, the wife of one of the most prominent citizens, and has left behind her many works which will live in the city's history.

While still very young Charlotte T. Blow married Joseph Charless, founder of the St. Louis Republic. She was a beautiful girl and became known as one of the most beautiful women in the West. The position in society to which she attained, according to persons who remember the days before the civil war, has never been attained by any other woman.

Her husband amassed a fortune and she took place at the head of charitable movements. Her daughter, who became Mrs. Louis Le Bourgeois, was considered the most beautiful woman the city ever knew.

In 1857 her husband, then the president of the Mechanics bank, was fatally shot without warning on Market street, between Third and Fourth streets, by a man named Thornton. An hour before he died he sent a message to the mob which surged about the jail intent upon lynching his murderer, asking that the law be allowed to take its course. The mob dispersed and Thornton was executed within two months.

After her husband's tragic death Mrs. Charless moved to New Orleans, to remain until her death. Up to her ninetieth year she retained the queenly bearing which had characterized her early years, and to the last her faculties were unimpaired.

Charlotte's Obituary reported in the
Duluth, [MN] News-Tribune
February 19, 1905

ADÈLE'S STORY

Adèle Le Bourgeois Chapin

1862-1938

(All quotations in Adèle's Story, except where noted, come from Adèle Le Bourgeois Chapin's *"Their Trackless Way": A Book of Memories.*)

1

When the Union officer threatened to bombard the house in 1863, Adèle was the baby cuddled in Lizzie's arms on the balcony at Belmont. The plantation survived the war unmolested, and life went on largely unchanged. Slaves were released from servitude, but most remained to carry on their former duties in return for wages, housing and meals. Sugar cane was still grown, cut and processed. For Adèle's family, the discontinuity between antebellum and post-war was small, except for the financial losses.

Belmont Plantation

To Adèle, Belmont was paradise. Her first memory was sitting up in an old-fashioned baby carriage, with large wheels like a small buggy, near the house. From her vantage point, she surveyed a large section of the garden, whose sights and smells stirred a life-long love of flowers and shrubs. She watched the mimosa tree, with leaves like ferns, burst forth with wonderful pink puffs that smelled like peaches. In one direction ran an avenue of oaks from the house to a grove of cottonwood trees that stood along the banks of the river. There among the cottonwoods during sunset she heard the cooing of doves.

Scents were especially important to Adèle. She loved magnolias, which were abundant around the plantation, including the small and very fragrant magnolia friscata (banana magnolia shrub). On either side of the house there were three large sweet olive bushes that bloomed nearly all year long. Their fragrance on a frosty morning in the southern sunshine, as she stood between the columns of the house, was something for her to remember. Amidst a group of laurels nearby grew patches of winter sweet. Adèle would gather it in bunches to make sachets to put in her mother's chest of drawers. She was also especially fond of the yellow acacia whose odor was subtle but exquisite.

The garden was divided into twelve large beds with a set of great Cape jasmine bushes guarding the four corners of each. Among the beds Adèle admired the small Persian lilacs and the occasional white hyacinth, which always reminded her of death, for her mother told her that she had placed a bunch of the delicate white flowers in the hand of Adèle's sister Charlotte who had died as a baby the year before Adèle was born. Near the peach orchard in a remote part of the garden, La Marque roses grew on a trellis that was at least one hundred feet long. One of Adèle's secret delights was to stand behind the trellis and "watch the sunset through it when it was covered with white roses that fluttered and dropped their petals in the summer breeze."

Elsewhere there were great bushes of white myrtles covered with feathery blossoms, and a grove of sour orange trees near the pigeon house. Adèle's mother made syrup from the orange flower petals, which was delicious with ice water on hot summer days. Two great white oleander bushes stood at the front of the house; their blossoms came early in the spring and lasted but a short time. Pomegranates symbolized the beginning of summer. Adèle liked to wear a pomegranate flower in her hair. Only once did the night-blooming Ceres send forth a blossom. The children were awakened in the middle of the night to see it emerge.

Adèle, born 13 January 1862, was the middle child (not counting baby Charlotte who died when not quite one year old). "There were," she wrote in her memoir, "seven of us: Charless, the gentle-eyed peacemaker; Louis, the strong-willed, dominant person; Edward, the gallant and heroic; then I, then Will, the twinkling-eyed *raconteur*, and gentle George, and last of all a baby sister came when I was nine years old and revealed a new world to me." Until Elizabeth arrived, Adèle was absorbed in a world of boys. She did what they did, and liked it very much.

"There were times," she wrote, "of thinking we were wild Indians and of catching the horses that ran wild on the batture [the natural levee made by the river], and of riding them bare-backed, clinging to their manes while they ran with us ... till they were tired, or we were, when we would slide off." During the muddy winter weather she and her brothers made a sleigh. They hitched it to an old mule, named Polk after the general and later president, and went sleigh riding in the mud, which they found "a delightful sensation." On other occasions they had "stage-coaching times when we would get out the old family coach, lined with white brocaded satin, with a seat behind for a postilion, and we would drive four mules tandem." Adèle was happy to have a minor role as errand runner, passenger or simply looker-on. It was also great fun to sit on the fence of the back pasture and wave red rags to excite the black bull that terrorized them.

On the plantation there was a large shed where old window shutters, firewood and other odds and ends were stored. One of the children's more exciting sports involved the shed, which had a mossy roof that sloped to within five feet from the ground. Adèle and her brothers built small sleds to slide down the slippery moss on the roof to land in a big clover patch at the bottom. "The bump," Adèle confessed, "was rather severe but we scorned such things."

76

During the harvest season, carts passed the house on their way to the sugar mill, which gave Adèle and her brothers the chance to hop aboard for rides and feel the excitement of cane grinding and sugar boiling. "The smell of the hot sugar, the sound of the machinery and the songs of the Negroes at the carrier where they loaded the cane for the mill were all rare delights," she wrote. They also liked to gather pecans and swoop through the air on swings that hung from the trees. One swing hung near a tall wash-shed. The children would climb to the roof and jump off on the swing. The children called it "the Winnequah swing," named for one they had enjoyed at a summer resort on the shore of Lake Monona in Wisconsin following one of their visits to see their grandmother Charlotte in St. Louis.

On rainy days they often went to play and explore in the attic. There they found all kinds of treasures. They discovered their mother's wedding dress made of white brocade depicting trees and bridges across streams. They came across old fans, high backed shell combs, swords, Indian shawls, a Freemason's apron and other insignia, and their grandmother Erasie's rosary. In the attic a small flight of stairs led to the cupola that crowned the roof. From the cupola, they looked out over the tree tops to see the vast fields of sugar cane in the distance. They saw the almost mile-wide Mississippi River, and, in the opposite direction, a line of cypress swamps spread against the sky.

One day the children discovered an odd packet wound up in a towel yellowed with age in a cedar chest in the attic. Unwrapping the towel, they found a stained suit of old-fashioned clothes. Only much later, Adèle learned that it was the trousers, shirt and jacket that her grandfather Charless wore the day he was murdered.

When she was older she joined her brothers on hunting expeditions. She earned the privilege by making shot over the nursery fire in the evenings. She would gather bits of lead, melt them down in a shovel, and pour the liquid into molds. On their outings, with their tutor and the dogs, Adèle carried the shot and powder flasks strapped over her shoulder. She learned to load the guns and became skilled with the ramrod. Now and then she was even allowed to shoot. The advent of cartridges, which came into widespread use in Adèle's childhood, was a major revelation to her.

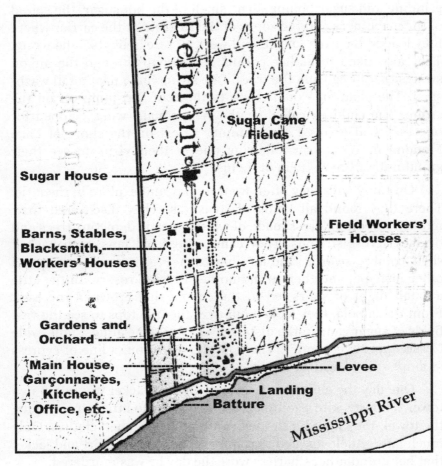

Belmont Plantation from map prepared by the Mississippi River Commission in 1882, which shows the general layout of the buildings on the plantation. The plantation fronted about three-quarters of a mile wide on the Mississippi River and was about three miles deep (extending about twice as deep as shown on this map).

For all her tomboyish activities, Adèle was bookish and open to culture. The library at Belmont held a large collection. Her parents, Lizzie and Louis, were great readers and encouraged their children to read. Louis took a particular interest in her education and introduced her to some demanding texts. Adèle read aloud to her father from the works of most of the important English and French intellectuals of the day: Charles Darwin, Thomas Huxley, Frederic Harrison, Charles Augustin Sainte-Beuve and Auguste Comte, among others. Lizzie preferred history and novels, so Adèle read with her the histories and essays of Macaulay, Carlyle, Froude and d'Aubigné and the novels of Dickens, Thackeray, Walter Scott and George Eliot. Lizzie loved Thomas Hardy. Adèle remembered that the last book she ever read with her mother was *Far from the Madding Crowd,* first published in England in 1874. On rainy days when they didn't feel like exploring the attic or some other adventure, she and her brothers would lie on the library floor looking at folios of Audubon's birds and Catlin's Indians.

John J. Audubon drew a major part of his bird illustrations during the 1820s while living at Oakley Plantation up the river from Belmont. When his first Double Elephant (pages slightly larger than three feet by two feet) edition of his *Birds of America* came out between 1827 and 1839, many plantation owners, like Adèle's father, bought copies of the great book. George Catlin's two volume edition of colored engravings entitled *Manners, Customs and Condition of the North American Indians*, published in 1841, was equally popular and highly sought after by those who could afford to buy it. In the drawing room, across a wide center hall from the library, there was a piano. Though she never learned to play very well, Adèle liked to practice Beethoven's sonatas. Lizzie had a wonderful voice that she inherited from her father, and Adèle loved to hear her sing Scotch ballads, French songs and pieces by Schubert.

In their early years, Adèle and her brothers were taught at home. Mr. Blackman was their principal master. He was punctual, strict and a bit humorless. To encourage his students, he constantly reminded them: *"Tempus fugit, Tempus fugit"* [time flies]. It was a drumbeat that was, as Adèle observed, a little out of place in the slow-moving South. Louis, however, endorsed Mr.

Blackman's decorum and sense of discipline, so the children obeyed him. Monsieur Richard, their French teacher, was *tout autre chose* [someone very different]. "He had no order, no precision, no discipline," Adèle wrote, "but we learned French and our brains were quickened by him and we loved him. He was silent and shy with our elders, but with us full of sympathy and interest." The two teachers rarely spoke to each other.

Monsieur Richard "had a history." He was a son of Auguste Richard, a Minister of Fine Arts under Napoleon Bonaparte, and had been educated for the priesthood. Before being ordained, he fell in love with a cousin. Too weak to face up to his father and too lively to submit, he ran off to Mexico with the Emperor Maximilian. Mexico had experienced a period of turbulence following the Mexican-American War, which had forced its government to cede a large portion of its territory to form parts of California, Nevada, Utah, Arizona, New Mexico, Wyoming, and Colorado. With the consent of conservative elements within Mexico, the French government under Napoleon III invaded the country and installed the Archduke of Austria as Emperor Maximilian I. When the Emperor's government fell six years later in 1867, M. Richard escaped and went to St. Louis thinking it would be like a French provincial city. Disheartened, friendless, ill and impoverished, he worked his way downriver to New Orleans on a steamboat. Eventually, Adolphe Ferry, who owned a plantation near Belmont, discovered him. Ferry found that he was "a man of unusual knowledge and culture." Hearing that his friend Louis wanted a tutor for his children, Ferry recommended Richard. The Frenchman remained a teacher at Belmont for eighteen years.

Life on the plantation was self-contained, but never isolated. Steamboat traffic on the river frequently brought visitors to Belmont. Often they arrived unannounced and occasionally they were distinguished. In 1871 the Grand Duke Alexis of Russia, the son of Tsar Alexander II, began a grand tour of the United States. After shooting buffalo on the southwest plains of Nebraska with General Sheridan, Colonel Custer, Buffalo Bill and the Indian leader Spotted Tail, Alexis went to New Orleans to celebrate Mardi Gras. As he was curious to see a sugar plantation, the Grand Duke and his entourage stopped at Belmont. Adèle, who had just turned ten, remembered "the calm with which my mother received them, the lack of confusion and excitement and yet the dignity and simple elegance." Adèle presented Alexis a large bouquet. She thought him handsome, but also "very merry and free and easy with the young ladies in his suite." The visit, though striking, made little lasting impression. Adèle couldn't remember that anyone in the family ever spoke about the Russians after they left.

2

What made a bigger impression on Adèle were the Negroes at Belmont. Those she remembered were mainly the ones who worked in or around the plantation house. "I can see their kind black faces now," she wrote nearly sixty years later, "and hear their peculiar dialect and the soft inflection of their voices."

First, there were the cooks – both named Martha. Big Martha, who by her size and demeanor overawed the kids and kept them from the kitchen, came infrequently, only as Little Martha's replacement. Little Martha, on the other hand, was their friend. Small and thin, wiry and quick with perhaps a touch of Indian blood, Little Martha "was very patient with us," wrote Adèle, "and even made us feel we helped her when we rolled the dough with a rolling pin and cut the biscuits with a round tin and pricked them with a fork." If Little Martha felt overwhelmed by their presence, she would shoo them out of the kitchen, like they were chickens.

Little Martha had many suitors. One was Varice, the plantation foreman in charge of all the field hands. Adèle saw him infrequently, but she remembered once hearing Varice talking to Little Martha through the kitchen window. "Look here, woman," he said in a gruff voice, "is you gonna marry me or ain't you? I'se tired a hanging round here coatin'." Adèle remembered Little Martha's soft, gentle reply: "I ain't sputin with you, Mr. Varice, but law, Mr. Varice, you is got a coase voice!"

Another favorite was Kit, the ostler, who ruled the stables. He loved his horses, and the children talked with him for hours while he did his work. He described the sturdiness and surefootedness of Ben, the western Mustang, and remarked on the charm of Silver Heels. He appreciated the wildness and swiftness of Fox and the whimsicality of Jessie, and on and on. Sometimes he lapsed into another world and would make up crazy rhymes, like "Wha did ya come from? Pass pa tank. Where de bullfrogs jump from bank to bank." Adèle was captivated; such catches would run through her head all day and into the night. They were still in her head late in life when she remembered her childhood.

Big Lucy, who had nursed Adèle as a baby, did laundry. Enormous, *une vrai colosse*, she accomplished the most delicate work ironing fine linen and lace. She also had many admirers and was continually getting married, for her marriages never lasted very long. "La, Miss Lizzie," Lucy confessed to Adèle's mother, "I don't care noden for dem men but I do like a weddin' veil and a cake!" Adèle loved to go the ironing house where Lucy would let her iron handkerchiefs or sit with her on the gallery and help polish brass. "It was Big Lucy," Adèle wrote, "who always brought me a little tiny red tin cup full of raisins when she came back from her Sunday outing!"

Some of her memories were more disturbing. Ma Melite told the children scary stories at night about Old Arp and Loupgarou, the bogeymen of the cypress swamps, so that they couldn't sleep. Adèle remembered lying awake certain that she could hear Time move. Ma Melite's rhyme, *"La nuit fait Loupgarou, vaut mieux rentrer en vos doux!"* [Loupgarou comes at night; you better keep quiet] would run through her head. She also remembered the dreadful evening that one of the field hands, Stephen, beat his son and hearing the boy's shrieks in the night. The next day Stephen disappeared from the plantation.

One evening after Adèle and her mother bid some guests farewell and were walking home from the landing on the river, they met a group of black men carrying guns. "It was about eleven o'clock at night," Adèle wrote. "They seemed to pause and I was frightened, but my mother's cheery voice saying, 'Good evening men,' reassured me and must have reassured them for they passed on." The next day they learned that the group had robbed a small store a few miles up the river and killed a young man who was sleeping there.

Still, most of Adèle's memories of Negroes at Belmont were happy ones. Zenon, the plantation's mechanic, could fix anything.

He repaired the mowing machine, wagon-wheels, even the sugarhouse engine when it broke down. Smart, accurate, and business-like, he was also tolerant and kind to the children, and much admired by them. Peter Harrison, who hauled water, was their friend, and they loved Edmond, the butler, who saw that the children had at least some of their favorite food at dinner. Edmond also warned Adèle when she was eating too much. Like her brother Louis, Adèle grew to a large size in adulthood.

Marie was the maid the children loved the best. Considerate and gentle, she possessed "a true ministering spirit" and proved a great support to Lizzie. The family was saddened when she married Thomas Miller and left Belmont, never to return. But the person who most impressed Adèle was her father's previous foreman, who was an old man when she was a child. She described John Blunt as "a great, tall, stalwart, white-haired negro, with a face like George Washington, a person of importance on the plantation." Her father, who had more faith in human nature than most slaveholders in the antebellum South, believed that a bad master made a bad servant, and was willing to buy a stout man with an iffy reputation. On one occasion, however, he made a mistake. When his new slave ran away within a few days, Louis and John Blunt set out to find him. While they were looking through the high reeds along the levee, the runaway bounded out from his hiding place and swung at Louis with a large cane knife (used for cutting down sugar cane). "Quick as a dart," wrote Adèle, "John raised his arm and thrust it between my father and the knife, and received the blow." The man escaped and was never captured. John Blunt, however, lost his arm saving his owner's life. In gratitude, Louis gave his foreman his freedom. "I believe," Adèle added, "my first idea of heroism was learned from the story of John Blunt."

3

Adèle's childhood ended in 1875 when she turned fourteen. The dynamics of the household had begun to shift when her brother Charless left Belmont three years earlier to attend Yale College. Soon after, Louis and Edward followed him to Connecticut where they enrolled in boarding schools before entering Yale themselves. Left behind, Adèle grew morose. Lizzie decided she needed a change and sent her to school in Connecticut as well.

Miss Porter's School in Farmington had been founded thirty years earlier, so when Adèle arrived its reputation of offering a serious education for young women in both the humanities and sciences was well established. At first Adèle hated the school; she felt totally out of place and alienated. "The school routine, the school happenings, the school gossip, all were strange to me," she wrote. It didn't help that her cousins Augusta and Lutie (Taylor and Henry Blow's daughters), who were two and one year older than she, were there, and that Miss Porter had chosen Lutie to be Adèle's roommate. In fact, her acute homesickness was aggravated by Lutie's grief. Lutie's mother Minerva had died in June, and then her father fell suddenly ill and died in September just as the new school year began. Adèle suffered through "an ascetic phase," imposing various kinds of strict discipline on herself. If she got too interested in a book, she forced herself to put it down and leave it unfinished. She refused to comb her hair in a becoming way. She dressed as plainly as she could. She stayed aloof from anything, anyone and any group at school that might be a "contaminating influence." She was awful.

Before long, however, she began to lighten up. She reached out to make friends, and woke up to the fact that Sarah Porter was "a woman of rare qualities of mind and heart." With the approach of Thanksgiving Day, Miss Porter urged her to accept an invitation from Edward Everett Hale and his family. Hale, a prolific writer of stories, essays and sermons, was a prominent clergyman and pastor of the Unitarian Church in Boston. He and his family had actively opposed slavery before the Civil War. His wife Emily's aunt was Harriet Beecher Stowe, whose book *Uncle Tom's Cabin*, published in 1852, graphically illustrated the horrors and complexities of human bondage.

Earlier in the year, Hale had visited Belmont for a few days, accompanied by his twenty year old daughter Ellen, who later studied art at *l'Académie Julian* in Paris. Hale had been impressed with what he saw at Belmont. In a letter written in April, he had described Adèle's father as "one of the most satisfactory men I have ever known." Noting that he was born four days before himself, Hale observed that Louis was engaged in dealing with "the greatest social problem of the age," namely, changing "untaught Negro slaves into voters" and transforming a feudal system of agriculture into a modern wage-based capitalist system in a state (Louisiana) notorious for political corruption. "Of course," added Hale, "he could not approach these duties, but that he had a cheerful, active, intelligent, prudent, careful spirited wife, who is also very pretty." At the end of their visit, Adèle kept Hale and Ellen company for a good part of the evening while they waited for the riverboat to fetch them at the Belmont landing. Though unprepared to leave home for boarding school, she was ripe for intellectual stimulus. In his diary Hale recorded, "Religion, philosophy and literature with Miss Adèle till 1 a.m. all the time walking on the verandah." (Hale, v. 2, 230-31.)

The holiday with the Hales proved a great success. Adèle had never experienced a Thanksgiving dinner before. "I sat and wondered – a strange awkward figure I must have been," she wrote, as she faced a bountiful feast of roast turkey and chicken pies. After dinner, her brother Edward and a friend from Yale, Robert Chapin, arrived to join the company. She was introduced to charades, a game she had never heard of. In one round, Adèle got into a laundry basket, was turned over in the middle of the living room, and had a blanket thrown over her head. She had played the part of Lord Ullin's daughter from a poem by Thomas Campbell. "Years after," she wrote, "on coming across the poem, I realized that the clothes basket was the boat and the blanket the flowing tide." Though feeling slightly foolish, Adèle knew she had been a hit, because everyone was amused and laughed heartily, including Edward's friend.

At Christmas Adèle remained at school with her cousin Lutie, who at age fifteen was now engaged to Adèle's brother Charless. Charless and Edward came down from Yale to spend a part of the holiday in Farmington. Edward invited Robert Chapin to come as well, and one day Edward, Robert and Adèle took a drive to Hartford together. In her letters home to Lizzie, Adèle wrote to tell her about Robert, as she did about everyone and everything that interested her.

In the winter term she went to New Haven with several other girls from school to attend one of the many receptions given by Yale's President Noah Porter, who was Sarah Porter's brother. Edward introduced Adèle to many of his fellow students, but she was on the lookout for Robert. When he finally came through the door, she felt the blood drain from her face only to rush back in again. They spoke just for a few minutes before he had to leave. It was only much later that Adèle learned that her mother had written Edward after Christmas telling him "not to take that blue-eyed Mr. Chapin to Farmington any more."

On Washington's Birthday, Adèle's new school friend Grace Potter invited her to New York to visit her family. Her father, Howard Potter, a successful businessman and philanthropist, had helped found the New York Orthopedic Dispensary and Hospital and was a major contributor to the Children's Aid Society. The Society supported several lodging houses for abandoned and orphaned boys and girls, who scrabbled for small jobs like shining shoes, sewing, washing, running errands and delivering newspapers. The boys' homes were called Newsboys' Lodging-houses, though not all the boys delivered papers. The girls' houses had no such identifier, but were simply called a Girl's Lodging-house. The houses provided kids a place to eat and sleep, but they were expected to work during the day. As she expressed interest, Howard Potter took Adèle to see one of the boy's houses. It might have been more appropriate for him to take her to a Girls' house, but Mr. Potter was especially popular among the boys as a counselor as well as a benefactor. Although she may have visited the Home of the Friendless that her grandmother Charlotte had founded in St. Louis, the Newsboys' Lodging-house was the first charitable institution for children Adèle had ever seen. The visit made a vivid and lasting impression on her.

Adèle also met for the first time a world-famous musician. Miss Porter, valuing a rounded education for her students, offered courses in art and music. She had hired Karl Klauser as the school's music director to teach music the way it was done in Germany. Klauser invited outstanding performers to play for the students, including his good friend Hans von Bülow, the German pianist and conductor. Two years before he went to Farmington, von Bülow had performed the world premiere of Tchaikovsky's First Piano Concerto in Boston. The critics had greeted the new work with jeers and ridicule but the audience was enthusiastic. When Miss Porter introduced Adèle, the pianist asked her if she played and offered to hear her do a piece. She played – apparently not very well – the Funeral March from Beethoven's Piano Sonata No. 12. Von Bülow cried out: "No! You will never play, you will never possess music, it will always possess you! You cannot give what you cannot hold."

When the school year ended in early summer, Adèle, now fifteen years old, left Farmington and headed home.

4

"My return to the South was one of the great sensations of my life," Adèle wrote. Everything seemed so familiar but at the same time so strange. She arrived in New Orleans on the train and met Lizzie at the St. Charles Hotel where they stayed the night before heading upriver to Belmont. When she saw her mother she "felt for the first time her individuality apart from mine. It was the same with the plantation."

The summer of 1876 was not a good time. The weather was unusually hot, and everyone fell ill. Yellow fever, a viral disease transmitted through mosquito bites, had broken out. Lizzie was already unwell, and Adèle's three brothers (Louis, William and George) caught the fever in the autumn. She helped her mother care for the boys by sitting beside them and then, as their fevers began to break, served them sips of champagne followed by small amounts of egg white or milk. As the boys improved, the disease struck her five-year-old sister Elizabeth. Adèle spent many nights sitting up, rubbing her with quinine and lard and keeping watch. The yellow fever eventually got Adèle as well. It was January before everyone had recovered and felt better again. They were fortunate, for many died. The disease spread along the Mississippi River between St. Louis and New Orleans, eventually killing an estimated 20,000 people in 1878, one of the worst outbreaks of yellow fever in the 19th century.

As a consequence, Adèle did not return to Miss Porter's school in the autumn. Instead, her parents hired a tutor from Yale to replace Mr. Blackman. Adèle studied chemistry, classics, physics, and, most importantly, Noah Porter's hugely popular book on philosophy, *Human Intellect*, published in 1868. Her discussions of Porter's book with her new tutor led Adèle to formulate her own religious views. "We sat up late at night, talking philosophy, and so it came to pass that we drifted into religious and theological questions, and I reached conclusions from which I have never departed."

Adèle's religious upbringing until then had been decidedly mixed. Her father, brought up as a Catholic, was more interested in the classics, philosophy and science than religion, and ceded control of the children's religious education to his wife. Lizzie held family prayers every morning at which she read passages from the Bible, and she and the children sang hymns. She said little however about doctrine, except to tell her children "God is Love." Her grandmother Charlotte, on the other hand, was stricter. She took the children to Sunday school and grounded them in the main principles of the Presbyterian faith – predestination and sanctification, which she tempered with her favorite text – "All your righteousness is as filthy rags." Nonetheless, Adèle found the Catholic faith appealing in several respects. She liked its ritual, mystery and sociability. She often went with her Aunt Noémi (her father's brother's wife) and her Catholic cousins to church at St. Michael's in the nearby town of Convent.

Stimulated by her discussions with her tutor, Adèle formulated a theory of the Trinity that satisfied her. She began by imagining a hypothetical first human person, who first sees "things outside himself;" then becomes conscious, seeing "something inside himself" perceiving "the outside things;" and finally recognizes something unseen outside himself and outside things, "something which transcended the actual." The first of these "three dimensions", she likened to God, the Father, "outside of matter, creating it." The second dimension, she identified as the "indwelling God," synonymous with Christ. The third dimension, she named the "transcendent God," whom she found analogous to the Holy Ghost. Adèle wrote all this down in the spring of 1878. Looking back over it some fifty years later, she still found it a satisfactory distillation of her religious belief.

In the early spring Adèle also had a near death experience. She went horseback riding with her brothers and a friend from Miss Porter's who had come to visit. Adèle rode the whimsical and unpredictable Jessie that day. While racing down a lane that led by a gate to the stables, Jessie turned and tried to jump the gate. Adèle pulled on the reins, the horse stopped, and Adèle pitched head first into the bottom of a ditch, which was baked hard as a brick by the sun. She was unconscious when her brother Louis picked her up. He revived her by dunking her head into a water trough. A few hours later she fainted and collapsed. Her mother put her to bed where she was forced to remain quiet for several weeks until she recovered from what was probably a bad concussion.

When Adèle was better, Lizzie decided that Adèle and Charlotte should spend the spring and summer in New London, Connecticut before returning to Miss Porter's for her final year. Adèle was delighted. She knew what her mother – she thought – didn't know: that the Chapins owned a summer home there. After they arrived, Charlotte told Adèle, "I find that my friend Mrs. Clark lives near here, with her daughter Mrs. Chapin, and I propose to drive to see her this afternoon and wish you to accompany me." Caught off guard, Adèle begged to stay home, complaining that her head hurt. Charlotte told her the drive in the country would do her good. Along the way Adèle wrung a promise that she could stay in the carriage when they arrived. As soon as she got inside, Charlotte told Henrietta Clark that Adèle was outside. "Almost immediately, the tall form of Robert Chapin appeared at the [carriage] door, and my heart gave the jump it gives to-day when I see him!"

Adèle was unaware that Charlotte and Henrietta had known one another for years. Both were born in Virginia and moved with their families to St. Louis. Henrietta's sister Irene had married Colonel John Emerson and their brother John Sanford had fought to preserve Irene's ownership of Dred Scott, while Charlotte's family strove to see their former slave become a free man. More than twenty years after the case was decided, the two warring clans would soon agree that, if Adèle and Robert were truly in love, they should marry. Seeing the chemistry between them, the two maternal grandmothers, Sanford and Blow, blessed their engagement, which was formalized in the following year in the spring of 1878 when Adèle finished school.

Educated and engaged, Adèle went to St. Louis in the summer after her graduation. The family gathered at Charlotte's house for the marriage of Adèle's brother Charless to their cousin Lutie on the first day of October. Not long after the wedding, a telegram arrived telling Charless (who had just begun to practice law in St. Louis) and Adèle (who had stayed on at Charlotte's house) to hasten to Belmont as their mother was seriously ill with a weakened heart. Lizzie's condition was accompanied and perhaps precipitated by acute stress.

Elizabeth "Lizzie" Charless Le Bourgeois

Lizzie had promised to endow the Charless Professorship of Physical Science at Westminster College just days after her father died. She had given the college two notes dated 1 July 1859 for $10,000 each payable in four years and bearing 10% interest payable semiannually. By the time the notes came due in the summer of 1863, her financial position had deteriorated as a result of the ongoing Civil War. Unable to pay the principal, she continued to pay the interest, which at some point was renegotiated down to 8%. Then, in 1869, a huge explosion at the family drug firm, now styled Blow, Curd & Co, destroyed several buildings and $100,000 of pharmaceutical inventory. Charlotte and Lizzie jointly owned the Blow building, which was valued at $35,000 but covered by only $15,000 of insurance. During the Long Depression of the 1870s but before April 1878, Lizzie stopped paying any interest at all on her promissory notes to the college. Her default was terrible, but not unique. Other donors to Westminster had reneged on their promises as well. From a high point just before the outbreak of the Civil War, the college's endowment – made up largely of notes like Lizzie's – shrank by nearly fifty percent in sixteen years. Several times the school nearly closed for lack of funds. The post-war years were difficult throughout the Mississippi River valley.

Pressed by the college to make good on her promise, Lizzie turned to her mother for help. In what was clearly a heart-wrenching request, Charlotte asked the board of trustees to return Lizzie's promissory notes and cancel the gift. "The request," the college Treasurer wrote in his report for the year ending 1 June 1879, "was founded upon the fact that Mrs. Le Bourgeois had met with losses in the depreciation of her landed estate, and consequently a depreciation of rents accruing therefrom; and also that the endowment of the Professorship made was a gift," meaning that the debt did not arise from cash previously received from the creditor. The college balked at the request, but a prominent board member, Edward Bredell, negotiated a compromise. The school would return Lizzie's notes on receipt of a cash payment of $10,000. (M. Fisher, 287, 291.) Lizzie was relieved but broken-hearted. She had failed her father, and was deeply grieved.

Adèle went with her mother to New York in early 1879 to consult a specialist. Unfortunately, the doctor had no effective remedy for Lizzie's illness. In Manhattan they also saw Robert, who was studying law at Columbia University. Finding comfort in his "quiet strength and judgment," Lizzie was deeply pleased that the two had chosen one another. The couple quietly decided to put their wedding on hold until Lizzie recovered, or didn't.

In the summer, when her mother felt a bit better, Adèle accepted her aunt Susan Blow's invitation to spend a few weeks with her in Concord, Massachusetts. Susan, Henry Blow's eldest daughter, had studied German philosophy, founded the first successful public kindergarten, joined the small circle of Boston-based intellectuals, and was probably responsible for Adèle's going to Miss Porter's school. "I stayed with my cousin in a boarding house where the philosophers were assembled, and I attended the lectures with much interest," wrote Adèle. "I especially remember the conversation at meals when, it seemed to me, everything was discussed both in the heavens above and the earth beneath, not to mention the blueberry pie." Susan introduced her to Alphonso Taft (father of the future President William Howard Taft), Amos Bronson Alcott (father of Louisa May Alcott, the author of the immensely popular book *Little Women*), and the venerable Ralph Waldo Emerson (Bronson Alcott's brother-in-law and the father of Transcendentalism). After impressing the sages and several other elders by translating a passage in Latin that had stumped them, Adèle returned to Belmont to nurse her mother, who, despite a brief respite, resumed her slow decline.

Toward the end, the family accompanied Lizzie to Newport, one of her favorite places, where she died and left them "a heart-broken household" in the summer of 1881. Her father "seemed crushed" and her little sister, now nine years old, was distraught. Her brother Charless and his new wife lived in St. Louis, her brother Louis had been running the plantation for the past several years, and her brothers William and George, eighteen and sixteen years old, had yet to go out on their own in the world. Though engaged to Robert, Adèle felt compelled to step into the role of *materfamilias.* She described her situation soon after Lizzie's death:

> In the autumn I engaged a tutor [for her younger brothers and sister], packed the family up and went South to the plantation. I felt that I must devote my life to them, and used to sit up late into the night playing poker with my brothers for fear that they would play elsewhere. But it was bitter to leave Robert Chapin, for I had already grown to depend upon him. I shall never forget the loneliness at Christmas time, filling stockings and trying to make it cheerful for the others.

After the Christmas holidays she decided that she could not abandon her family at Belmont, and so wrote Robert to tell him "it was my duty to give him up."

5

Though quiet in demeanor and gentle in character, Robert Chapin would hear nothing of it. He immediately hastened from New England to Louisiana. He asked Adèle's father to confirm his engagement, which he did. Robert even persuaded him to take the youngest children and come with him and Adèle to live in New England.

Adèle had wanted to have her wedding at Belmont, but Charlotte refused to revisit the place that had sapped the health and wealth of her only child. So, on the first day of June 1882, they were married at Charlotte's house in St. Louis with her father, five brothers, little sister and M. Richard, her old French tutor, standing by her.

The next morning Adèle and Robert, her father, brother George, and sister Elizabeth boarded a private car at the train station and arrived the next day at four o'clock in the morning at Pittsfield, Massachusetts, where Robert had taken a house for the summer. "I had never been amongst the [Berkshire] hills before," she wrote. "When we arrived they were purple with an impending storm and the apple trees upon their slopes were in full bloom." Thus began "the ten happiest years of my life."

They spent their first summer exploring the area around Pittsfield. "I remember long drives through the hills," she wrote, "my father and husband on the front seat of the wagon and I sitting between my brother and sister in the back. Just the consciousness of my husband's presence filled me with an inexpressible joy." She and Robert visited his ancestral home in Springfield, Massachusetts, where he introduced Adèle to his Chapin grandparents. Accustomed to Southern manners, Adèle embraced and kissed Robert's grandfather unaware that his own children never did. There she learned that their ancestor Deacon

Samuel Chapin had come from England around 1630 and helped establish the town of Springfield.

In the meantime, Robert found a house in New York and asked Adèle to choose furniture for it. It was a daunting task. Nothing suited. Having grown up on the plantation with old furniture imported from France, Adèle "could not buy black walnut or ebony furniture or plush hangings." She searched in vain. "Mother Chapin," she wrote, "thought me quite mad, for I was not limited as to money and why was I not satisfied?" Eventually, on a trip to Boston, she stopped at a little shop, J. F. Bumstead & Co., where she found furniture, hangings and wallpaper that she wanted. She had discovered, quite by accident, the work of William Morris, the British poet and interior designer, who had only just begun to export his designs to America.

After they were settled in Manhattan, Adèle went with her father, brother and sister back to Belmont to meet with brothers Charless, Louis, and William to settle her mother's estate.

During the war years and afterwards Adèle's father had borrowed heavily to maintain the plantation. When the burden of debt became too great, Lizzie mortgaged her own real estate properties in St. Louis, largely inherited from her grandfather, to pay off Louis's obligations, buy the mortgages on Belmont, and absorb the losses. As part of the transaction, Louisiana law required Louis and Lizzie to legally separate their shared property and for Lizzie to foreclose on his debt to her, in an amount of about $48,000. As a result, Lizzie acquired the title to her husband's plantation a couple of years before she died. Despite her desire to let her husband inherit Belmont, Louisiana law required that her estate be divided among the seven surviving children, due to the earlier separation of property. In her will, Lizzie stipulated that Belmont and all of her properties in St. Louis were to remain undivided for at least five years so that the revenues generated by the plantation could pay off the mortgages on her Missouri properties. At their gathering at Belmont, the siblings decided on how much money to give their father as an annual stipend, since he was now without property or income.

When it was time to leave the plantation, her father announced that he would not return to New York, but stay in the South. Adèle anticipated his resistance. "I simply took the stand," she said, "that I would not go until he came with me." She listened while he protested. He told her she ought to go back to her husband. She waited. Louis finally relented and never lived in Louisiana again.

Louis Sosthène Le Bourgeois

The following summer of 1883 Adèle and Robert rented another house, called Broadhall, near Pittsfield. They invited Charlotte to visit. It was a busy season. "Fired with zeal, I put up preserves and pickles," she wrote, "and busied myself about household duties, trying to give my sister and brother, and Grandma and my father a happy time" as well as finding time to spend with her good husband. Some unwanted excitement occurred when Adèle and Charlotte took Adèle's new carriage, a gift from Robert, out for a test drive:

> On our way home, coming down a steep hill the iron on either side of the pole broke, and threw the Victoria on to the horses' legs. The coachman was instantly thrown from the box and the horses tore down the hill, kicking and plunging, until they came to a turn in the road bringing the side of a mountain before them; unable to turn the carriage they rushed into the mountain side, throwing my grandmother and myself out. Apparently neither of us was hurt. We were picked up by a passing wagon and taken home and the next day we felt the effect of the shock very much. One horse was instantly killed and it was necessary to shoot the other.

Charlotte, who had survived a near deadly bout of cholera, out-lived her husband and only child, and was now seventy-three years old, walked away from a serious accident that killed two strong horses and destroyed a brand-new Victoria.

6

As a married woman, Adèle found outlets for her tremendous energy. She threw herself into the social life around her and she began to have children. She gave birth to her first child in December 1885. He was named Louis Le Bourgeois Chapin, after her father. During the summer as her pregnancy developed she began to feel herself "a part of the creative force of the world, when buds and blossoms and trees, and flowers and birds, all seemed akin to me; when the meaning of life seemed clear to me though its mystery was deeper than ever. I felt a part of all the great world forces." She was startled, however, when her boy finally appeared. "I had thought of a child as a beautiful curly-haired being with an angel face, and when my baby was shown to me I tried to conceal surprise, and for a long time I did not know that all babies are like that."

Feeling unwell after her delivery, Adèle decided to go south in the spring. Accompanied by the baby, her father and her sister, she went to Belmont in April. It was a hideous trip; the baby cried the entire time. Once there, however, all was peace and joy, as Adèle proudly showed off her son to her brothers and the old servants. The baby began to relax as well. They remained in Louisiana for nearly two months. When they returned north in June they went again to the Berkshires. Unable to get the house he wanted in Pittsfield, Robert chose one in Lenox, called the Dorr Place. It was a beautiful spot in the hills, but neither Robert nor Adèle was aware that Lenox had become a fashionable resort. "Here," Adèle wrote, "began the claims of society upon me, which I have never been able entirely to escape, though I have never conformed to them and have fought them all my life."

When Robert and Adèle married, the Gilded Age in American history was in full swing. A term coined by Mark Twain in the early 1870s, the Gilded Age reflected the immense economic growth that took place in the nation in the years after the Civil War. Huge fortunes were amassed by Andrew Carnegie, John D. Rockefeller, Jacob Astor, Cornelius Vanderbilt, Andrew Mellon and many others, and the country witnessed a wave of ostentatious living. The wealthy built magnificent mansions up and down the East Coast and throughout the major cities and secluded countryside. From a rich family himself, Robert was able to join the urban aristocracy described in the late 19th century novels of Henry James and Edith Wharton.

In the autumn of 1886, after Robert moved the family to a large and beautifully furnished house on 54th Street, Adèle enjoyed her first ladies' luncheon as the guest of honor. It was there – she claimed – that, aside from her girlhood experiences at Miss Porter's, "I heard the first gossip I had ever heard." One of the ladies at the party told how a gentleman had treated another woman very rudely. Each lady said what they would have done if the incident had happened to them. What Adèle told her friends was somewhat different from what the others had to say. "I would have told Papa, and he would have shot him!" It was a boast, however, that hardly matched her father's character.

Adèle's second child, also a son, was born a year after the first and named for his father, Robert Williams Chapin. It proved a difficult time. Louis, now one year old, succumbed to scarlet fever two days after Robert was born. Until then little Louis had slept in his mother's room and now he had to be taken away. Separated from his mother in a bedroom on an upper floor of the house and cared for by a trained nurse, Louis cried constantly while Adèle fretted. "I hated everything," she wrote, "and only longed to see my boy." In her anxiety she began to lose her milk. The doctor decided little Robert needed a wet nurse. It was a fortuitous intervention.

The wet nurse, a young woman with ample milk, was totally untrained in childcare. Watching how the trained nurse who tended Louis taught the untrained one gave Adèle an idea. She would start a school for the proper training of young women to care for babies. Adèle turned to her new friend Dr. William H. Draper for advice. Draper, who had just become the President of the New York Academy of Physicians, endorsed the idea. He told Adèle that she should talk with his former student and young colleague Dr. L. Emmett Holt, who was just then trying to start a special hospital for babies-only in the city. At Draper's urging, Holt called on Adèle soon after. He "came and showed such sympathy with my idea," Adèle wrote, "that I was enabled to outline my plan and try it in connection with the Babies' Hospital then in embryo."

The Training School for Children's Nurses became a successful and integral part of the new hospital, which had its official start the next year, 1887. The hospital was first located at Lexington Avenue and 55th Street. Today it is known as the Children's Hospital of New York. For her work in conceiving, planning and raising funds, including her personal donation of $40,000, for the nursing school, Adèle attained immediate recognition. (*Good Housekeeping*, 4 January 1890.) The following year she was elected a member of the Board of Supervisors of the Orthopedic Hospital, which was founded by Dr. Draper and funded by, among many others, Howard Potter, who had introduced Adèle to the Newsboys Lodging-houses ten years earlier. When Dr. Holt published his famous book on childcare, *The Care and Feeding of Children – a catechism for the use of mothers and children's nurses,* he dedicated it to Adèle. He wrote, "To Mrs. Robert W. Chapin, through whose efforts the first practical training school for children's nurses in America was established, this book is respectfully dedicated by the author." The book went through twelve editions from 1894 to 1924, and remained in print as late as 1940.

It amused and gratified Adèle that she made such a substantial contribution to healthcare at an early age. She was twenty-five years old when the Training School got off the ground in conjunction with the Babies' Hospital. One day not long after the opening of the hospital, a lady called and asked for Mrs. Chapin. When the woman was shown into the living room, she asked Adèle, "Is your mother at home?" Adèle replied that her mother-in-law, who happened to be staying with Adèle and Robert at the time, was out. The woman then told Adèle that she had come to inquire about the Training School for Nurses. When Adèle answered, "I founded that school," the woman was stunned. "I shall never forget her look of amazed scorn," Adèle wrote, "as she said, '*You?*'" Adèle soon convinced her visitor that she indeed had started the school. Though the woman was an experienced and well-known, though unidentified, philanthropist, she listened to Adèle, took her advice and started a similar school elsewhere.

7

Adèle remained restless even as she became pregnant with her third child, her daughter Julia who was born in September 1888. Not satisfied with conceiving, organizing and raising the money for the Training School, Adèle wanted something more. As she put it, "I longed to get closer to suffering humanity, for I never thought one got the human touch out of a committee." Once, at Belmont, Adèle had asked her father to identify her greatest faults. He had told her, "*Une seule, mon enfant; trop de zèle, trop de zèle*" [Only one, my child, too much zeal, too much energy].

She asked William Rainsford, an Episcopal minister in New York and later big game hunter, if he knew any place "where no woman would go" but where she could be of use. "Yes!" he replied, "the epileptic and delirium tremens ward in Bellevue Hospital." And, off she went. At Bellevue she helped an epileptic who, she said, "was never quiet except when I held his hands," and who, she felt, did more for her than she for him "in giving me an outlet for that human longing to express sympathy which the world stifles."

Another patient she visited was a man named Moore. He was consumptive and, she feared, near death. After seeing him one day, she had trouble falling to sleep because she had "said nothing to him about his soul and a hereafter." The next morning, though it was not her day to visit, she rushed back to his bedside. "Moore," she asked, "are you a Christian?" He answered, "Yes – and I am mighty glad too because I can pray for you every night." Beside spiritual aid, Adèle gave Mr. Moore, whom she obviously liked, red flannels and, ignoring the rules, some whisky.

Yet another was a journalist who had written for the *Missouri Republican*, the newspaper that her great-grandfather, the first Joseph Charless, had founded in St. Louis. He was reading *The Fair Maid of Perth*. When she asked why he liked the work of Sir Walter Scott, he replied, "Why do you like sunshine?" Adèle treasured her experiences as a volunteer at Bellevue. "I learned," she wrote, "that human qualities blossom and flourish amongst those the world calls vilest and lowest, and in that dreadful, smelly hospital ward amongst the dregs of humanity I found much to teach and to uplift me."

At the same time, Adèle, despite her reservations about "the claims of society," eagerly joined the world of the social, political and cultural elite. One of her earliest friends was Joseph Hodges Choate. Thirty years older than Adèle, Choate had established his legal reputation as an invincible litigator and had helped to destroy the system of political corruption that William Tweed and his followers had created in New York city in the 1860s and '70s. Choate's law partner Charles Cotesworth Beaman soon became her friend as well.

Early in her marriage Adèle was introduced to Charles de Kay and his sister Helena who had married Richard Watson Gilder. Charles and Helena were both artists; he was a designer, poet and translator and she a painter. Richard Gilder was the editor of the *Century Magazine* from 1881 to 1909, and also a poet. He had wooed Helena away with his romantic verses from her lover, the painter Winslow Homer. From these friendships, Adèle and Robert came to know the actors Joe Jefferson and Richard Mansfield, the artists John Singer Sargent, John La Farge and William Merritt Chase, and the writer and raconteur Samuel Clemens, better known as Mark Twain. Mansfield and Charles de Kay introduced Adèle to the world of Eastern art about the time that the Japanese artist Kazuko Okakura visited New York in 1886. La Farge had introduced Okakura to the Gilders and their circle of friends and helped assure his successful trip to America. Responding to her curiosity, Mansfield showed Adèle his collection of Japanese kakemono (hanging scrolls) and de Kay his collection of curios.

At a reception that the Gilders held in the spring of 1889, the Chapins also met Grover and Frances Cleveland for the first time. Like Joseph Choate, Cleveland was an ardent reformer. As mayor of Buffalo and then governor of New York, he worked to reduce the worst excesses of political corruption and bossism. His reputation for honesty and common sense helped him get elected President of the United States. When the Gilders introduced the two couples, Cleveland had just finished his first term in office as President. He and Frances were the first and only presidential couple to be married at the White House. Considerably younger than her husband, Frances was two years younger than Adèle, and the youngest First Lady in American history. The two twenty-plus year old women soon become fast friends.

The President and Adèle moreover hit it off right away. For several years, during the interim between his terms of office, the Clevelands saw the Chapins frequently. Often Adèle sat next to him at dinner parties because he enjoyed her company so much. Adèle, in fact, was a talented conversationalist. She listened carefully, thought clearly, spoke vividly and could take a round, sympathetic but objective view of things. She was also invariably upbeat and always candid. Her ability as a talker was recognized early and gave rise to one of her husband's few *bon mots*. At a dinner party that included the Clevelands, Gilders, Choates, Beamans and Rainsfords, Charles Beaman proposed a toast to the health of "his dear friend Mrs. Chapin," which obliged Robert to rise to his feet and say a few words in response. Adèle watched as her shy husband got up and said, "Gentlemen, I am exceedingly embarrassed; I very rarely have an opportunity of answering for Mrs. Chapin, she generally speaks for herself."

In the autumn of 1890 the Clevelands tightened their friendship with reciprocal visits. Frances came to the Chapins at their "cottage" (read, country mansion) in the Berkshires and Adèle and Robert visited the Clevelands at their "camp" (rustic, but comfortable house) in the Adirondacks. It was Adèle's first experience of "camp life." She remembered, "We were in a charming little log cabin, and the long talks I had there with Frances Cleveland began the friendship which has lasted for life."

8

Just as they reached the pinnacle of their position in society, the Chapins encountered a series of events that altered their lives.

Robert, who had begun his career as a lawyer, bought a large stake in the Ingersoll Company sometime in the mid or late 1880s. Ingersoll manufactured mining and rock-drilling equipment. The company had suffered a series of crippling strikes and lost much of its value before Robert bought in and took control. As his first important act, he introduced a novel profit-sharing scheme that included the workmen as well as the managers. The plan alleviated the strain between capital and labor, and profitability soon returned. Robert also elevated the inventor of the company's principal drilling devices into ownership, renaming the business the Ingersoll Sargent Rock Drill Company.

For a while everything went extremely well, perhaps too well. Robert borrowed heavily and over-invested in a string of copper mines in Canada. When the mines failed to produce, he had to liquidate his ownership interest at a significant loss to cover his debt. He and Adèle were forced to downsize immediately. They reduced their staff of household servants from ten to three and cut their living expenses fivefold. They gave up their home in Manhattan and retreated to a much smaller house in Short Hills, New Jersey. There, their son Robert, not yet five years old, died in July 1891.

A third unhappy event occurred soon after. Fifteen years earlier, Adèle's brother Louis, on leaving Yale, decided to return south to throw his enormous energies into making the plantation in Louisiana successful. Belmont was her brother's great passion. Louis, who never married, loved the place, "as a man might love a woman." In her will, his mother had recognized the "great interest taken by Louis and the valuable services rendered by him in our efforts to work Belmont Plantation profitably and successfully," and bequeathed him an additional one-fourth share, "provided that he remain on the plantation and continue to manage it until the debts are paid." Louis remained. Substituting rice production for sugar, he began to generate profits that helped to relieve the family's burden of debt. In June 1892, however, their worst fear materialized when the Mississippi River, swollen beyond capacity with the torrential rains of half of North America, rose and knocked a hole a quarter-mile wide in the levee in front of the plantation house. The turbulent waters flooded the house to the second floor and plowed up the new rice fields and all the old gardens. Many of the magnificent magnolias and oaks were destroyed, replaced by a wild profusion of unwanted willows. The place never recovered. Two years later a fire destroyed the abandoned mansion and Belmont was sold, passing out of the family.

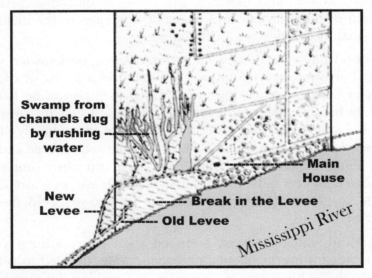

Belmont Plantation shown on a Mississippi River Commission map from 1893. Once the river returned to normal levels after the crevasse of June 1892, a new levee was built that encroached on the plantation grounds. The levee was constructed around the mansion, which had withstood the floodwaters. Deep channels dug by the rushing waters created a swamp, which remains to this day. After the house burned in 1894, the columns remained standing but a new levee was soon constructed behind the foundations of the house, leaving the columns standing on the batture and in the river for many years.

Still Adèle and Robert were fortunate. Robert retained his position as president of Ingersoll for a while before he stepped down and assumed a role as business promoter. More importantly, their friends did not abandon them. The Clevelands invited them to Grey Gables, their country place at Cape Cod for the summer of 1892. At the time Mrs. Cleveland was helping Adèle's brother George obtain a position at the Edison Electric company in New Orleans, which was rapidly expanding as it replaced the city's gas lighting with electric bulbs. The following winter when they could finally afford a small apartment in New York, George Vanderbilt, who was then in the midst of building his great mansion, Biltmore House at Ashville, North Carolina, offered Adèle a ticket to hear the Polish pianist Ignacy Jan Paderewski perform.

Adèle was thrilled by the concert. Afterwards her friend Grace Arnold, an amateur singer and prominent socialite, invited her to meet the pianist. Adèle and Paderewski, who was enormously popular with New York audiences, conversed in French. She remembered telling him that, "*votre musique a soulage mon coeur blessé*" [your music has healed my wounded heart]. "After this," Adèle wrote, "I seemed to come back to life again, and the numbness and indifference which I had felt since my boy's death seemed to grow less."

When her friend Frances La Farge returned from a trip to Europe, she brought Adèle a seal – a beautiful stone, on which was engraved a heart with a sword through it and the words "*non sine dolore*" [none without pain]. The seal became one of Adèle's most treasured possessions. In her thank you note to Frances, she penned the lines:

> Not without pain are we born, nor yet without pain
> do we live, nor without pain do we die or attain
> highest joy. Dolores, Dolores is the open sesame to
> every real experience.

As their financial situation improved during the year, Adèle resumed her work on the committees of the Orthopedic Hospital and the Training School of the Babies' Hospital. The Clevelands, back in the White House following his second election as President, offered the Chapins their place in New York, but the house was too large and expensive for Adèle and Robert to accept. They did however return in the summer to Lenox. It was there in the autumn that Robert told Adèle that he was going to England to pursue some business developments for Ingersoll Sargent. A month later, he sent her a cable saying he was heading for South Africa and couldn't predict when he might return. Early in the next year Adèle accepted an invitation from the Clevelands to visit the White House. With her son Louis in school, she went down to Washington with her daughter Julia. "I remember it," Adèle wrote, "as a happy oasis in that desert of a winter."

When Robert eventually returned, he surprised Adèle. "Never shall I forget the night he said 'Del, would you go to South Africa with me?'" The idea of moving from America to Africa had never entered her head, but she didn't hesitate making her reply. "I would go to the ends of the earth with you," she said.

9

Adèle and Robert, their children, and her father and sister departed for Europe in October 1894. They landed in England for a short layover. Robert sailed for South Africa to find a suitable home for his family while the others went to France. Adèle found schools for Louis and Julia in Paris for the year, which allowed her to explore the city and northern France. At a tea in Paris she met Anne Douglas Sedgwick, a twenty-one year old American from New Jersey living in London, whose career as a popular novelist had yet to emerge. The first of Anne's twenty novels, *The Dull Miss Archinard*, appeared four years later. Her work, which often compared the differences between American and English attitudes, won wide attention. She became one of the best selling novelists in the first three decades of the twentieth century. She married the British essayist Basil de Selincourt, who, after Anne's death in 1935, would marry Adèle's daughter.

In June 1895 Adèle and Anne journeyed west from Paris with a letter of introduction to Claude Monet, the artist and leader of the Impressionist movement. Monet had been living for the past twelve years in a pleasant country house in the village of Giverny. At first a renter, he bought the place in 1891 as the surging popularity of his work finally made him a well-known and wealthy man. It was a lovely, sunny morning when the two women arrived. Adèle recalled that poppies were blooming all through the surrounding fields of wheat. As they approached the farmhouse gate, they saw a middle-aged man wearing a panama hat and a mauve blouse. He came towards them and they asked whether M. Monet lived there. He replied: "*Je suis M. Monet.*"

When Adèle presented their letter, he invited them to see his studio and offered to answer their questions. Adèle asked him to tell them a little about the evolution of impressionism. He replied in French:

Have you ever noticed a pair of checked trousers? At a distance they are gray, near by they are black-and-white; but there is a point at which they have ceased to be grey and not definitely black-and-white, when the colors seek to mingle in the eye and produce an almost dazzling effect. Rembrandt has said the last word about light, but no one has successfully before painted motion, and it occurred to us that if we caused the colors which were usually mixed on the palette to be mixed in the eye, by placing them side by side on the canvas, we could make poppy fields quiver, poplar trees blow, and even the atmosphere to have that *tremblement* which you see on a hot summer's day. We do not pretend to have arrived, but we have made a great new departure in art which it will take generations to perfect.

Monet had recently begun to produce a single subject in a series of paintings done in different seasons and at different times of the day. He had exhibited the first series, his famous *Haystacks,* in the gallery of his dealer Paul Durand-Ruel four years earlier. Adèle asked him what that was all about. Monet told her:

It's an accident. I start to paint the façade of Rouen cathedral in the early morning; while I paint, the light changes and grows more beautiful. Quickly, I take another canvas and begin again – and so on, until I have many canvases begun and I must finish them all, waiting for the lighting of each to return.

Emphasizing the temporality of objective reality, he also acknowledged a professional weakness: "I cannot paint children, because I should lie unless I painted the same child a thousand times."

Monet invited Adèle and Anne to stay for lunch. The trio had a delightful time together.

10

In the fall Robert returned to gather his family for the voyage to Africa. Adèle's father and sister chose to stay in Paris. Robert and Adèle, young Louis and Julia, and a French governess with the unlikely name of Mlle. Cretin boarded the *Moor* and sailed from Southampton, England in December 1895. They arrived in Cape Town at the southern tip of Africa on the eve of an incendiary event.

Robert had gone to Africa to sell mining and drilling equipment. Fields of diamonds had been discovered around Kimberly and gold near Johannesburg. The precious stones and metal lay in areas controlled by the Boers, descendants of Dutch settlers who first went to Africa in the 17th century. Wealthy British and American adventurers who wanted to extract the natural resources found themselves blocked by the intransigent Boers who were predominantly farmers, less interested in worldly riches, more attuned to an austere way of life, and fiercely independent. As more and more outsiders entered their space, their starchy leader Paul Kruger galvanized the Boers to pass laws restricting the outsiders' rights. The Anglo-American outsiders, called *Uitlanders* by the Boers, finally got fed up and fomented a rebellion, which they launched two days after the Chapins arrived on the continent.

A group of mercenaries led by Leander Starr Jameson and backed by the resources of Cecil Rhodes planned to overthrow the Kruger government in Pretoria, the capital of the Transvaal. They intended to force reforms that would lead to rapid exploitation of the country's natural resources. Rhodes had already amassed great wealth in diamond mining in other areas of South Africa, and garnered substantial political power in becoming Prime Minister of the Cape Colony, the southernmost region of Africa and a vital part of the British Empire. He was in a strong position to succeed in his planned land grab. Mistiming and bad communications, however, resulted in a quick and decisive defeat. The Jameson Raiders were intercepted at the border by a Boer militia and forced to surrender. British and American conspirators in Johannesburg were arrested and imprisoned. The attempted coup was a total failure and a major embarrassment in England and the United States.

Among those imprisoned were Cecil Rhodes's brother and several prominent American entrepreneurs, most importantly John Hays Hammond. Hammond was a successful mining engineer who helped Cecil Rhodes form the diamond mining company De Beers, which today remains the largest producer of diamonds in the world. Hammond was also Robert Chapin's classmate at Yale and Robert's most important prospective buyer of Ingersoll Sargent equipment. Hammond's arrest and subsequent conviction derailed Robert's expectation of huge sales in Africa.

On their arrival, Robert had planned to take his family directly north to Johannesburg, but the trauma and uncertainties accompanying the Raid kept them in Cape Town. It was an awkward time as many refugees from the north swarmed south. The hotels were full and therefore expensive. When they finally found an inn, there was only one room available and it was not ready. Declaring Africa a horrible country, the Chapins' French governess had a nervous collapse. Adèle settled her down with smelling salts and took the children to the hotel's piazza. Sitting with her back to the ocean, with one child on either side, she read stories from Kipling's *Jungle Book* and sipped tea. When Robert, harried and distracted, arrived with their luggage, he exclaimed, "What are you doing?" Adèle replied quietly, "Creating an atmosphere."

They were detained in Cape Town for two weeks. When they arrived in Johannesburg, they found that prices were extremely high there too. Adèle remembered that they "paid £50 a month for a corrugated-iron house. Eggs were six shilling a dozen, vegetables almost impossible to obtain at any price. Cabbages were considered a great luxury." Eventually they found a nicely furnished, comfortable house that was also affordable. Robert went immediately to work to aid John Hammond and his friends in jail in Pretoria, a short distance from Johannesburg. Just then the American consul decided to return to the United States. President Cleveland quickly appointed Robert to the post, which allowed him official access to the prisoners. The jail, built to house blacks charged with petty crimes, was squalid; the food was barely edible; and the prisoners, unaccustomed to hard conditions, began to fall ill. Robert did what he could to supply decent food and bolster spirits.

The moment of crisis came when court was convened to try the prisoners. On 28 April 1896, the judge found the prisoners guilty of treason and, despite assurances to the contrary, condemned to death. The next morning Robert told Adèle that he must see President Kruger before he cabled President Cleveland. He also said, "You had better come with me."

Aside from a keen concern for its incarcerated citizens, America's interest in the Transvaal was slight. The Cleveland government was more worried about its on-going dispute with the British over the boundary separating Venezuela and British Guiana on the Caribbean coast of South America and preserving the sanctity of the Monroe Doctrine, which sought to keep foreign influence out of the Western Hemisphere. Apart from the boundary problem, the United States was inclined to side with the British against the Boers. Americans didn't see Kruger as a national hero trying to preserve his people's independence against British tyranny, nor did they think of him as an ugly oppressor of black Africans. Kruger – like Sitting Bull when gold was discovered in the Black Hills of South Dakota – was just a stubborn rock in the road of progress.

When Robert and Adèle entered Kruger's house, the President of the Transvaal was sitting "all in a heap, his chin resting on his chest, smoking a pipe." An attendant placed two chairs facing his where they were directed to sit. An interpreter stood behind Kruger's chair. They sat in silence for several minutes, expecting the President to speak first. Finally Robert spoke up. He explained why he had come and asked what message he should send to the President of the United States. Silence. Like a great Sphinx, Kruger said nothing. Adèle could stand the tension no longer. She burst out. "President Kruger – Christianity stands for mercy, and a Republic should stand for freedom. You claim to represent both, and we expect both from you."

"Was sagt die Frau?" [What did the woman say?], he shouted. The interpreter explained. Kruger became agitated. He stood up and with "his head thrown back and, in a voice like thunder, intoned in Dutch, 'Speak, Lord, for Thy servant heareth.'" A moment later, he said, "God has not yet spoken." He sat back down and Adèle nearly fainted. She thought he must have said, "Off with her head!" There was another long pause. Then Kruger spoke again. "I tell my generals to show mercy on the battlefield; but the penalty of murder is bloodshed." And that was all he said. The interview was over. The next day Kruger commuted the sentences, though the prisoners did not learn for a long time what their penalties had been commuted to. It is unclear what, if any, influence the Chapins' visit had on Kruger's thinking.

A month later Mark Twain, arrived in Pretoria. He was near the end of a year long, round-the-world journey. Highly popular and successful as a writer and speaker, Twain had made a lot of money during his career. But he was also very extravagant and had a knack for making terrible investments. His worldwide tour had the purpose of generating income to pay down his debts. Having known the Chapins in New York and very curious about the American prisoners, he asked Robert to arrange a visit to see the men. Intending to be amusing, Twain annoyed some of the prisoners by joking that, in a world of charlatans and entrapments, they were better off in jail than running around free.

Four days later the Chapins threw a dinner party for Twain with about twenty British and American guests. Toward the end of the meal Adèle thought to ask Twain to talk but couldn't bring herself to do it. Instead, she proposed a toast: "To the United States and to South Africa – England's oldest and youngest children. The first has defied parental authority, and the second is just learning how to kick!" The toast accomplished what Adèle wanted. Twain rose to speak. He told the gathering that, if England of 1776 had been the England of 1896, the States would have done better to remain her colony. What the colonists revolted against was not the mother country but a party faction within Parliament that was narrow-minded and mean-spirited in its governance.

Shortly after, the same evening, another group of roughly twenty Boer men arrived. Robert had invited them to come in after dinner with the idea that the Anglo-Americans and Boers could get to know each other better and to "lessen the bitterness of feeling" that divided them. The dour Boers, dressed in plain clothes and wearing long beards, contrasted sharply with the natty *Uitlanders* decked out in evening dress. "In the charged atmosphere of the room," Adèle recalled, "talk soon became intense, and I remember feeling like a salon of the French Revolution." Twain took her aside. He said, "You have no idea what an impression you have made upon those Boers. Why, they have never seen a woman before in an evening dress. Anything you say would have great influence. I want you to speak to them."

Adèle was appalled at the notion. It was one thing to give a short toast before a small group of friends and familiar faces, but something else to address a bunch of strangers so unlike herself. "I beg you," she said, "not to let me do anything foolish, anything I should regret." Twain assured her, "You can trust me. Come and say to these men what you said to me to-day." Twain led her into the drawing room and rapped on the piano to get everyone's attention. "Gentlemen," he called out, "this is not a moment for logic − it is a moment for sentiment. A woman expresses that better than a man, and I have asked Mrs. Chapin to speak to you."

Adèle spoke for about twenty minutes. When she finished, some of the Boers came forward, kissed her hands, and asked her what they should do. She had no exact idea what she had said. Nor do we, except that it was stirring and conciliatory. Twain thought her brilliant. He sent Adèle a note the next day, 30 May 1896. "You got at the deep places in our hearts," he wrote. "It was a strong, moving speech. It made me want to follow and endorse and applaud."

Samuel Clemens (Mark Twain), ca. 1900
(Courtesy of the Library of Congress)

11

With his business plans in disarray, Robert determined to leave South Africa and head back to England. Before going, he and Adèle saw Paul Kruger one more time, and again urged leniency for the prisoners. Kruger indicated that he cared little for the men in jail. "If a man sets a dog on another man, one does not wish to kick the dog, but the man," he told them. "I want Cecil Rhodes."

Early in 1897 they departed from Cape Town on the *Dunraven Castle*. They were surprised to find both Olive Schreiner and Cecil Rhodes on board. Adèle had met Schreiner earlier in the year and thought she was like "a pure flame." Born in South Africa of English parents (her father was a Wesleyan missionary), Schreiner was well known for her book *The Story of an African Farm*, published in 1883, which openly criticized organized religion and the treatment of women in society. Educated in England and a few years older than Adèle, she had returned to Africa in 1889 and struck a brief alliance with Rhodes, but now stood firmly for the right of the Boers to remain independent of British imperial ambitions in the south of Africa. As for Rhodes, Adèle met him for the first time on the ship to England.

She had already determined that Cecil Rhodes was a bully and a troublemaker. Aside from wanting to be the dominant player in the precious stones and metals field, Rhodes desired to force the diverse political units in southern Africa into a grand Union of South Africa under British dominion. On board the *Dunraven Castle*, she tried to avoid coming into contact with him, a plan that worked well until they reached Madeira off the northwestern coast of Africa. One day she was writing letters when Rhodes approached. After standing beside her for several minutes, he addressed her, "Why haven't you spoken to me?" She asked why she should. "Because," Rhodes replied, "nearly everyone else on board has, and I wanted you to." Not to be intimidated, she asked, "Do you always have what you want?" To his answer, that he generally did, Adèle told him, "You have had it too often, Mr. Rhodes."

Taken aback but clearly intrigued, Rhodes pursued the conversation. She obliged by asking him about his motives. Was he trying to stir up war in South Africa? No, he answered, he was "merely moving my wheel to where there was a current – you can't make a current, but you can move your wheel." He then asked her why the Jameson Raid failed. After a few moments to reflect, she gave an answer: "I will tell you, Mr. Rhodes. It failed because men will fight for their homes, they will fight for their country, they will fight for their God; but they wouldn't fight for Cecil Rhodes, and they wouldn't fight for money." Rhodes conceded that she was right. "Good God, that's true!" he exclaimed.

When they arrived in England, Joseph Chamberlain and his wife Mary invited Robert and Adèle to dinner. Mary was Chamberlain's third wife and considerably younger than he. In fact, she was three years younger than Adèle, who was the same age as Chamberlain's oldest daughter Beatrice. Chamberlain had met Mary when he headed a British delegation to the United States to resolve a dispute between the two countries over fishery boundaries off the coast of Newfoundland. The two had married in a private ceremony in Washington in November 1888. Mary was the daughter of William Crowninshield Endicott, a well-known figure in Boston, who had been Grover Cleveland's Secretary of War in his first administration. With connections in common in New England and Washington and their shared interest in Africa, it was natural enough that the Chamberlains made friends with the Chapins.

Chamberlain, now the British government's Colonial Secretary, was responsible for what happened in the country's widespread Empire. He wanted to get an American view from Robert and Adèle about the past year's events in southern Africa. When he finished asking questions, Adèle asked him one – a question that everyone at the time wanted to know: "What do you think of Cecil Rhodes?" Chamberlain did not hesitate to reply:

> I will tell you a story. A man sat in his study and lifted his eyes to high Heaven and said: "Great God, this is Thy work." Then he touched an electric button and called his butler, gave him a large cheque and said: "You go do it." The butler muddled the whole thing, and when the man was accused, he shrugged his shoulder and said: "It's none of my business; it lies between high Heaven and the butler."

Adèle wondered if Chamberlain had told the story because he thought he could trust her to keep a confidence. "Not entirely," Chamberlain replied. "But if anyone ever wants to know what Joe Chamberlain thought of Cecil Rhodes, you can tell that story." Adèle understood the parable as Chamberlain intended, taking the man in the story to be Rhodes and the butler Jameson. Today, based on historical research, we read the tale differently, taking the man for Chamberlain and the butler for Rhodes.

12

As soon as they were settled in London the Chapins re-connected with Mark Twain, who had reached England several months earlier. On his arrival, Twain, who had undertaken his long worldwide trip with his wife Livy and daughter Clara, learned that his favorite daughter Susy, who had remained in Connecticut, was sick. Mrs. Clemens and Clara immediately left to return home, while Twain stayed in London, hoping Susy's illness was not serious. But, it was. She had contracted meningitis and died in August 1896.

Twain sank into deep mourning. He declined opportunities to lecture and kept a low profile, seeing only a few friends. "He was alone in London," Adèle remembered, "and he used to come and see me quite often." He was extremely unhappy and restless, and she worried about his state of mind. "He would walk up and down the room and say: 'If I was God, I would be ashamed to treat my children so. Don't talk to me about a Heavenly Father; no human father would behave as God does.'" There was nothing that Adèle could say or do that seemed to help, except listen. "I believe," she wrote, "the fact that he could talk out what he felt was a relief, and I suppose I showed the intense sympathy I had with his great and bitter grief, for one day, quite suddenly, he said to me: 'Do you know, I believe I would do almost anything you wanted me to do.'"

Twain unwittingly opened an opportunity that Adèle was quick to exploit. When she arrived in London, her own children, Louis and Julia, were sickly, suffering from pneumonia and whooping cough and general malaise. She found a wonderful physician in Dr. Thomas Gilbart Smith who practiced at the London Hospital. Smith and his colleague Mr. Treves revived the children through patience, tenderness and good care, including exercise and massage. Extremely grateful and still very much interested in the field of healthcare, Adèle volunteered as a visitor to Dr. Smith's ward.

When Twain offered to do anything she asked, Adèle said that she wanted him to go with her to the London Hospital to tell stories to the sick men she visited. Twain was caught off guard. He tried to backtrack. Giving Adèle "his inimitable, quizzical" look, he pleaded that he had never spoken to such an audience in his life. "Besides," he added, "you're asking me for a cool thousand dollars. I was offered that yesterday to give a lecture, and I refused." When Adèle persisted, he worried that the newspapers would hear about it and that the people he had turned down would get after him. She promised him that wouldn't happen – and it never did. Reluctantly, Twain agreed.

Gilbart Smith, who also enjoyed a reputation as a witty raconteur, was delighted with the idea. On a beautiful spring day in late April or early May 1897, he escorted Adèle and Mark Twain to the Fitzgerald Ward of the hospital. The ward was comprised of elderly men, many of whom were terminally ill. In "his slow, mellow way," Twain drew from his vast collection of stories. He told the story of how he had stolen an unripe watermelon and how, after eating it and getting sick, he demanded that the farmer give him a ripe one to compensate him for his indigestion. He also told a tall tale about his grandfather who once lost a ten-cent piece in a field patrolled by a ram of "pugnacious propensities."

Smith, who was also the director of the London Hospital Musical Society, arranged for a pair of young ladies to accompany Twain's stories on piano and violin. Very skillfully the two women punctuated the watermelon story's "gastric crisis." With "a paean of joy ending in a crescendo in B flat," they celebrated the ram's defeat. The patients enjoyed the performance immensely, and gave Twain a loud round of three cheers. Said one of them, the show "was a bit of orl right, I give yer my word." On their way home, Twain confessed to Adèle, "I have never had such an appreciative audience." (Le Bourgeois and Evans, 344-7.)

Toward the end of the year Robert went back to Africa while the rest of his family – Adèle, her father, sister and children – returned to the United States in order to enroll Louis in boarding school. Eton College in England had offered Louis a place, but Adèle heeded the advice of a young Eton student. "No, Mrs. Chapin, don't do it. If he's a good sort and stands up for his country," he told her, "we'll have to put him down; and if he's a snob and imitates us, we'll despise him."

They spent the winter and the following spring and summer in Lenox visiting family and old friends and preparing Louis to enter the Groton School in Massachusetts in the fall of 1898. One day during the summer a young woman came to the house with a letter of introduction. The friend who had written the letter explained to Adèle that her visitor was interested in dancing and asked her to do what she could to help. Absorbed as she was with her own children, she thought immediately of dancing lessons. "I think I could organize a dancing class – twenty children or more," Adèle told the young woman. "Would Tuesdays suit you?"

No, lessons would not suit. "That is not what I understand by dancing," the young woman replied in a sad and dreamy way. "I look upon dancing as Theocritus looked upon dancing." Adèle, uncharacteristically, was at a loss for words. "Where did you study?" she finally thought to ask. "I gaze upon the great statues of the world," came her reply. "I dance to Greek choruses; study the poses of Botticelli figures. I interpret the dawn and the sunset; I dance the *Rubaiyat of Omar Khayyam*; I dance bare-footed on the lawn. Let me dance for you, any day you choose."

Adèle knew little about professional dancing, but gave in. "I was dazed but charmed," she wrote. "She was very lovely to look at, very girlish and natural and unspoiled. So I had said: 'I will see what I can do and let you know.'" With the help of her friend Mrs. John Winthrop, she arranged three lawn dances for Isadora Duncan. The first took place in mid July at Mrs. Winthrop's summer residence in Stockbridge. Isadora danced her interpretation of Shakespeare's *Midsummer Night's Dream* to the music of Mendelssohn. Her performance served as a fundraiser for the Red Cross. Tickets were sold for $2 each and nearly two hundred people showed up.

Duncan performed a second time a week later at the country house of Mrs. Oscar Iasigi where she interpreted Ethelbert Nevin's music, dancing to his compositions "Narcissus," "Ophelia," "Water Nymph" and "A Shepherd's Tale." She gave her final performance at Mrs. Winthrop's again in early August, giving her rendition of the *Rubaiyat of Omar Khayyam*.

Adèle remembered her first appearance. "Suddenly," she wrote, "we saw, flitting from tree to tree, a figure in diaphanous draperies – grey, mauve, pink – with loosened hair to which loose flowers clung. Emerging from the shade, she danced, or posed, a dance of dawn – quite exquisite." Nearly everyone was charmed, but a few old ladies were shocked. Adèle confessed that she was "not entirely prepared to be responsible for it all."

Isadora Duncan had just turned twenty years old in May and was virtually unknown. She and her family (mother, sister and two brothers) had left San Francisco and traveled to Chicago and then to New York City, where Isadora began dancing minor roles for Arnold Daly's troupe. She hungered for the chance to dance in her own style, unconstrained by precedent, choreographer or costume. Immediately after her triumph in the Berkshires, she received several invitations to dance at Newport, a richer and posher community than Lenox. In August, Mrs. Calvin Brice asked her to dance on her balcony for a half hour. "But thunders of applause," a newspaper reported, "recalled her. Over and over was she brought back and Miss Duncan on the occasion of her Newport debut danced not a half hour but two hours for Mrs. Brice's guests." Swiftly she was asked to dance for Mrs. Hodgson, Miss Mason and Mrs. Fred Lee Pierson. Mrs. John Jacob Astor IV, married to one of the wealthiest men in the nation, watched her perform and invited her to dance at her grand villa at Newport in the winter. It was the kind of invitation that she dreamed of. "Mrs. Astor," Isadora wrote in her autobiography, "represented to America what a Queen did to England." (Duncan, 43.) The delightful Miss Duncan wowed the wealthy elite in Newport. The next year she sailed to Europe where her career skyrocketed. She conquered London first, then Paris and on to Munich and Berlin, and St. Petersburg and Moscow.

Adèle quickly forgot about the young girl who had knocked at her door in Lenox, but ten years later, she knocked again. Adèle was sitting in her drawing room in her house in London when her butler announced Miss Isadora Duncan. "For a moment," Adèle wrote, "I was perplexed, and then a memory came back to me; so that when she said: 'Mrs. Chapin, I have come to thank you. I am the most famous dancer in Europe and I owe it all to you,' I knew what she meant – though what she said seemed incredible."

Isadora Duncan
(Courtesy of the Library of Congress)

13

Robert determined to make another try at business in southern Africa. When he and Adèle arrived in England in late 1898, Joseph and Mary Chamberlain invited them to spend Christmas with them at their house in Highbury. It was a very special occasion. Adèle remembered that in the afternoon Chamberlain, who was known to be a bit stiff and chilly, played games with her ten-year old daughter Julia, and how "full of fun and friendliness" he was. As she was observing them, she suffered a terrible premonition that war would soon breakout between the British and the Boers. "I do not know why it was but a sort of terror seized me then that this African war was coming, and I begged him not to let it come, saying, 'If it comes, it will cost millions of pounds and thousands of lives.'" Chamberlain brushed her anxiety aside. He laughed and said, "Mrs. Chapin, don't be dramatic. There will be no war." Even if it happened, the Boers, he predicted, "will yield to us like chaff before the wind."

Robert and Adèle departed England in January 1899. On board they met Sir Alfred Milner, whom Chamberlain had appointed Governor of the Cape Colony two years earlier. Milner faced the difficult, ultimately impossible task of persuading Paul Kruger to accept British rule. Milner had risen rapidly through the British civil service because he was judicious, confident, clear-headed and energetic. Adèle took an immediate liking to him and they became close friends. She believed that he combined all the great qualities necessary for diplomacy and might yet resolve the approaching conflict in the Transvaal. But that was not to be the case. In the ensuing months discussions between the Boer President and British Governor foundered.

When Adèle returned from Johannesburg to Cape Town just before the final break between the two sides, she called on Milner to talk over the political situation. Ever an optimist, Adèle recommended that he adopt an easier and more conciliatory style with the Boer leader. "If you would treat Kruger as you treat me," she told him, "I believe you could do anything with him." Her suggestion infuriated Milner. "Kruger," he retorted, "shall have every chance and the best possible terms shall be offered him. But I should despise myself if I cajoled him; that I could never do!" Milner understood that Kruger had to yield if he were to succeed. At their final meeting at the town of Bloemfontein, Kruger rejected the British terms that Milner brought to the table, terms that amounted to a scarcely concealed ultimatum. Milner demanded that the Boers enfranchise the foreigners in the Transvaal and accept British control. On his return to Cape Town, Milner wrote Adèle a short note in June, summing up his encounter: "And so it was a failure – as I anticipated .... I am fearfully tired and disappointed, but *not beaten*."

Before Bloemfontein, Adèle had described Milner to her father in this way: "Plato said, 'He shall be as a god unto me, who can define and decide.' I have met such a man." But after Milner's meeting with Kruger, she wrote her father a more somber assessment: "The sympathy, interest and open-mindedness with which he had always listened had gone – the die was cast." It was a dark time for Adèle as well as for Africa. Her son Louis had fallen ill with scarlet fever at school several thousand miles away. Franklin Delano Roosevelt wrote to his mother and father on 28 May 1899 that his classmate, Louis Chapin, had only a mild case of fever. "Still," he added, "it is hard on him as his parents are in Johannesburg South Africa, and old Mr. LeBourgeois in London, but he has some other relatives over here." (Roosevelt, 301.) Louis quickly recovered though it was sometime before the news reached Adèle. Then, soon after she sent her letter about Milner, her father died in London (23 June 1899) at the age of seventy-seven.

Louis Le Bourgeois had lived with his daughter and son-in-law for most of the seventeen years following Lizzie's death. Adèle and her father had been close since childhood and the intimacy continued until the end. Louis had been obliged by war and indebtedness to give over the reins of his plantation-empire.

Unlike King Lear, Adèle wrote, he "accepted defeat and circumstances like one who condescended, full of tenderness, full of dignity, keeping his faith and his love of humanity, and his grace and charm unsullied by the grossness of the fight." He remained "a fountain of wisdom, gentleness, and patience, creating a beautiful atmosphere, which is greater than ruling a kingdom." Adèle remembered quite clearly his telling her brothers that, "a gentleman is a man who never allows his interests to influence his convictions." Louis practiced what he preached; he advocated the doctrine of Free Trade and, specifically, argued for lifting import duties on sugar even though doing so would have undermined the family sugar business. As one of the delegates elected to the state constitutional convention in Louisiana to consider an ordinance of secession from the United States, Louis was one of the few members to vote against the proposal. But, once the secession was inevitable, he ultimately voted with Louisiana to join the Confederate States of America. Even for Louis, slavery and secession presented difficult contradictions.

In October hostilities broke out in Africa and the war – bloody, expensive and long as Adèle feared – lasted until 1902, when the British finally beat the Boers into submission. Once again Robert's business prospects were ruined. They decided to return to England to wait out what they hoped would be a war of short duration. In London Adèle found a 17th century house to rent in Chelsea known as Queen's House since it was thought at the time that Christopher Wren had designed it for Queen Catherine of Braganza, King Charles II's wife. Adèle was delighted to learn that the 19th century poet and painter Dante Gabriel Rossetti had also lived there from 1862 until his death in 1882. Somewhat eccentric Rossetti had given the house a racy reputation. He kept a mistress as well as a menagerie of animals that included his favorite, a wombat. When Robert bought their daughter Julia a dog, Adèle decided that it should be called Dante Gabriel Rossetti, to Julia's disgust. The dog's name was soon reduced to Ro.

Adèle made the most of her short tenancy. In May 1900 Richard Watson Gilder and his wife Helena came to visit. Adèle put on a round of parties that included the elite of American culture, most notably, Mark Twain, John Singer Sargent, Cecilia Beaux, James Whistler, Henry James, and Joseph Choate. Appointed as the American ambassador to England by President McKinley in 1899, Choate remained in the post until 1905. Sargent, seeing Adèle in a dress she had just made for herself, observed, "How Jacobean you look in this Jacobean room." She then realized, "how like a Holbein my full black satin sleeves and my white cape were." And, added, "To be stout and plain also helps a Holbein effect!" When her sister Elizabeth became engaged to Doctor Eugene Crockett of Boston, Adèle insisted that they should come to England and be married from the Queen's House. The wedding took place in the Old Church in Chelsea in July. Three months later, Adèle delivered her fourth child, whom she named Adèle Christina.

16 Cheyne Walk, Chelsea, London, "Queen's House"
Etching by Walter W. Burgess ca. 1895

It had been a busy two years, but not a very productive time business-wise. Robert and Adèle decided to move back to their country house in Lenox, Massachusetts in the autumn.

Adèle and Christina By Cecilia Beaux

14

Early in the year 1901 Adèle visited her friend Ellen Barlow in New York. Mrs. Barlow was nearly thirty years older than Adèle; she had married Francis Barlow who had served as a general in the Union army and later a politician in New York. Ellen's parents Sarah and Francis Shaw had been prominent abolitionists before the Civil War and advocates of equal rights for Negroes afterwards. Ellen's brother Robert Shaw had lost his life in the war commanding the all-black 54th Massachusetts Volunteers.

During her visit, Mrs. Barlow invited Booker T. Washington to dinner. "Out of consideration for what she thought might be my Southern prejudices," Adèle wrote, "she gave me an opportunity of dining out that night." But Adèle preferred to meet the remarkable Mr. Washington, whom she already knew as an impressive force. Born a slave in 1856, Washington believed that Negroes could better improve their position in society through education as opposed to confrontation. When he was twenty-five years old, he had been appointed the first head of the newly founded Tuskegee Institute in Tuskegee, Alabama, and remained its leader until his death in 1915. Adèle eagerly engaged Mrs. Barlow's guest. She gave a brief account of one of their exchanges over dinner:

> In our conversation that evening I was struck by his sense of humor and by his justice to the slave-owners. He told me that the slave-owner was the greatest friend the Negro ever had, for no one else would have taken the trouble to train and educate him; and that the only native races that would survive were those that had passed through slavery! And I remembered often saying that, hitherto, the only two methods of dealing with native races had been extermination or slavery – and that certainly slavery was the less cruel of the two.

Adèle was impressed with Washington. When his autobiography, *Up from Slavery,* was published later in the year, she sent a copy to Alfred Milner.

Washington was invited to another, more important dinner several months later. Shortly after President McKinley was assassinated in September, his successor Theodore Roosevelt asked Washington to the White House, where he dined with the President and his family. News of the event caused a national furor, particularly in the South. The image of a black man sitting at dinner with the President in the nation's capital was bad enough, but it was, for many, intolerable that he should eat at the same table with the President's wife and young daughter. The uproar subsided, but it left many, on both sides of the issue, deeply disturbed.

Earlier in the year Mark Twain, upset by the rising number of lynchings of blacks throughout the country, wrote an indictment of the murderous practice that he entitled "The United States of Lyncherdom." Twain never published the essay, but the intensity of his feeling was still white hot when he received an honorary degree at Yale during its bi-centennial celebration in October 1901. Twain arrived in New Haven with many dignitaries and other important people, including President Roosevelt and Booker T. Washington. He immediately re-connected with some old friends. He met the Chapins and Ambassador Choate and his wife, and they all had lunch together. Afterwards Robert and Adèle went to Twain's lodgings where they spent the next hour or so "deeply engrossed in talk." Some of the talk was evidently about the maltreatment of Negroes and their friendship with Booker Washington.

Twain and Washington had first met in London at the American embassy on the fourth of July 1899 at a reception for Choate as the new Ambassador, but came to know each other better through their mutual friend and benefactor Henry Rogers. Extremely wealthy, Rogers had partnered with John D. Rockefeller in the success of the Standard Oil Company. He had met Twain in 1893 when the author's business affairs began to unravel and had advised him to make his round-the-world speaking tour to shore up his finances. Rogers had sought out Washington the following year after hearing him speak in New York and began providing substantial funds to the Tuskegee Institute and other Negro schools in the South. Both Twain and Washington became frequent guests on Rogers' yacht *Kanawha*, as it cruised along the East Coast.

Engrossed in conversation, Twain and the Chapins lost track of the time. Suddenly they realized that they were about to miss the reading of the bi-centennial Poem. As they rushed off to the auditorium, Twain got a bright idea in his head. He wanted the Chapins to sit on the stage with him. As neither was invited to be there, Robert demurred, but Adèle decided to do it. "He marched into the great hall, giving me the open sesame by a wave of the hand;" she wrote, "and, beckoning me to follow, he walked on to the platform and seated me between himself and Booker Washington." The idea was simple and perfect: show the world that it was all right for a white woman to sit next to a Negro, whether in a private dining room or before a large audience. "I was the only lady on the platform," Adèle recalled, "and an object of much curiosity."

Shortly after the Yale celebration, the Clemens family invited the Chapins to visit them at Wave Hill, an estate up the Hudson River that they had just leased for a year at the beginning of October. As they had done in the past, Twain and Adèle engaged in long and absorbing conversations. Livy Clemens admonished them in a gentle voice one evening, "It is twelve o'clock. Mr. Chapin and I are ready to go to bed." But the two continued to talk into the night. "Next morning," Adèle wrote, "he and I were down before Mrs. Clemens appeared, and were again deep in conversation. She always insisted that we had been talking ever since she left us, and had not gone to bed at all!"

15

Robert continued to sell for the Ingersoll company, and saw a new opportunity in Canada again in 1904. Adèle decided to fortify herself by spending the summer in the Cotswolds in England before joining him in Montreal. Before she left, she heard that Livy Clemens, long ailing, had died in Genoa on the fifth of June. Aboard the steamship *Minnehaha* two days later, Adèle wrote Twain to say how sorry she was to hear of Livy's death, and that she wished she were in the Berkshires – where Twain and his daughters Clara and Jean had just leased a house in Tyringham for the summer – to speak to him in person. "I beg you to know," she wrote, "that you have my sympathy, dear friend, and believe if I knew a word to say that would help I would say it or a deed to do that would help I would do it – I am thankful to have known her." (Twain Papers.)

On her return to the Berkshires in the fall, she ran into their friend Henry James. Although James spent most of his adult life in England, he had come back to the United States for a lecture tour and to visit his family. Like Twain, James had run into some financial difficulties after experiencing a creative dry spell. When he heard they were moving to Canada, James asked Adèle, "*Why* Montreal?" His tone echoed Adèle's feeling. Why, indeed?

Soon after her arrival in Canada, she was delighted to hear the news of the appointment of Lord Grey as the country's new Governor-General. "We had known him and Lady Grey in England and we admired, as later we grew to love, his great personality," she later wrote. "These were my keys to Montreal, and they unlocked many doors." Adèle quickly observed the sharp separation between the French and English communities in Montreal. "It was much as it had been in New Orleans before and immediately after our Civil War," she remarked. "There the French quarter and the American quarter were separated from one another by Canal Street, and there was no intercourse between them." With connections to Lord Grey, and her own French heritage, Adèle determined that she could help bridge the gap between the two communities in Montreal. She set about inviting the leading women of both sides to her drawing room and began a new women's club, based on the Fortnightly Club in New York. With thirty women, half English and half French, "I introduced them to each other," she wrote, "and I had a longing to make them understand each other better."

On the occasion of the first meeting at her home, Adèle chose "patriotism" as the subject for discussion. "I started off by saying that I had so many patriotic emotions – having been taught to love France by my father and England by my mother – in my childhood having learned to love the South, and my husband having taught me to love the North; that in France I sang the 'Marseillaise' *de plein Coeur.'* and in England 'God Save the Queen'; in Germany, the *'Wacht am Rhein,'* in memory of my great-grandmother; and in Ireland, 'Erin Go Bragh'; and I questioned whether I had lost or gained by these patriotic emotions." She noted that she "was encouraged by Dr. Osler who said in his speech, 'we must begin by being denationalized and every problem in life should be faced from a cosmopolitan point of view.'" The leading French and English ladies of Montreal proceeded to discuss the concepts and offered their own perspectives to the mix, as Adèle peppered the discussion to "draw out conversation."

Her first meeting was a success and the club flourished for a while – "but," Adèle wrote, "my husband's affairs were not going satisfactorily, and in June [1905] it was decided that we should leave. It was a wrench again, but when an opening in England had been offered to my husband I was not altogether sorry to go back." Robert accepted a position as a director of the Farwell Trust Company in Chicago, which entailed operating an office in London under his own name. Granger Farwell, who formed the firm, was Robert's classmate and close friend at Yale. Robert, Granger, and Adèle's brother Edward took their degrees in Yale's Sheffield Scientific School, and belonged to both The Cloisters and Sigma

Delta Chi scientific fraternity. Unable to afford to rent the Queen's House in Chelsea, Adèle found a rather worn but agreeable place in Kensington Square. Once settled, the Chapins continued to see and entertain their friends. Alfred Milner and Henry James were frequent visitors as were Lady Cynthia Asquith and her husband Herbert.

Adèle also resumed her charitable efforts. She conceived a plan to establish a day nursery connected with each elementary school in London. Working mothers would leave their toddlers at the day nursery, which would be run by a trained nurse. Older girls in school would spend a certain amount of their school time in the nursery for practical training in the care of infants. The experience would awaken the girls to a sense of responsibility, motherhood and the joy of childcare. Adèle succeeded in obtaining provisional approval from the London County Council after several years of hard work. She then formed an oversight committee and eventually raised sufficient funds to hire a nurse to set up a model nursery. All was ready to go when she was obliged to return to the United States.

In the meantime, her daughter Julia, who reached the age of twenty in 1908, followed in her mother's footsteps. She and her friend Paulina Cockerell began volunteer work at the Great Ormond Street Hospital. They noticed that many children returned repeatedly to the hospital. It soon occurred to them that better care at home could reduce the number of the children's visits. They devised a scheme to inform the district nurse in each neighborhood when a child left the hospital so that proper follow-up could take place. The plan worked remarkably well. When Julia married a couple of years later, her job at the Great Ormond Street Hospital became a fully funded, paid position.

Though she was like her mother in her desire to advance charitable causes, Julia was in one respect very different. One summer she and her mother were invited to the horse races at Royal Ascot. Built in 1711 by Queen Anne, the race course was located near Windsor Castle. The high point of the racing season was and still is the week of competition referred to as Royal Ascot.

A very posh and dressy social event, Royal Ascot was the place to see and be seen. When they were alone Julia turned on her: "Mother, what do you mean by bringing me to a place like this? Don't you suppose I know that all these young men are betting and gambling? And just think what the women have spent on their clothes – just think what the money might have done for the poor of London!" Adèle was stunned, and found it hard to defend herself. Brought up in a nineteenth century Southern tradition of *noblesse oblige*, Adèle awakened to the fact that her daughter was a young woman of the new twentieth century.

Julia Chapin
By John Singer Sargent, 1909

16

"For six years we lived this happy life," Adèle wrote about their time in London between 1906 and 1912. One of the highlights of this period was an invitation from the Special Ambassador to Great Britain appointed by President Howard Taft to view from the balcony of the Stratton House the coronation parade of King George V. The Special Ambassador was John Hays Hammond, Robert's good Yale friend who had been imprisoned by Paul Kruger as one of the Jameson Raid traitors. But the six year period of contentment passed. Lack of financial progress brought it to an end.

"My husband's affairs," she revealed, "were going badly, and in the midst of all this fullness of life and interests and work we were obliged to give up our house and go to America, expecting never to return." A few years earlier the Chapins had bought a modest farmhouse in Tyringham, ten miles from Lenox. "Never shall I forget arriving there at dusk and walking through high grass to the old front door with its worn stone steps, and feeling the homely welcome as we went in. How can I describe it? It was the welcome of simplicity and peace."

Alfred Milner paid a visit of three days to Tyringham in the autumn of 1912. After the British defeated the Boers, Milner had become the first Governor of the Transvaal and Orange River Colony, which consolidated the two previously autonomous territories into one administrative unit under the British crown. For his work, King Edward VII had elevated his loyal servant to the peerage as a baron. To Tyringham, Lord Milner brought welcome news from England about all their friends. He and Adèle talked far into the night before the log fire – "good, uninterrupted talk, with no engagements waiting." Milner also provided good company for Adèle's youngest daughter, now twelve years old. He and Christina, who was known as Babs within the family, sprawled on the floor studying maps of the Berkshire countryside. Milner was amused that the British general William Howe, having marched through the area during the American Revolution, named the town of Tyringham after his country house in England.

Henry James wrote Adèle from London, saying how much he missed her company and wished she were nearer. He imagined her enduring an austere and unpleasant exile from civilization:

> ... it comes to me, as somehow, a dreary drop from Kensington Square to a Massachusetts winter shanty – and you don't trace for me the shades of transition. What you enable me to see on the other hand is that your courage and *ressort* [resiliency] are of the same high order as ever. Only one doesn't like to be, or to see one's friends ... thrown back on the test of these virtues .... I wish you, at any rate, a bright rebound, in due course, to Kensington Square.

The return to England came soon enough, but not as a result of planning or good fortune.

At Christmas 1913 all the family gathered at Tyringham. The Chapins' married children, Louis and Julia, came with their babies as well as Adèle's sister Elizabeth with her daughter Kitty, who was a year younger than Babs. Everything was festive. They covered the fireplace mantel with pine boughs and decorated the Christmas tree with lighted candles. Babs was handing out presents when the sleeve of her Santa Claus suit caught fire from one of the candles. In seconds she was enveloped in flames. Adèle wrapped her in her arms and threw her to the floor; her son-in-law Reese Alsop tossed a rug over both of them to smother the fire. Babs suffered severe burns to her face. Making matters worse, the house caught on fire a few days later when the exhaust pipe connected to the stove burst into flames. They sought refuge in Manhattan.

Adèle later reflected that, "The only two times in my life when I have tried to renounce the world and get down to the absolutely simple life and extreme economy, I have been over come by disaster." Soon after the house fire, her son Louis accepted a job to represent Redmond & Company in London. When the doctor suggested that Babs would recover more quickly from her burns in a milder climate, Adèle decided that she would fare better in London than in New York, and they could help Louis and his family get settled. She and Babs sailed away in February 1914.

17

Arriving in England on the eve of the First World War, they found the atmosphere palpable with anxious foreboding. Everything seemed out of tune and out of order.

After the assassination of the Austrian Archduke Ferdinand in Sarajevo in June, American citizens were advised to return home. Herbert Hoover organized an exodus of over 100,000 Americans from Europe during the summer and fall. Adèle decided to stay in London with the idea of helping out. She didn't have to wait long. With the German invasion of France through Belgium, the First World War began. Soon Belgian refugees began to flood into London. They needed everything – food, clothing, money, healthcare and housing. Adèle called on her friends for assistance; they responded generously and quickly. Six years before, on one of her many Atlantic crossings, she had met Alexander Cochran, a wealthy American carpet manufacturer and philanthropist. He had graduated from Yale in 1896 and later established the Elizabethan Club at the college, donating a building, a large sum of money and an outstanding collection of late 16th and 17th century English books. Learning that Adèle was engaged in aiding the refugees, Cochran sent her a check for £1000 to carry out her work.

With her Belgian relief work largely wound up by the spring of 1915, Adèle thought it was time to go home. She booked passage for Babs and herself, and began telling friends good-bye. At the American embassy she had tea with Florence Page whose husband was the U.S. ambassador to Italy. Florence told Adèle that there was a severe shortage of beds in England for wounded soldiers. "I could not believe it!" Adèle wrote, "I made enquiries and was told there was an urgent need." She wrote to Alexander Cochran again. He cabled back right away, saying: "If you will undertake to run it, I will support a hospital."

Tired and torn, she went to see her friend Sir William Osler for advice. Born in Canada, Osler had been on the medical faculties of McGill University in Montreal, the University of Pennsylvania in Philadelphia and John Hopkins University in Baltimore before accepting the appointment as the Regius Chair of medicine at Oxford University in 1905. Adèle told Dr. Osler that she was ill; she wanted to see her family; she wanted to go home. "Don't let me do this unless it is necessary;" she said to him, "but if you think it is necessary, I must stay and do it." Osler was emphatic. "It *is* necessary. The need is desperate. You *must* do it."

Adèle with Sir William Osler (center), Robert Chapin (back right), and others
(Courtesy of Robert Alsop)

Osler gave Adèle a letter of introduction to Sir Alfred Keogh, a general and physician who had risen to prominence for advancing medical practices in the British Army. Sir Alfred endorsed Adèle's proposal to organize a primary hospital for convalescents and authorized a special grant for the project. Adèle then searched for a suitable facility. She finally found the place she wanted. It was a mansion, called Caen Woods Tower, with lovely views, overlooking twelve acres of gardens near Hampstead Heath. The rooms were airy and large, and there was a long balcony, ideal for convalescent strolls. But there was a problem: the owner had already offered it to the Red Cross. Adèle discovered that the building provided more space than the Red Cross needed, so she worked out a deal for cash. "This they were delighted to do;" she wrote, "and I, too, was delighted to feel that in getting my house I was also able to help the Red Cross."

Caen Woods Tower

Adèle then went shopping for beds, linen, china, kitchen utensils and all the other household items a well-equipped facility required. The hospital opened in October 1915. William Carnegie, Canon of Westminster, performed a service to celebrate the occasion in the mansion's small chapel. Adèle's friends and main supporters, Lord Milner, Sir William Osler, Alexander Cochran, and Florence Page, were there. Many other distinguished visitors came later – most notably the King and Queen – to see what was soon hailed as a model of good management, successful recoveries and overall cleanliness. In October 1916, Adèle's cousin Martha Blow Wadsworth traveled to London to volunteer her services to the hospital.

Adèle Le Bourgeois Chapin
passport photo from 1917
in her hospital administrator's uniform
(Courtesy of the U.S. National Archives)

During the war, over 2000 British soldiers passed through the facility, which became known as the American Hospital for English Soldiers. For establishing the hospital and overseeing its success, King George recognized her efforts after the war by making Adèle a Member of the royal Order of the British Empire. The order was created in 1917 especially to recognize individuals who made valuable contributions to the Empire during the First World War.

18

Just after the cessation of fighting in Europe (Armistice Day, 11 November 1918), Adèle's friend Beatrice Chamberlain died. Her brother Austen, a member of the British government's War Cabinet, asked Adèle to write her obituary for the *Times of London*. "This touched me deeply," Adèle wrote, "I received the message late in the afternoon, after returning exhausted from the hospital. It was to be inserted the next morning. I felt inadequate, and threw myself on the sofa in a sort of despair." She picked up a book of French poems and found one that she and Beatrice once had read together. "This gave me my clue." Adèle then produced a plain but perceptive portrait of a dignified and dedicated woman.

"By the death of Miss Beatrice Chamberlain," she began, "many people's lives and many people's causes are the poorer. One who was not a friend, and who differed from her on all the questions of the day, said of her that she considered her one of the greatest of Englishwoman; and one who was very near to her writes, 'I feel that the great prop of my life has been taken away.'" Adèle drew a portrait of Beatrice that captured her strong character without making her appear monolithic. "It is certain," she continued, "that she had the heart of a great woman and the mind of a great man. Her vivid personality, her brilliant intellect, her sense of humor and her warm heart kindled many fires. She was a splendid antagonist; but however sharp her blade and however straight her home-thrust the wound was a clean one that quickly healed and left no scar."

Without betraying her own antipathy to late Victorian imperialism, Adèle didn't equivocate about Beatrice's support for her father's colonial policies, but relied on Beatrice's own voice. She quoted directly: "'The Empire has stood together. My father is vindicated,' were her first words at the beginning of the War. Almost her last were, 'The Armistice is signed.' Between these two moments she had no other thought but to serve the Empire that her father loved. It was the passion of her life." Adèle made it clear that her friend was not inflexible. Though she had been adamantly opposed to female emancipation, Beatrice turned her energies to making women informed and effective voters once it was granted. "She was a patriot," Adèle wrote at the very end, "and died for England as truly as any soldier in the field." Her obituary revealed the combination of clear analysis, sympathetic understanding, and rich but succinct language that made Adèle a strong writer and a sparkling conversationalist.

After the war she sailed back to the United States in April 1919 on the *Aquitania*. She saw her grandchildren, whose number had increased to seven, for the first time in five years. It was wonderful to be re-connected, but the weight of the war years had left her exhausted. She fell ill with pneumonia, which dampened the family reunion. At first she thought that she and Robert would remain in the States, but Babs, who had returned to America in 1915, was homesick for England and thought she wanted to study classics at Oxford. So, back they went in the autumn, arriving on the first anniversary of Armistice Day.

They lived mainly in England in the ensuing years, but traveled nearly every year to Massachusetts to spend time at Tyringham and see their grandchildren. Adèle gradually relinquished her social and charitable activities, contenting herself with fewer visits but much letter writing. By the end of the Great War most of her most important male friends had died. Her father (1899), Charles Beaman (1900), Grover Cleveland (1908), Richard Gilder (1909), Mark Twain (1910), Joseph Chamberlain (1914), Booker Washington (1915), Henry James (1916), Joseph Choate (1917) were all gone as were three of her brothers Edward (1899), Charless (1905) and George (1910). She still had enough energy to amuse and sometimes embarrass her younger friends, children and grandchildren with her renditions of Negro stories and dances that she learned as a child at Belmont. Past the age of sixty, she could show her audience the subtle movements of the Turkey trot. With her hands curled in her armpits and elbows extended to the side, she could stoop down, gently move her elbows up and down, like turkey wings, and lift and slide her feet across the floor – a big *adagio* bird in rhythm with life.

Adèle Christina "Babs" Chapin
By John Singer Sargent, 1921

As Adèle slowed down, Robert picked up. He finally discovered the right combination of talents and interests to create a livelihood that provided both joy and a steady stream of income. After the war, their friend Christopher Turnor, a wealthy landowner and social reformer, engaged Robert to manage his agricultural businesses. Robert created an accounting system that provided Turnor with a clear picture of the financial position of his several farms at any moment. Turnor recommended Robert to other wealthy landowners. During the last years of his life, he ran a successful estate management business, and prospered.

Despite various ailments, Adèle's curiosity and initiative remained strong. In 1898 she had met Lord Kelvin who at a dinner party showed her how a piece of radium – a basic element whose properties had been recently discovered by Marie Curie – glowed in the dark. Adèle at once became an avid backer of Marie Curie and her Institute in Paris. Thirty years later her friend John Fulton, a young researcher at the Yale University Medical School and serious book collector, introduced her to Abraham Flexner, who had published a famous report sponsored by the Carnegie Foundation in 1910 that led to the complete overhaul of medical education in North America. When Adèle met him in 1929 Flexner had worked for more than a decade at the Rockefeller Foundation and was about to found the Institute for Advanced Studies at Princeton. Adèle urged him to provide financial support to the Curie Institute. In a letter to Fulton in March 1933, she wrote, "Did you know that your little deed of kindness in Paris when you put me in touch with Abr[ah]am Flexner has resulted in $10,000 a year for the years to my French doctors at the Radium Institute from the Rockefeller Foundation? It took 4 years to do it but it was worth doing!" Fulton was delighted. "I shall never cease to be grateful to you," he replied, "for bringing me into contact with this phase of French medicine. I am inclined to look upon it as perhaps the most fundamental thing that they are now doing in France." (Fulton Collection.)

In November 1937, Adèle wrote Fulton again, thanking him for a copy of a speech he had given. "We are battling with colds and old age and the many infirmities of the flesh which is dreary," she said, "but the spirit is still willing." It was one of her last letters. Six months later, while visiting their daughter Julia at her cottage in the little village of Kingham in the Cotswolds in England, Adèle died. Robert, at age eighty-two, was himself in frail health. The shock of Adèle's death brought on his. A devoted husband, who lived a good part of his life in his wife's shadow, Robert Chapin died four days later.

Robert W. Chapin and his grandson Robert

NELKA'S STORY

Nelka de Smirnoff Moukhanoff

1878-1963

(All quotations in Nelka's Story, except where noted, come from Max Moukhanoff's *Nelka: Mrs. Helen de Smirnoff Moukhanoff. 1878 – 1963, A Biographical Sketch,* with the additional exception of quotations from Susan Blow's letters to Dr. James Putnam, which come from Blow (Susan) Letters.)

1

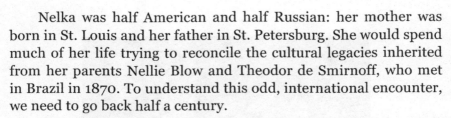

Nelka was half American and half Russian: her mother was born in St. Louis and her father in St. Petersburg. She would spend much of her life trying to reconcile the cultural legacies inherited from her parents Nellie Blow and Theodor de Smirnoff, who met in Brazil in 1870. To understand this odd, international encounter, we need to go back half a century.

Nelka's grandfather Henry Taylor Blow was two years old when his parents Peter and Elizabeth sold their family plantation in Virginia for the large sum of $5500 in 1818. By the time the Blows arrived in St. Louis twelve years later, the family fortune had gone from riches to rags. Fortunately, Henry was endowed with a high level of energy and intelligence and his sister Charlotte had married a successful businessman. Henry went to work for his brother-in-law Joseph Charless, who, recognizing his abilities, made him a partner in his paint and drug company when Henry was nineteen years old. The panic of 1837 and the ensuing recession nearly destroyed the company, but the brothers-in-law managed to survive. When the economy recovered, they decided to split the firm, Joseph taking over the wholesale drug business and Henry the white lead works.

Henry experienced another setback nearly a decade later when two large fires in St. Louis burnt down first his house and then his castor oil factory, part of the white lead works, in 1849. The *Weekly Herald* (of New York) reported his factory loss at $120,000 with insurance covering less than half that amount. With pluck and luck, he started afresh. A rich family friend, George Collier, provided funds to rebuild the factory, forming the Collier White Lead and Oil Company. Henry became the President and a substantial stakeholder. He streamlined the process for refining raw ore into white lead, and formed a partnership with his brother Peter and Ferdinand Kennett in 1857 to mine lead at Granby in the southwest corner of Missouri. When Kennett quit the business, Henry and his brother co-opted several others to create the Granby Mining and Smelting Company in 1865. As Henry accumulated wealth, he rose to political prominence in Missouri and then on the national scene, first as a State Senator and later as a Member of Congress.

Before all of this, when he was still a young man working closely with Joseph Charless, Henry married Minerva Grimsley, the oldest daughter of Susan Stark and Colonel Thornton Grimsley. Orphaned as a child, Thornton Grimsley had become an apprentice in the saddlery business to his foster father, John Jacoby, in Bourbon County, Kentucky. He eventually moved to St. Louis where he became a successful saddle merchant, bought property, and became active in politics. He opened the National Hotel on Market and Third Streets in 1829, the year before Peter Blow began to run the Jefferson Hotel. The National was considered the finest hotel in the city at the time, which helps explain in part why Peter Blow's operations of the Jefferson failed.

Minerva Grimsley Blow
(Courtesy of the Missouri History Museum)

Henry Taylor Blow by Mathew Brady
(Courtesy of the U.S. National Archives)

Before ever meeting Minerva, Henry had asked his sister Elizabeth Rebecca to help him find a suitable wife. In a letter dated

18 May 1837, he charged her "to look out for a young lady whose intelligence, amiability of disposition lights up every feature, not too large or too small but with a pretty foot and a soft hand – a beautiful and good set of ivory and whose 'little' waist has never been 'tortured' by 'tight lacing.' I am very particular about this." (Blow Family Papers.) Presumably Minerva fit the description, though her waist did not stay little long. She and Henry had nine children, but only six survived childhood. Of the four surviving girls, Susan, born in 1843, was the oldest child, and Martha, born nineteen years later, the youngest. The third daughter was Lucretia (called Lutie) who would marry Charlotte's grandson Charless Le Bourgeois; the second was Ella (called Nellie), the mother of Nelka. The children grew up in a household that knew wealth and valued education.

Portrait of Minerva with Susan and Nellie

After the destructive fires of 1849, Henry moved his family to Carondelet, a suburb of St. Louis, where he later built a grand mansion, which he called Southampton, after the county in Virginia where he was born.

Despite his roots in the South, Henry was an early, active and vocal supporter of Abraham Lincoln, and then Ulysses Grant. From both Presidents he received diplomatic assignments. Lincoln appointed him Minister to Venezuela in 1861, and considered a plan to send him on a special mission to Chiriquí (now a province of Panama). The President struggled to conceive an acceptable solution to the problem of emancipation. He abhorred slavery but resisted the notion of freed slaves becoming citizens on an equal footing with whites. Voluntary but incentivized transplantation of freed slaves to Africa and Latin America seemed an attractive option. Henry would go to Chiriquí to check it out as a possible destination. In the end, the plan was shelved as more important concerns overwhelmed the Lincoln administration.

When President Grant took office, he appointed Henry Minister to Brazil. Relations between the United States and Brazil had languished during the 1860s and Grant wanted Henry to mend them. In July 1869 the Blow family – Henry, Minerva, Susan, Nellie, Lutie, Martha, sons Peter and John, and niece Alice (the daughter of Henry's deceased brother Peter), and a nurse – sailed on the steamship *Merrimack* from New York to Brazil. Henry had his first audience with the Emperor Dom Pedro II in late August and began the task of diplomatic restoration.

The forty-four year old Dom Pedro had been emperor of Brazil since he was five, when his father abruptly abdicated the throne and left the country to protect the reign of his daughter Dona Maria da Gloria as Queen of Portugal in 1831. Benefiting from a constructive regency, Dom Pedro developed into a strong governor, capable of balancing competing interests while developing positive policies. In 1852 he abolished the importation of slaves, and in 1871 encouraged the national legislature to pass a law decreeing that every child born of a slave was a free person. An avid reader and master of more than a dozen languages, the Emperor promoted the advancement of science and education. He carried on an active correspondence with people from all areas of public life around the world – Richard Wagner, Louis Pasteur, and Henry Wadsworth Longfellow, for example. In 1869 the Emperor and Henry Blow became good friends.

In Brazil Henry's daughter Nellie, twenty-two years old, met Count Theodor de Smirnoff and fell in love. A member of the Russian nobility, de Smirnoff had been educated at the Imperial Lyceum in St. Petersburg and had graduated first in his class in 1862. A brilliant linguist, he had joined the Russian diplomatic service. When he and Nellie met, he was serving as Secretary at the Russian Embassy. In 1871 Theodor led the Grand Duke Alexis on his tour of America that included the Duke's visit to Belmont plantation where Nellie's cousin Lizzie Le Bourgeois lived. The next year, he and Nellie were married in St. Paul's Episcopal Church in South St. Louis.

The wedding was posh but circumspect. It took place "in the presence of a few appreciative friends, the affair being so very private and exclusive that only those were admitted who were furnished special cards for the occasion," the *St. Louis Democrat* reported. Fourteen pairs of attendants and Nellie's sister Martha as a flower girl preceded the bride and groom down the aisle. "The little Gothic church," the newspaper continued, "is small and unpretending; but the bride had a preference for it, she having contributed the greatest portion towards its erection, and therefore felt more at home within its friendly walls in consideration of this proprietorship." As a wedding gift, Henry bought his daughter a small house across the street from St. Paul's so that she and Theodor would have their own home for return trips to St. Louis. After the wedding, the couple travelled to New York before returning to Munich, Germany, where Theodor held the post of First Secretary for the Russian Legation.

Theodor's career looked promising and the two adored one another. They had two children, a boy and girl, in quick succession, but neither destined to live very long. In financial terms, the couple were a disaster together. Nellie liked to spend and Theodor – it was alleged – liked to gamble. The family soon learned that Theodor had borrowed heavily against his property in Taroslav on the Volga River. In a long letter to Minerva, dated 10 September 1874, he explained his difficulty. He pleaded that without help he would be unable to accept a better and more expensive post to a major capital city and his career would stall, as diplomats in Russia were expected to cover a portion of their costs out of their own pocket. The timing of his request was particularly bad as both parents were more ill than anyone knew. Making matters worse, Henry was back in Washington, having been appointed by President Grant to a thankless position as one of the commissioners governing the District of Columbia after Congress abolished the Territorial government run by Alexander Robey "Boss" Shepherd in June of 1874. Henry resigned from the position at the end of the year primarily to attend to Minerva during her illness.

After a long and painful battle with cancer, Minerva died in June 1875. Her demise affected the community as well as the family. "St. Louis mourns with sad sincerity, not as a polite conventionality, the death of Mrs. Henry T. Blow. She has been the Lady Bountiful of the city; using culture and wealth as opportunities for Christian charity; and more than a quarter century she has been connected with all beneficent schemes in this city and state," printed *The Springfield Daily Republican* in Massachusetts. Among her many good works, Minerva helped her sister-in-law Charlotte establish and manage the Home of the Friendless, serving on its Board of Trustees from its incorporation until the time of her death.

After the funeral, Nellie and Lutie went with their father to Saratoga Springs, New York, arriving at the United States Hotel in early September, while Susan and Martha traveled to Hagerstown, Maryland. Exhausted from sitting long hours at Minerva's bedside, Henry planned to enjoy the spring waters, relax and recover. His plan was upset by a letter from Theodor. Writing to Susan on 7 September 1875, Henry explained:

> Nelly's letters from Mr. Smirnov have made her very contented, he is now writing me most assiduously to get me to raise 75,000 francs [about $15,000] for him. I replied sending him money to pay Nellie's bills, which should have been paid from money previously sent him. I also said some very plain things to him, copies of which I enclose. Please preserve them carefully. (Blow Family Papers.)

Henry's candid reply is now lost, but he was clearly upset. Four days later, feeling exhausted after a short walk, he went to his room to lie down. A little before the dinner hour, he felt worse. Nellie and Lutie called for a doctor, but it was too late. According to the coroner, Henry died of cerebral congestion (likely a stroke or hemorrhage). The children were stunned – both parents dead within three months of each other.

After returning to Germany, Nellie came back to America the following year for two happier occasions. Dom Pedro, the Brazilian Emperor, and his family were making a three-month tour of the United States and would be stopping at St. Louis. And her sister Susan was going to have an exhibition at the United States Centennial Commission's International Exhibition in Philadelphia.

Like Nellie, Susan had fallen in love in her early twenties. Her parents, however, found the man she favored unsuitable. Although William Coyle, a Colonel in the Union army, had been wounded (a gun shot through the shoulder at Pea Ridge) during the war, he offended Henry and Minerva by corresponding with their daughter without an introduction or their permission. When Susan persisted, Henry checked into the Colonel's background. In a long and forceful letter, he explained to Susan that he had found friends and even members of Coyle's family who attested to his unsatisfactory character. Whatever romantic spirit Susan had, she never found another man to love. Instead, she discovered fulfillment in philosophy. She learned German and became a leading member of the stout group of Hegelian philosophers centered in St. Louis. After the failure in 1848 of liberal revolutionists to shake off the shackles of repressive, ultra-conservative governments in Europe, a large number of German immigrants arrived in St. Louis. The intellectuals among them brought their knowledge and admiration of Georg Wilhelm Friedrich Hegel, who in the late 18th and early 19th centuries developed an idea of historical progress that many found compelling and attractive. Hegel's notion implied that the human world was getting inevitably better. Susan made Hegel's philosophy her own.

Susan Elizabeth Blow
(Courtesy of the Association for Childhood Education International (ACEI) archives, Special Collections, University of Maryland Libraries)

Susan was very pleased when her father took the family to Europe after their year in Brazil, allowing her to spend time in Germany. There she met the disciples of Friedrich Froebel, another German idealist and contemporary of Hegel, who advanced the importance of childhood learning and the concept of the kindergarten. On her return home, Susan established in Carondelet the first successful public kindergarten in the United States in 1873. Now, three years later, her work would be featured at Philadelphia's World Fair.

In May Dom Pedro and his entourage arrived in St. Louis. They saw Susan's kindergarten and visited the Blows at home. With the death of her mother and father, Susan had become the senior member of the family. She greeted the Emperor at Southampton and talked with Dom Pedro for two hours about the education of children.

Southampton, ca. 1876
(Courtesy of the Missouri History Museum)

Afterwards the Emperor and the Blows traveled to Philadelphia for the great exhibition. Impressed by her work, the Commission judges awarded Susan a medal. In their citation they commended her for the "large and excellent exhibit of kindergarten work in the kindergartens of St. Louis." After a few triumphal days celebrating the Nation's hundredth anniversary and Susan's accomplishment, the Dom Pedro and Blow families (Nellie, her husband Theodor and children, and her sisters Susan, Lutie and Martha) boarded the steamship *Russia* in New York bound for Europe on 26 July 1876.

Sometime after their return to the Continent, Theodor and Nellie's son and daughter died in St. Petersburg. Years later when she published her book *Letters to a Mother*, Susan dedicated the work to "my sister Lizzie Charless and my niece Athena Feodorovna." Athena, named for Minerva, was Nellie's daughter and Lizzie was Nellie and Susan's sister who had died in childhood. A bright spot finally arrived when Nellie's third child was born on 9 August 1878 in Paris. Nellie and Theodor named her Elena Feodorovna de Smirnoff, but always called her Nelka.

Nellie with Nelka, 1878

2

Nelka was six when her father died of tuberculosis in Berlin. His death was no doubt hastened by his arrest in Munich some months before. An anonymous and unfriendly writer, reporting his decline and death to the *Missouri Republican*, declared that, "possessing nothing more than an empty title of count" and having squandered his wife's fortune, de Smirnoff had resorted to forgery.

Theodor with Nelka, ca.1881

The Blow family was chagrined. Theodor's attorney immediately responded to the newspaper, emphatically denying the accusations. A family friend answered that the report "does a grievous wrong not only to the departed, but to the members of one of our most esteemed families." An heir of Prince Gortschakoff had accused Theodor of the crime and had him detained in prison. Theodor knew the Prince and his family well. As Tsar Alexander II's prime minister for twenty-five years, Gortschakoff oversaw the diplomatic corps and had negotiated the sale of Alaska to the United States in 1867 during the Grant administration. The grievance was quickly aired in court. The charges were dropped and Theodor released. Nellie's aunt Charlotte also rose to his defense. "My niece's husband, Mr. de Smirnoff," the newspaper quoted her, "although unfortunate, was a polished gentleman and an honorable man, as all who knew him can testify." Despite his difficulties, Nellie remained loyal. "His accomplished wife," the family friend wrote, "who clung to him with heroic devotion until the end, respected and esteemed as she is by a host of friends, deserves the warmest sympathy."

After the funeral, Nellie returned to St. Louis to collect Nelka, where she had left her in Susan's care during Theodor's last illness. Their trip back to Europe began a pattern of forty years of trans-Atlantic travel for Nelka, and a conflict of loyalties between America and Russia. The conflict would not have arisen if Nellie had been less devoted to Theodor. She wanted very much to raise Nelka as a Russian. Her desire was, in a way, capricious, because she had never learned to read or speak the language. Her connections with the de Smirnoff family, moreover, had been few and tenuous while her attachment to her own remained strong. At one point, Susan met Theodor's brother in England but failed to make a lasting connection. As it was, most of Nelka's childhood was spent in the United States and western European countries rather than Russia.

The details of her early years are sketchy, but the general lines of her development are clear. She first attended an exclusive and "rather advanced" school in Brussels where she learned German and became fluent in French. During the summers she and her mother returned to St Louis.

When she was nine she spent the holiday with her great-aunt Charlotte and others at a resort at Lake Bluff north of Chicago. The following year she and mother returned to St. Louis to attend the wedding of Nellie's sister Martha to Herbert Wadsworth, a scion of a wealthy family from New York.

Martha Blow Wadsworth
(Courtesy of the Missouri History Museum)

Herbert Wadsworth
(Courtesy of the Martha Blow Wadsworth Photographs
Collection, Milne Library, SUNY Geneseo)

Like her sister Lutie and her cousins Adèle Le Bourgeois and Augusta Blow, Martha had gone to school at Miss Porter's where they graduated in three consecutive years. After her parents died, Martha lived with Lutie and Charless and then Susan before she met Herbert. The couple was married in Christ Church in St. Louis on 2 April 1888.

Ever vivacious and frequently provocative, Martha orchestrated a blow-out event. She chose the music, choreographed the events, and even drilled the choir herself. She hired Ernest Richard Kroeger, a young concert pianist, to arrange specific pieces and play the organ. Kroeger would later provide with great success the complete programming of music for the St.

Louis World's Fair in 1904. Martha wore for her wedding dress a silk wrap-around gown that was so fine that, she claimed, she could thread it through her wedding band. A Chicago newspaper wrote, "All who were so fortunate as to witness the impressive ceremony united in praising the beautiful and unusual music that rose and fell like a song of spring, while the bride and groom advanced to the altar, and burst forth in a grand chorus of joyful triumph as man and wife returned united down the aisle."

Following their honeymoon, the couple lived in Avon, New York, in the Genesee Valley, in Herbert's rambling mansion of a house, which he had wryly named, Ashantee (pronounced 'a shanty').

A few months after Martha's wedding, a creditor foreclosed on twenty-two properties that Nellie had inherited from her father. In his will, Henry had carefully divided his estate for his six children in a way to guarantee a steady stream of income accruing from rents and dividends. He divided his real estate holdings into six discrete parcels, each valued at a bit more than $50,000, and also gave each child equal shares in stock in various companies. Over the years, Nellie mortgaged her properties to help finance her lifestyle at home and abroad.

A week after the foreclosure, Nellie and Nelka went to stay with Martha and Herbert at their home in the Genesee Valley. Despite the financial setback, Nellie moved to Washington, where she became active in diplomatic and social circles, hosting occasional parties and musicales. Often Martha would come down from New York to help out. In the meanwhile, Nelka developed a passion for reading. "I read very much now whenever I get a chance to," she wrote to her aunt Susan in 1888. "I think it is splendid and always amusing." She had also grown fond of music. "I can play lots of little duets on the piano with Mama," she added. "I love it."

Nelka traveled with her mother to Louisiana to visit her Le Bourgeois cousins at Belmont plantation when she was thirteen. She grew quite close to her aunt Lutie's two girls, Liz and Lucretia, who were two and four years younger than she. In one photograph taken at Belmont, she is sitting on a swing hanging from one of the great old pecan trees. In another, she is seated at the base of one of the large columns that surrounded the manor house. She wore a full-skirted dress, stockings and flat shoes. Her hair was light-colored and the tresses cascaded to her waist. She held a book on her lap.

Nelka de Smirnoff at Belmont, 1892

The idyllic pictures were taken only days before the Mississippi River broke through the levee and crashed through the plantation. Nelka and her cousins had to be evacuated from the second story balcony and ferried to safety in skiffs.

Nelka de Smirnoff at Belmont, 1892

After the flood Nelka went back to Brussels, where she returned to school and ruminated on the aging process. "When I was ten," she wrote Susan, "I thought it would be dreadful to be eleven, but when I was eleven I was quite satisfied if I did not have to be twelve, and so on .... But ever since I have been fourteen I have thought it was awful and have *never* become reconciled to it." She also began to take an interest in general history.

She and her mother toured the battlefield at Waterloo where Napoleon Bonaparte met his final defeat at the hands of the Duke of Wellington in 1815. "We went by carriage all the way [about eight miles from Brussels], first through the *Bois de la Cambré* and then on through the most perfect woods imaginable." Along the way, they saw "a little mound in the middle of the battlefield with a huge lion on the top as the emblem of victory." She was tickled to find that there were "three little birds nests one in the lion's mouth and one in each ear. Wasn't it nice?" The lion, cast in iron weighing thirty-one tons, stands on a stone pedestal about twelve feet high at the peak of a very steep and large hill built for the purpose. Nelka's sight was keen to see three small nests because the only good view of the lion is from afar. At the battlefield museum, she bought a photograph of Napoleon and one of Wellington. It was perfectly natural for her to praise the latter and despise the former, whose French army had ravaged Russia in 1812. "I have such a contempt for Napoleon, and I take pleasure in comparing [his photograph] with the frank, open face of the Duke of Wellington."

When she turned sixteen, Nelka began to pick up her pace and excel academically. "I am first in grammar, literature and physics," she wrote Susan. She also became increasingly serious and critical. She read Victor Hugo's *Le Dernier Jour du Condamné* and found it compelling. "I would like to see some persons who have lived and who live. It makes me crazy to see people vegetate." In another letter, she repeated Jean-Jacques Rousseau's classic pronouncement, *"Une injustice qu'on voit et qu'on tait, – on la commet soi même."* [An injustice one sees and says nothing about, – one commits it oneself.] To this, she added, "I wish more persons could or would recognize that truth."

She finished school in Brussels just before she turned seventeen in 1895. Nellie then took her to St. Petersburg for a quick immersion in Russian culture, even though what Nelka most looked forward to seeing was the Imperial collection of Dutch and Flemish paintings at the Hermitage Museum. When the visit was over, they returned to Paris to further her education. Nelka teased Susan (who, like all the Blow sisters, had been raised as a Presbyterian) by telling her, "I am going into the Convent of the Assumption next week." Warning her not to be "horrified," she quickly explained that the convent was really a finishing school for young ladies, some of whom, like Nelka, came from rich and well-connected American families in the Midwest. Her friend Marion Cockrell, whose father Francis served as senator for Missouri for thirty years, attended the Convent about the same time Nelka did. Marion had the honor of christening the battleship *Missouri* when it was launched in 1901.

"The Assumption is an exception to all convents," Nelka reassured Susan. It offered a slate of regular courses on foreign literature, history and art, reinforced with special lectures by professors from the Sorbonne and other colleges in Paris. She heard one of her first lectures at the *College de France* on the early 19th century French author Henri-Marie Beyle, who wrote under the pseudonym Stendahl. Best of all, the convent provided an atelier with drawing courses featuring live models, men, women and children. "Of course," she continued, "Mama never imagined such a thing possible in a convent – the general idea of convents not going beyond wax flowers."

With tongue in cheek, she enumerated the privileges she would enjoy as a Convent resident: "1) Clock-like life and no time lost. 2) No risk of disagreeable associations as they are most particular who they take. 3) I will see Mama almost every day." In addition, "I shall have to go to bed at eight! – just fancy that !!!, but then I have an astonishing capacity for sleeping and eating just now." Besides her regular studies at the Convent, Nelka also began playing the violin. Jeanie Lea Southwick, visiting Paris, painted Nelka's portrait in 1895, showing her holding her violin. In time,

Nelka became fairly proficient, but eventually gave it up. On the other hand, her interest in art and painting continued strong.

Portrait of Nelka By Jeanie Lea Southwick
(Courtesy of the Missouri History Museum)

Nelka returned to the States for the winter season 1897/8 to make her debut in Washington. In her coming-out photograph, she wore a late Victorian gown with huge mutton chop sleeves and a high ruffled lace collar. The gown was cinched at the waist with a wide ribbon and her skirt flared widely to the floor. Her hair was parted in the middle and pulled back; she held a bouquet of two-dozen roses. Fashionably dressed *à la mode*, she made a comely debutante. She stood out at one party when – instead of singing or playing a song – she delivered a recitation in both French and Russian.

Nelka, 1897

When Tsar Nicholas II appointed Count Arthur Cassini ambassador to the United States in 1898, Nelka found herself a comfortable spot in Washington society. The new Russian ambassador brought with him his daughter Marguerite to serve as his official hostess. She and Nelka immediately became friends. The Cassinis had arrived from the Chinese imperial court at Peking where Marguerite acted as her father's interpreter. A remarkable linguist, she spoke six languages. She was also vivacious and often mischievous. When Nelka turned twenty in August, Marguerite organized a birthday party for her. "Mama and all our little Russian colony," Nelka wrote to Susan, "drank my health, wishing me each in turn to find myself each year one year younger, till I had to stop them less they eclipse me altogether."

Although happy in the company of her new friends, Nelka was distraught. "It is terrible to be twenty," she told Susan. She knew she was intelligent, but felt inexperienced and hesitant. "I have absolutely no facility for expression – that is what is the matter," but other people were not much better. "I see persons so clever, so talented, genuine in their line and with absolutely distorted points of view." But, being unable to see things clearly herself, she knew she was not in a position to combat the errors of others. She felt overwhelmed with "mental indigestion" and a total sense of incompleteness. She knew she couldn't model herself on Susan as a strong philosopher. The world of ideas was not for her; she needed something tangible to sink her teeth into. She wanted to "exhaust" herself. "I need to work," she told Susan.

Soon after her birthday, Nellie and Nelka traveled to the fashionable resort at Newport, Rhode Island. One afternoon, not long after they arrived, while they sat talking together, Nelka saw her mother slump in her lawn chair and without a word pass away.

3

For some time, Nellie had been sliding into ill health with a weakened heart. Her death was not entirely unexpected. Still Nelka was shocked, for her mother was only fifty years old. It took her a long time to regain her equilibrium.

At loose ends, she accepted the Cassini's invitation to spend the fall and winter of 1898/9 at the Russian embassy in Washington. In the spring she went with them to visit her aunt Martha and uncle Herbert at their home in Avon, New York, before the ambassador and his daughter departed for their summer break in Europe. A newspaper article, written at this time about Marguerite and her father, mentioned Nelka as "one of the prettiest Russian-American maidens imaginable." Pretty as she was, she felt rootless and restless. Susan invited her to live with her in New York, but Nelka couldn't bring herself to accept. "No one could offer more generously what unfortunately I feel that I may never have [again]," Nelka replied. "Don't misunderstand me, dear Poodie [Susan's pet name within the family], but my 'home' was forever lost when Mama left me and I can never find it except with her. I am Mama's own, and my 'home' such as you meant it can only exist in memory and anticipation."

She decided to go back to Europe instead. In December 1899 she re-enrolled as a resident-student at the Convent of the Assumption and began taking a full slate of art courses at *l'Académie Julian*. When Rodolphe Julian started the art school thirty years earlier, he broke tradition by allowing women to enroll and – even more shocking – allowing them to paint men as well as women in the nude. Nelka was thrilled to be in Paris again and felt as if she were walking on air. "What beauty there is here!" she exclaimed. "The intellectual and emotional stimulus would make a cow tingle." She threw herself into painting. "I am so busy, I have my whole week planned ahead for almost every second. You see I am at the studio every morning including Saturday and have several lessons a week in the afternoon." She was delighted to find a Russian Orthodox church nearby where she could go on Sundays. She also began studying Russian, which she told Susan, was "getting on." "I will be very glad," she added, "when I have mastered the language, – then I am going to begin Italian."

Excited to be active and in charge of her own life, Nelka continued to search for meaning and direction. She worried that she couldn't adopt Susan's optimistic view of the world or build a sensible philosophical structure of her own. "Where," she asked her aunt, "can I read something holding your point of view which would be more within my range of understanding than Hegel?" Nelka simply couldn't grasp an idea of progress in a world that engendered so much violence. Referring to the Spanish-American and Boer Wars that broke out in Cuba in 1898 and Africa in 1899, she told Susan, "I am disgusted with the ending of the century with two wars, – it is a disgrace." In a fit of repudiation, she told Susan, "I think the whole world is very horrible anyhow and I don't believe in worldly goods and possessions, or countries, or governments and I don't see why everyone inhabiting tropical climes couldn't dispense with clothes."

The problem, she felt, was that "the whole organization of everything is abominable and I don't believe it is a necessary state of development." Life, in a way, was just one damned thing after another. "Most ordinary lives," she continued, "are the quintessence of artificiality and the grossest waste of time." She included herself in her indictment. "I am more than ever against the 'me' in myself. It is the source of all evil." On a lighter note, she concluded another letter by observing, "How madly busy all the little people are, buzzing over the planet, – and for what? How nice it is to go to sleep. I am going to bed. P.S. I think it is an intellectual crime to wear long skirts in the streets."

After six months in Paris, she began to feel more content as her life settled down. Reflecting on the year spent in America after her mother's death, she confided to Susan, "I am just beginning to feel the peaceful reaction of it all and I dread the idea of getting roused again before having fully got hold of myself. The total change I felt necessary proved a salvation and that complete absence of all reminders of the past year is the only thing where I can get quiet." As to returning to the States, she added, "Suffice it to say that I want to stay just as I am until after next winter when I feel like going back to America without regret.... I do not feel equal to any more emotions."

Bereft of her mother and separated from her favorite aunt, Nelka was not without family and friends. On New Year's Day 1900, she dined with her French cousins, the La Beaumes in Paris, who were related to the Blows in St. Louis. "There was just the immediate family," she wrote, "and we were twenty-three at table." Then, in the summer, her friend Louisette Bonaparte invited her to visit in Denmark. Five years older than Nelka, she was the only daughter of Jerome Bonaparte, the grandson of Napoleon's brother Jerome. She grew up in Baltimore and Washington and had recently married Adam, Count von Moltke Huitfeldt, a diplomat, whose father had been the Danish ambassador to Paris.

The journey to the von Moltke estate, Glorup Manor, on the island of Funen in Denmark was taxing but worth the effort. "We were still two days on the steamer getting to Bremen [Germany] and then changed trains and boats about fifteen times in 24 hours getting here. But once here it is beyond all words in delight." The manor house, which had been renovated in the 18th century, was a small baroque building standing in a large park. An allée of lime trees framed the garden that reflected an Anglo-Chinese influence. "The place is perfectly beautiful," she continued. "It is so quiet, so far away from everything. Beautiful forests that we drive through, deer all over, swans, fountains and all so *old*." Glorup traced its roots to the 14th century; the von Moltke family took possession of the estate at the end of the 18th century.

When she returned to Paris she tackled her painting with renewed vigor. "I work so hard," she wrote Susan. "My efforts alone deserve some results, but it is slow in forthcoming. This week however there is an improvement. I get up before seven every day and go to bed at nine and drink eight glasses of milk a day." But painting for Nelka appeared more a chore than a pleasure, and accomplishment seemed beyond her reach. "There is nothing so disastrous," she confessed, "as to be fooled by the appreciation where it is not deserved. How I wish I could do any one thing well."

It appears that Nelka broke off her studies in the early fall when she accepted an invitation from her mother's friend Mary Beale Bakhmeteff to come to Sofia, Bulgaria, where her husband George was serving as the Russian ambassador. Mary Beale and Nellie Blow shared a similar background. They were wealthy American women married to Russian diplomats, their fathers had been intimate friends of President Grant, and the President had appointed each to a ministerial post, Henry Blow in 1869 to Brazil and General Edward Beale to Austria in 1876. When Nelka was born, Mary accepted Nellie's invitation to become Nelka's godmother.

Traveling to Sofia proved even more trying than going to Glorup. "I was almost stopped at the Hungarian and Servian frontier," Nelka told Susan, "because I had no passport. By the merest chance I had a very old one in my bag which was absolutely invalid but which, added to my absolute refusal to leave the train, got me by three frontiers in the end." She had help from some of her fellow travelers. "I called a Turk and a Servian who were in the same compartment to my rescue and for an hour or more carried on a heated discussion in every language." Undaunted by the rules, Nelka rose to the challenge of traveling alone into eastern Europe. "The diplomatic corps have to depend almost entirely on each other and it is very interesting being thrown with people of so many different nationalities."

Nelka had been delighted with the cold, orderly atmosphere that she found in Denmark, but Bulgaria resonated more deeply with her basic temperament. Located in the southeastern corner of Europe, Bulgaria, short on economic resources and long on hostile neighbors, suffered a difficult history. Only recently, in 1878 after the Russo-Turkish War, the country had regained autonomy from the Ottoman (Turkish) Empire. Nelka was unable to adequately describe her sensations on arriving in Sofia, the national capital, to Susan. "How can I tell you how I feel at being here. It is an entirely new world. So interesting and so beautiful." Life in Bulgaria seemed simpler and less complicated than anywhere else. It was the Orient. It also helped that she was treated well. "No one could be lovelier to me than Madame Bakhmeteff," she wrote Susan. "She comes to my room every two minutes and asks me if I have anything under the sun and seems so pleased to have me here. It is really delightful. I have a sitting room next to my bedroom all to myself, filled with every book that I have been longing to get hold of." Moreover, she could go horseback riding every day.

Nelka stayed in Sofia for four months, which gave her ample time to read, ride and reflect. She continued to wrestle with the great issues of life. Civilization, she deemed, was largely an artifice benefiting the rich and powerful. In contrast, "Nature," she asserted, "is the only guide and I don't believe Nature is bad." She still felt handicapped by her ignorance and inexperience, but didn't doubt that her native sense of things was essentially correct. Organized education, in contrast, was worthless; it was "no better than the shoes that are put on Chinese female feet to stunt and deform them." At the same time, she saw that many of her own notions and feelings were often at odds with one another. "I am one mass of contradictions to myself," she confessed. Her one anchor of faith lay in her mother. "I believe," she told Susan, "I am level-headed and more or less reasonable, but that is not my merit. Any sanity of judgment I have comes from Mama. Whatever good there may be [in me] is due entirely to her."

In Sofia she resolved once more to get serious about her painting. She would work twice as hard as she had before. "If one would do anything the least in art," she argued, "one must give oneself to it 24 hours in 24 hours and live these 24 hours double." She set a very high standard, declaring, "There is no art but good art and what is not best is not art at all." On her return to Paris, as always, she found the city extremely stimulating. "You would not believe how waked up I can get," she told Susan. It was a sensation that she only felt in Paris. "I believe it is in the air," she said.

After working hard through the winter, she decided that she was strong enough to return to America. She had a choice of places to go: Susan's summer house in Cazenovia near Syracuse, New York, and Martha's summer place in Avon near Rochester, New York, about 120 miles west of Cazenovia. She went first to see her aunt Martha.

Martha and Herbert never had any children, but devoted their energies to sports, culture and cultivating friendships. Martha was an accomplished photographer and painter. Her watercolor studies of flowers are on permanent display at the New York Botanical Garden in the Bronx. Energetic and sometimes aggressive, she was much admired for her skill with horses, which she learned from her big brother, Johnnie.

John G. Blow, or Johnnie, was a handful. He was a favorite of Martha, but trouble to his parents. He hated school, bedeviled his teachers, and loved the outdoors, especially riding. He wanted to become famous in the world of horse-racing. At the age of twenty-one, when Martha was about twelve, Johnnie used part of his sizable inheritance to buy a stable of racehorses. The recently formed St. Louis Jockey and Trotting Club named one of their main events the "Blow Stakes" for him. Ambition overpowered common sense within a matter of months. He entered one of his best horses, named Bill Bass, in a Kentucky Association event at Lexington in May 1878. Johnnie's horse was expected to win, but just before the race, rumors began to circulate around the track "that a scheme had been fixed up to swindle the unwary," that Bill Bass would be held back. Sure enough, the jockey slowed the horse to a standstill at the halfway mark. Despite the jockey's testifying he acted alone, the Association judges debarred Johnnie as well. (*Cincinnati Commercial Tribune*, 20 May 1878.) Johnnie died two years later of peritonitis. His early death did nothing to diminish Martha's enthusiasm for horses. He would have been proud of his baby sister when in November 1905 the magazine *Country Life in America* featured her as a champion rider, with a photograph on its front cover of her and her horse jumping a tall fence.

Martha in her turn encouraged her nieces to ride, having more success with Nelka than Lucretia Le Bourgeois, who resisted her aunt's policy of rising early and riding often. Martha didn't accept the notion that "it's a man's world," but competed head on. She particularly bristled against her friend Teddy Roosevelt's bumptious manliness, insisting and sometimes proving that she could do most anything better than he, especially horseback riding.

Herbert was a skilled painter, poet, and scientist. He invented a number of agricultural devices for which he received U.S. Government patents, including a design for a horizontal silo, an electrical switch, and a safety valve for a sugar boiler. He also held some unusual views for his social class. When the Panic of 1893 struck the country and brought on a six-year period of severe unemployment, Herbert was invited to address a Chamber of Commerce meeting in Rochester, New York, to discuss ways of alleviating the widespread distress. Advising that "furnishing employment" was better than giving alms to the jobless (which, he said, merely "encouraged poverty"), he added that, "The poor are not the immoral class. If you want to find the most immoral men go to the upper ten. Go among the high officials of the state and the leaders in society. This remark will apply to both men and women. They are the most licentious and immoral people we have. I consider, sir, that the poorest people of this country are the virtuous ones." (*Rochester Democrat and Chronicle*, 12 December 1893.)

During the year, Nelka experienced two unsettling but very different encounters. The first occurred in Sharon, Connecticut where Mildred Barnes invited her to visit. Mildred, a year younger than Nelka, was Martha's friend; Mildred and Martha shared many interests: art, music and riding horses. Nelka found Mildred enchanting and very attractive. One night in a moment of excitement they hatched a romantic notion to run off and lead a life immersed in Byzantine art. Writing from Avon after her visit, she told Mildred that their "plan which had a spasmotic birth upon [a] certain two feet square on the floor of my room at Sharon is taking a firm hold upon my mind. Mildred we <u>must</u> – and <u>completely</u>." (Bliss Papers.) Their idea of running away and living together was wild and impractical, but remembered by both long after.

Later the same year, Nelka experienced a more disturbing encounter at Avon. Writing a letter to a friend named Robert, she deliberately teased a young visitor named Cary into thinking that the Robert in question was Mildred's Robert (Mildred later married her step-brother Robert Woods Bliss). Nelka evidently misjudged the fellow and went too far. She told Mildred that Cary:

> <u>fell</u> upon me most literally and we had an awful struggle, all over the floor in which my brand new petticoat was torn to shreds by my stepping in it and the letter also torn with two photographs enclosed before I got away. I am glad aunt Martha was not there. She heard the shrieks and came in after I had escaped. I managed to send the remains of the letter however. (Bliss Papers.)

Mildred apparently mentioned the incident to her parents, because soon after Mr. Cary was declared *persona non grata* in the Bliss household. When Martha heard of her friend's banishment, she sought an explanation but never received one.

Whether this episode with Mr. Cary or the evaporation of her Byzantine dream with Mildred was a cause or not, Nelka grew increasingly edgy toward the end of the year. American social conventions and the trappings of wealth were getting under her skin. She and her cousin Liz Le Bourgeois traveled to Rochester in November 1901 where they "spent a disagreeable day" having clothes made for themselves. For someone who argued for short skirts in Paris and no clothes at all in the temperate zone, such an expedition was beyond the pale. "It is extremely painful to me," she wrote to Susan, "but all this kind of thing just pushes me more in the opposite direction and makes me firmer in my fast maturing resolution. I am exceedingly blue."

She didn't identify the resolution that she was reaching. But in another letter to Susan written in November, she suggested three alternatives to a career in art: "If I am not married by the time I am twenty-seven [she had recently turned twenty-three], I am determined to go into a convent or our Red Cross." A few weeks after she sent the letter, the first Nobel Peace Prize was conferred on Jean Henry Dunant, a Swiss businessman, who founded the International Committee of the Red Cross in 1863. The fact may have pushed her in the direction of nursing. But first she would look for a husband.

Nelka on horseback at Ashantee, 1903
(Courtesy of the Martha Blow Wadsworth Photographs Collection, Milne Library, SUNY Geneseo)

4

Herbert had inherited a legacy from a very rich uncle. With plenty of money and no children, he and Martha decided to build a grand mansion that would serve as a major center of social, political and diplomatic life in the nation's capital. It would also provide a home for their motherless niece and a platform for her to find a suitable husband. With very little help from anyone, Martha designed a beautiful Beaux-Arts style house on Dupont Circle. When its doors opened in 1902, the Wadsworth house at 1801 Massachusetts Avenue, N.W. became Nelka's principal address in the United States.

The Wadsworth House on Dupont Circle
(The American Architect and Building News, 29 September 1906)

Nelka re-entered Washington society in a big way. The year 1902 began with a bang. Theodore Roosevelt had succeeded to the Presidency a year earlier, after an anarchist shot and killed

William McKinley. With his daughter Alice coming of age, Roosevelt gave the first debutante ball ever held for a President's daughter at the White House. Seven hundred prominent people were invited to witness her debut into polite society. Nelka and her cousin Liz Le Bourgeois, whom Martha had invited to spend the social season, were among the selected guests. Alice's party was the first in a stream of movable feasts that carried Nelka for two years as she looked for a man to marry.

The New York Times recorded the most important events. In January Count Cassini and Marguerite entertained in honor of Nelka and Alice at the Russian Embassy. The German ambassador invited Nelka and Liz to a reception for visiting naval officers. In February Martha and Herbert gave a small dinner party in honor of Alice Roosevelt, Nelka and Liz; the next day the annual Assembly ball embraced the Capitol's political elite and the entire diplomatic community of four hundred, including Nelka and Liz. In early March the Westinghouses invited Nelka and Liz to a dinner for Earl Grey, a friend of Adèle's who would become the Governor General of Canada in 1904.

In March, Marguerite (created Countess in her own right by decree of Tsar Nicholas II in 1901) gave a dinner party for her twenty best friends. The party featured each woman wearing a headdress in a style not seen for at least 100 years; one hundred additional guests were invited to an after-dinner reception to witness and applaud the costumes. Marguerite dressed herself up as Francesca da Rimini (from Dante's *Purgatorio*), wearing "a white princess gown, pearl-embroidered, a filmy veil held by a pearl and diamond tiara, and long black braids twined with pearls." Ethel Barrymore appeared as La Traviata. Nelka attired herself to resemble "a cute young Queen Wilhelmina" (who became the queen of the Netherlands in 1815), Martha looked like an Alsatian peasant, and Liz, most likely at Marguerite's suggestion, went as a Chinese maiden.

In April, Martha held a singing recital of two score women, including Nelka, for the entertainment of an audience of two hundred in the Wadsworth's grand ballroom at their house on Dupont Circle. In May the Minister from the Austro-Hungarian Empire put on a diplomatic dinner that included Nelka. Later that month, the *Philadelphia Inquirer* reported that "the good-natured little Countess Marguerite Cassini, who has perhaps had more portraits painted than any beauty in Washington, is sitting for a new picture, this time to an amateur, the pretty Miss Nelka de Smirnoff, the niece of Mrs. Herbert Wadsworth, who is very gifted as an artist." Then, in October, she traveled to New Orleans to participate as a bridesmaid in Liz's wedding to John Richardson, where she also reunited with her great aunt Charlotte Charless, her cousin Lucretia, and others in her extended family. In December, Secretary of State John Hay hosted a party in honor of Herbert's cousin James Wadsworth, Jr. and his family, inviting some of their younger friends including Nelka, Mildred Barnes, and Josephine Boardman.

The social season of 1903 was just as busy. In January Count Cassini held a Christmas party, according to the Russian calendar, followed by a small dinner for twenty; Nelka was one of the twenty. She then went by special train to Charlestown, West Virginia, to be one of the bridesmaids for the marriage of Angelica Crosby to John B. Henderson. She attended a dinner for young people held by Senator Foraker and his wife, and another given by Senator and Mrs. Hanna. In February she presided at one of three refreshment tables at an afternoon tea party given by her friend Marguerite, the Countess.

Nelka was one of four bridesmaids at the wedding of Mlle. Irene des Planques of France to Alexandre de Pavlov, the Russian minister to Korea. Held at the new Russian embassy on Scott Circle in February, the wedding turned into a disaster. Pavlov had known Marguerite since their days in Peking where he served as her father's secretary. He had fallen in love with Marguerite and wanted to marry her, but had neither the approval of her father nor any encouragement from her. Irene, who was Marguerite's cousin, had taken a liking to Pavlov. It was convenient for Marguerite that their attachment should lead to a marriage.

Unfortunately, both bride and groom got cold feet at the last moment. While Marguerite, Nelka and the other three bridesmaids dressed her, Irene "dissolved into a storm of tears and hysterical protests." Marguerite finally had to call her father to Irene's dressing room. The Count commanded his poor niece to perform. "'No scandal,' he says in a terrifying voice. 'Down you go! Get married now you must, and go to hell afterward if you wish.'" (Cassini, 185.) The marriage lasted a year.

Nelka, Martha, and dogs Dis-Donc and Bonhomme
at the Wadsworth's house on Dupont Circle
(Courtesy of the Martha Blow Wadsworth Photographs Collection, Milne Library, SUNY Geneseo)

In March, Nelka visited Mrs. Sackett M. Barclay in New York, who gave a tea in Nelka's honor at her house on West Thirty-Seventh Street. (Several months before, Nelka's cousin Lucretia had noted in her diary that Mrs. Barclay's son Harold, who graduated from Harvard in 1897 and was in medical practice, was "one of Nelka's young men.") The Italian ambassador hosted a small dinner party honoring the French ambassador and included Nelka as a guest. President and Mrs. Roosevelt entertained the British ambassador at a small dinner at the White House. Nelka and three other unmarried women were invited as well as three single men.

For two social seasons in Washington, Nelka made herself visible and approachable to eligible bachelors, but nothing clicked. It wasn't that she lacked serious admirers. Over the years about thirty men of every nationality proposed marriage to her, including five in Bulgaria during her four-month stay in Sofia in 1900. Max Moukhanoff, who first met Nelka in 1905, enumerated her qualities. She was "pretty, with a lovely figure, always very feminine, with a brilliant mind and a sparkling personality, a great sense of humor, broad and diversified education, an understanding of art and good taste, cosmopolitan in her experiences and spoke four languages [English, French, German and Russian]." Her extraordinary charm and personality gained her favor with women as much as men. Nelka told Max's mother Veta that she would know that she had the right man when she experienced "a complete and overwhelming feeling" for him. Fifteen years would pass before she discovered her man.

Nelka decided to go abroad again after an unfortunate rupture in her relationship with Marguerite. For six years the two had been intimate friends. Increasingly unbridled, Marguerite had several outrageous flirtations in succession during the year – with Comte Charles de Chambrun, first secretary of the French Embassy, Nicholas Longworth who eventually married Alice Roosevelt, and Baron Ivan von Rubio-Zichy, second secretary of the Austro-Hungarian Embassy. When Marguerite turned her attention to Rubio-Zichy, everyone thought that he was already engaged to

Josephine Boardman, sister of Martha's good friend and neighbor on Dupont Circle, Mabel Boardman. Washington society quickly split between supporters of Josephine and defenders of Marguerite. Nelka at first sided with Marguerite, but when her behavior became erratic Nelka changed her mind.

In her memoir, Marguerite wrote:

> One day I thought Nelka had gone out of her mind when she announced she was going to have a court of love. But no. She had been reading about the troubadours and the courts of love of old Provence. She had decided to hold a trial, she to be the judge, the girls who were my closest friends the jury. I, the defendant, would be given a chance to reply to those who accused me of stealing Zichy from Josephine.
>
> When I walked into the Wadsworth's drawing room on the appointed day, the jury was all arranged in chairs. Nelka began at once: "Marguerite" – and she was stern – "don't you think you have behaved badly to Josephine?"

Marguerite surprised her friends by answering simply, "Yes." Nelka pressed on: "Well, then, why do you do it? And why do you go on seeing Zichy?" Marguerite gave another straight answer. "Because I love him. I can't help it." Her quick confession ended the trial, but not her agony. Her father and her friends disapproved of Zichy, and Zichy began to attack Marguerite for not loving him enough. Several days later, as she and Zichy walked down Connecticut Avenue, she bolted away and jumped into her carriage that had followed behind. Overwhelmed by a sense of "complete hopelessness," she swallowed a bottle of chloroform and ordered her coachman to take her to the Wadsworth house.

Nelka was looking out the window when the carriage arrived. Marguerite was semi-conscious. Nelka, the coachman and several Wadsworth servants brought her into the mansion. Martha summoned a physician, who after several hours declared there was nothing more he could do. Luckily, a few months earlier, having heard that Teddy Roosevelt was taking jiu-jitsu lessons from a Japanese master, Yoshiaki Yamashita, Martha rounded up a number of women, including Nelka, Lucretia, and Marguerite, to study the martial art with the master's wife, Fude. As soon as the doctor departed, Martha had Marguerite carried to the grand ballroom. Martha, who was small but tremendously athletic, went to work. There, Marguerite wrote, Martha "threw me all around the room, tied me in knots, banged me against the walls, bounced me off the floor, tossed me over her shoulder. When exhausted she would rest a few minutes then begin all over again." (Cassini, 211-14.) It took several hours before Marguerite revived. It took several months before she could reappear in public. In the meantime Nelka sailed to Europe in the summer of 1904.

She visited her friend Louisette, the Countess Moltke, in Denmark before going to Paris where she resumed painting and began taking classes with the French Red Cross. "I have painted a portrait of myself, grinning from ear to ear," she wrote Susan, "which you probably would not like, but it is the best I think I have done." Her mentor Julian urged her with "great approval" to submit the picture to the Salon, "but it was refused with *eight thousand* other masterpieces." She conceded that it was "a fearful blow to me but salutary for my soul no doubt." It also must have pained her that in March her cousin Lucretia, who had enrolled at Julian's school the year before, won the academy's prestigious Julian-Smith medal, the first woman ever to receive the prize.

5

Frustrated with her art, Nelka turned her full attention to medicine. The outbreak of war between Russia and Japan added urgency to her decision. In an era of Imperial expansion that saw much of Africa, China and the old Spanish empire carved up by the strong Western powers, Russia and Japan found themselves left behind. In February 1904 the two laggard nations started fighting for the remaining footholds in China. The world was surprised as the Asian country (Japan) defeated the European (Russia). To gain quick and practical experience Nelka volunteered at a children's clinic. "I go to the *dispensaire* every morning," she wrote to Susan. "I have got so much into it that I cannot get out. I enjoy it so much that I only remember once in a great while that I may be doing a little good in it as well." With reports of wounded Russian soldiers being transported from the Far East to St. Petersburg making news in Paris, "I have an unreasoning longing to be in Russia and doing something," she continued in her letter to Susan. "It seems such a useless ridiculous war and so much loss. I cannot understand the way people view things – the loss of life and the suffering just makes me sick. I see no dignity or sense in anything but quiet and peace."

Nelka worked hard and fast through the autumn. She received a diploma from the French Red Cross, which granted her the status of apprentice nurse, and was soon teaching other students. She then returned to Washington in early December. Instead of going directly to Dupont Circle, she spent her first few nights at the Russian embassy with Marguerite to mend their bruised relationship. Marguerite, still shaken by her wild flirtations, had kept a low profile since her chloroform debacle, but decided to come out with the New Year. Unfortunately, terrible news spoiled her plan. "You're going nowhere tonight," her father told her as she raced down the staircase in her evening gown. "Port Arthur has been surrendered." (Cassini, 215.) With the fall of Russia's last stronghold in the Far East to the Japanese on 2 January 1905, Arthur Cassini asked for and received a new assignment. He and his family left Washington for Madrid in May where he became the Russian emissary to Spain. For seven years, he had tried but failed to sway the McKinley and Roosevelt governments to support Russia in its Far Eastern ambitions.

Nelka meanwhile re-integrated herself into Washington society. She took a minor role in a play written by the Dutch ambassador that was put on in April at the New Willard Hotel. She then decided that she must go to Russia. She bade her family and friends farewell, and sailed for Europe on the *Lorraine* in October. In Paris Mrs. Winthrop Chanler and her daughter Laura invited her to dine at their apartment. They also invited Herbert and Martha's Washington neighbor and friend Henry Adams, whose book *Mont Saint Michel and Chartres* had just been privately printed. Adams adored Mrs. Winty, as he called her, and confessed that, were she willing and not already married with a dozen children, he would run away with her. Over dinner Adams congratulated Nelka on choosing to live in Russia where she could relish "a milder and cheerfuller climate." (Adams, iv, 721.)

When Nelka arrived in St. Petersburg, Mary Bakhmeteff provided her a place to stay and introduced her to her sister-in-law Elizabeth Moukhanoff and her family, including Elizabeth's son Max, who was then seven years old. Elizabeth, who was called Veta, had served as a lady-in-waiting to the Tsarina Alexandra and was the great-great granddaughter of Count Smolensky, who, with the aid of a frightfully cold winter, had driven Napoleon's great army from Russia in 1812. Another old friend of her mother, Mr. Pletnioff, helped Nelka find a nursing position with the Russian Red Cross, which was organized according to "communities of sisters." A prominent aristocratic woman governed each community, and each governess reported to the Dowager Empress, Marie Feodorovna, the August President of the Red Cross and mother of Tsar Nicholas. Pletnioff steered Nelka to the hospital of the Kaufman community in St. Petersburg under the direction of the Baroness Uxkull.

Nelka took an immediate liking to the Baroness, who, wealthy and worldly, seemed to take an interest in everything – the arts, politics and humanitarian causes. She was particularly keen on establishing international peace and reached out in all directions. When she and her husband were stationed in Rome, where he had served as the Russian ambassador to Italy in the 1870s, they frequently entertained their friend the composer Franz Listz. The Bakhmeteffs approved Nelka's joining her Red Cross community, but worried that the Baroness was "just on the edge of being a little 'advanced.'"

Nelka had arrived in Russia as major changes were taking place in the imperial government. Economic distress throughout the country and deep discontent over the nation's astonishing military loss to Japan led Nicholas II to create a new Duma to address the nation's ills. Like herself, most of Nelka's friends were deeply loyal to the Tsar, but still, she wrote to Susan, "the extremes are very great, – you see Pletnioff is somewhat liberal, but nothing in the sense that the word is used abroad and Mr. Bakhmeteff is for the strictest adherence to middle age regime. Between the two I must find the just milieu." However uncertain she was about her proper place on the political spectrum, Nelka was very happy to be in Russia and have the Baroness as her mentor.

She found the Kaufman hospital in St. Petersburg beautiful and perfect in every respect. Wishing only that she had arrived sooner, she was thrilled to be doing something useful at last and so different from her life in Washington. The soldiers "are so good and patient," she wrote to Susan, "but oh, Poodie, – it is so terrible to see them, many so young, without arms or legs and one whose head was almost blown off, – so grateful to have a new glass eye put in him the other day. Soon they are going to make him a nose."

Nelka shared quarters with four other sisters. While Nelka's mastery of the language was quite good, she was not totally fluent when she arrived in St. Petersburg. "I am managing to get on somehow with Russian," she told Susan, "but the other night when I had a conversation with Sister Swetlova on subjects that were not absolutely elementary it was awfully funny." Fortunately, another of her roommates, Sister Belskaya, spoke "every language and has helped me a great deal."

When the Kaufman hospital added a new wing, Nelka and her roommates were re-assigned temporarily to a large public hospital in the inner city. The new assignment proved more shocking than caring for her wounded soldiers. "Oh, Poodie," she wrote, "I cannot describe it to you. The hospital is all right enough, but the poor people! There are 3,000 there. We are in the surgical section for women. It is very various and valuable experience as you learn everything in a short while, but I would not care to prolong it."

Nelka with convalescent soldiers

In the early summer of 1906 Nelka accompanied a group of soldiers who were sent to Finland to recuperate in the countryside. After a year of practical experience, she was put in charge of both the apothecary and the operating room. Each day was full and varied. "I am on night duty after a strenuous day – assisted the doctor with the instruments and material for 25 dressings, put up eight prescriptions myself, dressed the wounds of five Finns, spent some time in the ward, went over the soldier's money accounts, did an hour massage, slept one hour and tomorrow morning I am going to take the temperatures at 6 A.M.," she wrote to Susan. After that, she continued, she would "start with two soldiers for Petersburg, – one who is to be operated [on] and the other who has been so ill for a week that they think it best to take him back as quickly as possible – neither of them can sit up." As soon as she delivered her patients, she was obliged to take the next train back.

Frequently exhausted, Nelka also felt energized. Life as a nurse in a distant culture broadened her perspective in ways she couldn't previously imagine. Ministering to wounded soldiers brought her physically and spiritually close to men who were often close to death. In particular, she came to recognize that "there are an indefinite number of experiences" that each person encounters, from which she observed "that one must abstain from any general conclusions upon the things of the world, owing to one's limited experience." Feeling calmer and more tolerant, she also gained confidence. "At last," she told Susan, "I seem to have found something where I am thought to be very useful." She regretted that she was "so far from Poodie and Pata [Martha's nickname]," but also confessed that, "I feel now so much at home."

Susan Blow told her friend and physician James Putnam that Nelka, though very happy in her work, was "postponing a final design of her life" until she returned from Russia, which she expected to do by the end of the year. She also told Putnam that "the Empress [Alexandra, wife of Tsar Nicholas II] has decorated her for war services and every one seems to think she has unusual gifts for the kind of service she has undertaken."

While she was in Finland, news appeared on the front page of *The Washington Post* (16 August 1906) under the headline "Girl Lashed For Taunt At Russian Soldier." According to the report, while the Chevalier Guards paraded in St. Petersburg, a young woman remarked, too loudly, that, "They are as gay as if they had captured Port Arthur" – alluding to Russia's recent defeat by the Japanese in the Far East. For her insolence, the officers of the Guards seized the girl and whipped her twenty-seven times for her impudence. *The Post* reported that, "The girl's clothing was cut as if by knives by the wire thongs of the whips and her flesh was horribly lacerated." The young woman was identified as Mlle. de Smirnoff. A sub-headline of the article asked, "Is She Mlle. Nelka de Smirnoff?" of Washington. The story was picked up in papers across the United States. Martha immediately sent Nelka a telegram and received a prompt reply. The next day *The Post* printed a follow-up piece on the front page, headlined – "Not Mlle. Nelka Smirnoff."

Article appearing in the Boston Journal 17 August 1906

For about twenty-four hours the family was in an absolute tailspin. "You can't imagine what a turn those awful reports gave us: Just were crazy!" Lucretia wrote to Nelka a day or two later. "It just seemed impossible yet all the papers all over the country said it was so." Lucretia, who had been visiting her aunt Elizabeth Le Bourgeois Crockett in Ipswich, Massachusetts, had read the story in the *Boston Transcript*. When she returned to Cazenovia, she "found Poodie very *ill*." By the time Martha arrived from Avon, Susan had mostly recovered and Martha was absolutely buoyant. "Pata is here now," Lucretia concluded, "looking very well and in a heavenlioso humor." (Van Horn Letters.)

It was an altogether unlikely event, for Nelka had grown more rigid and autocratic as she found her place on the political spectrum. She told Susan that Western liberalism could never appeal to the Russian character, yet she was alarmed by its spread. Fearing that her fellow nurses were becoming too liberal, she began to fight back. "I get perfectly outdone with the papers some of the sisters bring into the ward, and I quickly lay hands upon every one I find. There is no stemming the tide but I shall do what I can wherever I am, – for it is too stupid." Moreover, she added, her "soldiers are too uneducated" for that kind of thing. Responding to Susan's arguments in favor of liberty and progress, she wrote, "I don't suppose you can conceive how I *feel* the autocracy, the Emperor." Her loyalty to the Tsar was a spiritual matter that transcended human understanding. "I don't care what I think, I feel autocracy, and the Emperor [is] simply not a human being to me." After a year in Russia, Nelka had become an archconservative.

Replying to another letter from Susan, Nelka wrote, "You say in your letter that you understand that my father's country should be dear to me and yet you think that my mother's country might also mean something. What I feel, understand and see in America does not mean anything. I *cannot* feel as they do." Nelka found that, compared to Americans, "Russians are more sympathetic and comprehensible." She was also quick to emphasize that her two American aunts were the most important persons in her life.

"What I care for most in the world is you and Pats – that does not need to be said."

Susan Blow, drawing by Nelka de Smirnoff
(Courtesy of the Association for Childhood Education International (ACEI) archives,
Special Collections, University of Maryland Libraries)

6

After two years in Russia, Nelka felt it was time to see her aunts. Her soldiers had either died or recuperated and gone home. She felt exhausted. Baroness Uxkull tried to persuade her to stay; she wanted to send her to aid victims of a famine that was ravaging the country. Nelka decided, "the famine will have to wait."

Instead of taking a ship from St. Petersburg through the Baltic, she went south by train. In January 1907 she arrived in Moscow for the first time. She was bowled over. "O, it is so beautiful," she wrote to Susan, "so old and real Russia, so solid and so unforeign." She deplored ("I hate, loath and detest") any evidence of an alien influence in the city. It was also extremely cold. "But," she continued, "I was out all the time and only had my nose frozen once."

From Moscow Nelka went to Yalta where she boarded a boat for Naples. From there she went by train to Paris. After a short stay, she sailed from Europe for the States. Though she took a roundabout route, she was in a hurry to get home. "I am palpitating at the thought of seeing you soon," she told Susan. There was a lot she wanted to discuss. She had experienced a magical two years in Russia but now it was done. What would come next? "Everything has splendid possibilities but it is always the fearful alternative and its possibilities" that worried her. "It seems to me I am just living in gulps. How will I ever put my whole self into one thing?"

She arrived in Washington in the middle of April. The newspapers noted that Miss de Smirnoff, back from Russia, was the guest of Mr. and Mrs. Wadsworth on Dupont Circle. She caught the tail end of the social season and then went with Martha and Herbert to their house at Avon. Susan joined them in July and then brought Nelka to her place for the remainder of the summer.

Susan thought Nelka looked tired and depressed at first, but was pleased to see her perk up when she got to Cazenovia. "Now that we are at home again and that she is interested in making changes in our little house and improving our little garden," Susan wrote to her friend Putnam, "she seems much better."

Nelka persuaded Susan to go to Europe with her in the following summer, but when Lucretia announced that she would marry Captain Van Horn in the fall, they gave up the idea. After the wedding, which took place at Avon in October 1908, Nelka spent the winter with Susan in New York at her apartment on West 115th Street, where Susan lived while lecturing at the Teachers' College of Columbia University. There she came down with a series of colds, so that by the early spring she looked run down and miserable. Susan told James Putnam in March 1909 that, "Nelka does not seem well. It is partly her state of mind." She complained about having to get around town on street cars and subways, but, more to the point, Susan noted, "She dislikes and is repelled by America." Susan made no mention that Nelka may have felt eclipsed once again by her younger cousin. Lucretia had found her husband before she turned twenty-seven, but Nelka, now thirty, was still unmarried.

Nelka's health and outlook remained down through the year and into the next. Neither improved until Martha thought to give her a dog – a black poodle puppy, which Nelka named Tibi. She was fluffy, active, very affectionate and highly intelligent. Tibi and Nelka fell in love, each certain that she understood the other, perfectly. But, before she became totally attached to Tibi, Nelka went with Martha on a long horseback riding expedition out West in July 1910. "Mrs. Wadsworth has taken the trip before and is sure it is just what Nelka needs," Susan wrote to James Putnam. "I hope she may be right. Nelka herself is delighted to go."

General Robert Shaw Oliver had invited Martha to join him on a reconnaissance mission. Though he was twenty years her senior, he and Martha had become close friends through their shared love of horses. Oliver had served as a cavalry officer in the

Civil War and, more recently, as President Roosevelt's and, currently, President Taft's Assistant Secretary of War. He had decided that it was important to survey areas in Utah and Arizona near the Four Corners. The General also wanted to test a kind of compressed fodder that Herbert and Captain Nathan Shiverick had invented. Herbert and the Captain hoped to patent their product. The fodder apparently satisfied the horses, but was never awarded a patent. After three weeks General Oliver and his soldiers concluded their mapping project. He left Martha and Nelka with Captains Shiverick and McCoy and a handful of men to explore the area for another three weeks.

Martha was in perfect shape for the trip. The year before Teddy Roosevelt had challenged his cavalry officers by riding 98 miles in 14 hours. In June 1909 Martha beat the President's record by riding sidesaddle, using a relay of horses, 212 miles in just over 15 hours. The western journey was nonetheless jolting and arduous. The countryside was extremely rugged and the temperature was either too hot or too cold. During the night it neared freezing while in the heat of the day it hovered around 100 degrees. One day the thermometer hit 139.

In Utah they visited the Natural Bridge. Aside from the "difficulties and trials" of getting there, the terrain was "terrible." The landscape, Nelka wrote, "impressed one as the most godless place conceivable .... such a mass of turbulent, ruthless rock, all dark red, – hopeless, shapeless chaos – it all looked just as if there had been a smash up yesterday." There was, she continued, "No beyond, no nothing, nothing alive, nothing dead, every step of the way almost impassable." At one point a horse lost its balance, the rider jumped free, but "the horse fell over backwards several times, broke its neck, slid down sheer rock and fell about 50 feet over the cliff – the sound was awful." Afterwards Nelka went to the bottom of the canyon to collect her wits and cool her feet in the water. "I closed my eyes," she wrote, "and tried to forget."

Little relief came in the days that followed:

There was a question of moving the sleeping blankets to get out of a scorpion patch, but we finally stayed where we were. I refused to mount my horse firmly and flatly until we got out of the worst part of the canyon, so I walked 12 miles when I had to pick every step on sharp stones. On the way back, Pata's horse went head over heels down another steep place but was not killed. Still a few miles further my horse slipped going over a huge mass of rock as smooth as an egg and about the same shape and everyone thought he was about to be hurled to instant death, when by a miracle he screwed around, got himself up and caught his footing again.

"I don't know what impression you might get from my letter," she told Susan, but, "I am wound up to the last degree."

Leaving Utah and heading south into Arizona, conditions improved a bit: "We arrived here [in Keams Canyon] in the rain, the pack train with the lunch miles behind and a waste of thistles to sit on, but it cleared up soon after and everything got settled." In some ways, the day-to-day routine resembled her nursing responsibilities in Russia. "I get up at 5 and see the sunrise and generally take the things in before everything gets astir," she wrote Susan from Ganado. "We have breakfast at 6, 6:30 and start our marches at 7. It was so cold one night I got up at 4:30 and made up the camp fire."

In contrast to the frightening landscape of Utah the countryside of Arizona was much more appealing. In August they traveled through the Canyon de Chelly. Nelka declared it "too wonderful for words ....I wish you could see it." A few days later, they passed through the Painted Desert, which Nelka felt "was even more beautiful than the canyon," if not less dangerous. They camped nearby "at a kind of oasis on a little lake and were able to have a swim – though the desert was full of rattle snakes and the lake full of lizards."

One evening Nelka walked away from the campsite, and got lost. The sky was overcast and there was no moon. Soon it began to rain. When the ground turned to mud, Nelka took off her shoes and stockings and kept walking. After a while she decided to spend the remainder of the night next to a large cactus. Alarmed by her absence, the troops went out to look for her. The soldiers blew their trumpets; they hollered. Nothing availed. Eventually Captain McCoy's small white dog found her.

Nelka leading her horse down a rocky path
(Martha took the picture and hand-tinted the glass slide)
(Courtesy of the Martha Blow Wadsworth Photographs Collection, Milne Library, SUNY Geneseo)

In Arizona Nelka discovered a sharp contrast between the Native Americans and the new arrivals. "Every place where the Indians live in their natural mud huts it is clean and inoffensive," she wrote. In contrast, the white settlers were disgusting. "As soon as there is a sign of a real house," she continued, "or what you call civilization, there is dirt, smells, refuse heaps and flies – and of all the sights in my life, bar *none*, the washstand in Mr. Hubble's store, with wet newspaper, stagnant slop jar, dirty tooth brush, filthy basin, sloppy soap, – all humming with flies, – it is the worse I have ever seen and the most stomach turning." Even though his bathroom revolted her, Nelka must have cottoned to John Lorenzo Hubbell, who had started the trading post in the early 1870s and was in his late fifties when Martha and Nelka showed up in Ganado. He encouraged the Navajo Indians in their art and crafts and defended their rights. He also advocated for equality between men and women. In contrast, she was thoroughly put off by an officious East Coast, self-appointed social worker she met near Ganado. "There is some freak from Boston in a checkered suit and goggles," she reported to Susan, "who walks around with some ideas for Indian betterment. I think they [the Indians] have reached the highest pitch [of civilization] in the fact that they do not scalp him!"

Nelka preferred the simple, rough living of the natives to the filth and arrogance of her own tribe, though her description of how she took to eating seemed to blur the distinction: "I had coffee, oatmeal and bacon all out of one bowl. I drink water that looks like bean soup and never use a fork and a spoon at the same meal. Sand and cinders or charcoal flavor everything, and I have fished olives out of the sand where they had fallen and eaten them with perfect satisfaction." She told Susan that, "this certainly is the way to live," but conceded, "some shifting might improve it."

The trip west with Martha proved physically exhausting and at times terrifying, but it did have its positive side. Having never met any before, Nelka discovered, "There are lovely Indians here."

Nelka (top photo) and Martha (bottom photo) with soldiers and Native Americans
(Courtesy of the Martha Blow Wadsworth Photographs Collection, Milne Library, SUNY Geneseo)

7

On her return east, Nelka went to Cazenovia and reconnected with Poodie and Tibi. Susan found her niece's condition disturbing. She told her friend Putnam, "Nelka has not been well since her return from her western trip. Her physician thinks she is having a reaction after too great stimulus and recommends the sea level." So, Susan closed her summerhouse in late October and brought Nelka to Atlantic City where they stayed a month at the Glaslyn-Chatham guesthouse on Park Place. With her health improved by the ocean air, Nelka spent the winter season with Martha in Washington. The round of parties, embassy dinners, and invitations to the White House, however, soon shook her equilibrium again. She decided to go back to Russia, departing with Tibi at the end of February 1911. She might have decided differently had she known that in July George Bakhmeteff would be named the Russian ambassador to the United States and arrive in Washington with his wife Mary Beale (Nelka's godmother) in November.

The presence of Tibi in her life made Nelka realize that, excepting her aunts, she preferred animals to humans. Writing to Susan from St. Petersburg, she said, "If there was for one moment in my heart what I feel for dogs, cats, horses and animals in general, I would be a real sister of charity." She simply no longer loved humanity. "If all these crippled numberless that I have seen all these days," she went on, "had been maimed dogs, I don't know *what* I would have done. There is something in human nature that is so contemptible and poor that I can't feel the same way."

"How do you keep your faith in humanity?" she asked Susan. Ideas, conceptions, she felt, were "beautiful things" but their actualization amounted to no more than "an outrageous fizzle." The abstract world of possibilities existed "only to be ruined by fatal microbes this human nature puts into it." Outside the human race, the natural world was beautiful. Man himself – "dirty and unenchanting" – was "the instrument of hideousness all around." Even as she re-dedicated herself to the Red Cross, she found "these sick people" the most depressing examples of humanity.

The Baroness was delighted to have Nelka back at the Kaufman community, for she had a specific task for her in Montenegro. A small state on the Adriatic Sea, wedged between the eastern end of the Austro-Hungarian Empire and Serbia, Montenegro, like Bulgaria, had gained its independence from the Ottoman Empire as a result of Russia's victory over the faltering empire in 1878. Now, in 1910, the little country had just upgraded itself from a principality to a kingdom. The Baroness wanted to help King Nikola, but her plan presented a serious problem for Nelka: No dogs allowed. She wrote to Susan:

> I am undergoing the greatest disappointment at this moment. I was to be sent to Montenegro to establish a Red Cross sisterhood and overhaul the hospital, and to be given five sisters to take with me, – I as the head, – so interesting, – and in the part of the world which has always attracted me to the utmost, ever since I was in Sofia. And after it was all arranged and I was simply reveling in every detail, Baroness Uxkull decided that it was simply impossible to take Tibi.

Nelka caved in and Tibi stayed behind. She was disconsolate so her solution was to stay busy. "I can hardly believe, at least I wonder," she wrote Susan, "at myself being able to do so many things I dislike: – getting up *every* day so early, no walks with Tibi, sleeping between five and six hours, often only four, and yet I enjoy everything, – ice cream is a festival, a moment to sew a treat, and bed heaven."

The Baroness did provide five perfectly fresh sisters for her to train. Nelka relished the prospect of playing the drill sergeant: "I am going to make them march like pokers, copy every record each time they make a spot and count all the linen every two weeks." She was not worried how her trainees might react. "As they will not have been in any other ward," she wrote Susan, "they cannot make any comparisons or complain." Since she could never leave the ward in their untutored hands, Nelka also felt she had to stay on duty from eight in the morning until nine at night or even later if there were serious cases to attend. This kind of responsibility buoyed her spirits: "I am very well, sleep little, eat little and am flourishing."

Even so, Nelka continued to dwell on the discontinuity between Russia and America. She was very sorry that she and Susan had been unable to travel to Europe together as they had planned three years earlier. She was convinced that her aunt would see Americans as more limited in the context of the Continent. "You would see," she said, "what makes me *shrivel* with most Americans." Still, she was ambivalent. "If I did not care for Americans and if I did not have a great deal of sentiment and associations, ties and memories to America, it would be so easy to leave it alone and not think about it. But I know I am both [Russian and American]."

It was especially important for Nelka that she had a position in Russian society, even among people who didn't know her. "For instance," she explained to Susan, "they may not know me personally but the fact that Papa was in the [diplomatic] service, was *Gentilhomme de la Chambre* [official title at Court], was educated at the *Lycée*, *defines* a type, defines in a certain manner his daughter, if only externally." Russians, she thought, moreover, comprehended completely her split allegiance. "Knowing that Mama was American, the whole thing is clear in a natural way," she added. "My wanting to be here is understood, – my attachment to America is understood." But, in the States, she felt her loyalty to Russia was not understood.

After training her new unit in Montenegro, Nelka returned to the States for a brief visit. She spent part of the time making the rounds of Washington once again, but with the same negative reaction. Writing to Susan from Martha's house at Avon early in the new year, she lamented over the "bumps and jolts and frights and moans" of traveling thousands of miles to see "my two best friends" only to turn around and hurry away again. "Oh, what is it all about?" she asked. She felt terribly torn. She longed for her work and she pined for her aunts.

The contrast between the glitter of life in Washington and the poverty of her next assignment in Russia could not have been greater. Throughout its history Russia suffered cyclical famines. Inevitably hundreds of thousands of people died with each onslaught. The famine in 1906 that Nelka chose to skip was followed by another in the eastern part of the country in 1911. To combat starvation, the government established feeding stations administered by the Red Cross. Sisters were sent to small isolated villages where they dispensed provisions and provided medical care to the peasants. The Baroness assigned Nelka to the village of Kalakshinovka in the district of Samara on the outskirts of the Ural Mountains that separate Europe from Asia.

Getting there across the vast steppes was an adventure. The village seemed inaccessible as she traveled in a low sleigh over "a desert of snow." The ride, she wrote, was "even with the snow ... more rolly and bumpy than the worst sea ever dreamed of." All she could do was lie down on a pallet of straw and close her eyes as she was driven along for hours at a stretch. Her first few nights she slept on a bed that consisted of "two wooden benches side by side – one a little higher than the other." Eventually she found a small house of her own. There she kept supplies for 900 people in the area. Once settled, she set up shop and established a routine. During the day she distributed food and medicine. Sometimes the peasants came to her and sometimes she went to them. Occasionally she traveled as far as fifteen miles to visit a sickened family. As always her days were long. In the evening, if she had the energy or time, she would sew and mend, scrape the mud off her boots, and write a few letters.

Though she had a good supply of basic items, there were some things that she lacked. In one of her letters, she wrote, "I have at last attained my own bowl and spoon. I drink coffee and eat a piece of black bread in the morning. At 12 a bowl of buckwheat or some kind of grain with a wooden spoon, – a glass of tea and at night a glass of cocoa and black bread, or as a treat a dish of sour milk. I cook and iron and do everything myself, but it is very simple." She discovered that a neighboring village about nine miles off was "quite a center" with an open market every week. "I shall buy some sugar and a little flour and perhaps if it can be found, a piece of ham. I am getting awfully hungry," she wrote in a subsequent letter.

The famine was widespread and Nelka witnessed great suffering. She was particularly stricken by the plight of the animals, which were also starving. "I don't know what I would not do to feed all the poor cows and horses and sheep that are left," she confessed. One thing she did was to spend some money she was given in St. Petersburg to buy fodder. "Aside from my pity for them," she explained, "it will be terrible for the peasants not to have a horse to work in the fields as soon as the warm weather comes." She told Susan that, "One poor woman when I bought some feed for her horse and cow simply fell on her knees on the ground." It is hard to "dream of this life," she added, "if one has not been in it."

Nelka's misery was not totally unrelieved. Letters from home were treasures. A letter from Susan enclosing a letter from Martha with a photograph of Lucretia "was the reward of a walk of six miles with a ton of mud on each boot, a night on the floor and a return at dawn on a rickety horse horseback." She also discovered and immensely enjoyed the peasants' bathhouse. "One can climb higher and higher and lie on shelves in different stages of heat," she told Susan. "I got so steamed up I wanted at one moment to open the door and just fly out into the field without a stitch. When I look out on the plains here and then think of New York and the subway, my brain simply stops."

And she did think of New York, and made arrangements to return to the States in July. She stopped first to visit Martha in Avon, and then went to see Susan and Lucretia (who was spending the summer) at Cazenovia. "There was great joy in this little house on the hill when Nelka reached here last Monday safe and sound," Susan wrote to James Putnam on 25 July. "She looks exceedingly well and seems much settled in mind." Well, she might. She had great news to tell that she evidently decided to keep to herself until she got home. The Tsarina Alexandra *and* the Queen of Greece (who was also the Grand Duchess Olga of Russia and Tsar Nicholas's sister) had visited her facility in Samara, approved her work, and awarded her a distinguished cross.

With the outbreak of the First Balkan War in October 1912, Baroness Uxkull recalled Nelka to St. Petersburg. The Russian government, supporting the ambitions of its client states to the south – Bulgaria, Serbia and Montenegro – in their efforts to further expand their borders at the expense of the long-declining Ottoman Empire, directed the Red Cross to provide a small field hospital for the Bulgarian Army laying siege to the city of Adrianople.

In St. Petersburg, Nelka re-united with Tibi and visited the Moukhanoffs at their country estate. There she ate well and got some much needed rest. "Yesterday," she wrote Susan, "I went with Veta and Max to town. We came back in the evening and after dinner I had a most *delicious* sleep on the sofa by the fire – Max waking me up every few minutes." Max was preparing to take entrance exams for the Imperial Lyceum, where Nelka's father had gone to school. Besides Russian, Ancient and European history, he was learning Latin, German, French and English. After her nap, Nelka tested Max with a dictation in English. "He is such a nice boy," she wrote, "15 years, so boyish and yet so developed and such a casual culture, just from association with cultured people, – and yet a real country boy, loving the affairs of the estate and everything to do with the place, and full of fun and mischief."

On her way to Adrianople, Nelka stopped off in Sofia to visit Eleonore, the wife of the Bulgarian Tsar, and to get her certificate to travel to the battle front. Capable and practical but not noted for her beauty, Eleonore earned the admiration of the Bulgarian people for her direct role in nursing wounded soldiers during her country's various wars. "I have just come from the Queen," Nelka wrote Susan from Sofia. "She was ill and could not receive me before. She was very, very nice – much nicer than I expected and better looking than her pictures. It is now 3 A.M., and I am to get up at six."

Nelka with Tibi

Nelka reached her nursing station at Kara Youssouf in early 1913. It stood on the outskirts of Adrianople where the fighting soon became intense. Turkish shells began falling in front and behind the Red Cross tents. For the first time in her life, Nelka felt she might not come out alive. She quickly wrote several farewell messages, including one to Veta:

> Dearest Veta:
>
> We are under fire, – the projectiles are going over our heads, – one just fell on the other side of our tents, and the ground is torn up before our eyes. Perhaps we may miraculously escape, – if not, goodbye. Perhaps some one may pick this up and send it. I send you much, much love, – give my love to my friends in Petersburg, – it is terrible for the poor wounded. Love to Max. – Nelka.

Susan's reply to a letter from Nelka tells how scary it was:

> Nothing I can say suggests what I feel. The picture of you with those awful bombs bursting above you, before you, to the right and left of you and the other picture of you plunging knee deep in mud and battling with mud and rain, as you made your way from tent to tent will never leave me. And what pictures of horror must move in ghastly procession in your mind. You have always wanted first hand experience. Now you have had such experience of famine, of war, of religious enthusiasm, of patriotic devotion. How will it all affect the necessary routine of life?

The First Balkan War ended a month later when the Bulgarian 2nd Army broke through the enemy lines and captured Adrianople. "What I noticed the most," Nelka wrote after the Turkish forces withdrew, "was the air of proprietorship of the soldiers in the town and how one felt the immediate transformation of the Turkish town into a Bulgarian one." The victory resonated with historical significance. More than fifteen hundred years earlier, invading Goths had defeated the Roman army led by the Emperor Valens at

Adrianople, a turning point that opened the way to the eventual collapse of the Roman Empire.

With war over – at least temporarily – Nelka and her sisters took down their tattered tents and carried the wounded back to Bulgaria. From Sofia, Nelka wrote Susan with this observation: "It was terrible in many ways. Those first days at Kara Youssouf, but I feel it was the greatest privilege to be there. One felt helpless before such a demand but it was so *real* and every breath meant so much."

8

Nelka returned to St. Petersburg where she stayed several days with the Moukhanoffs at their country estate before returning to the States. There she tightened her relationship with the family in a way that she could not yet appreciate. Veta sent her a note afterwards:

> Max and I miss you very much. I was so happy to have you with us for a time, your visits are always so nice and cheerful. I always remember them with so much pleasure. We had a long talk with Max about you and decided you were a real friend for us and Max said: "we must always be real friends to her." He is very fond of you.

Years later when Max printed this letter in his book about Nelka, he wrote: "I was then 16 years old and very much in love with Nelka."

Nelka arrived in Washington in time for her cousin Henry Le Bourgeois' marriage in June 1913. Susan, now the matriarch of the family, headed the receiving line at the reception for Henry's family, where Nelka was able to reunite with Martha and Herbert, Lucretia and others in the family. This time she intended to stay in the States indefinitely, even as it became clear that Russia might soon be engaged with its friends England and France in a great war against Germany and its ally Austria-Hungary. She found that the double separation from Tibi and her aunts was too much to bear. She looked forward to settling down at last. But, just after the wedding, something terrible happened. Tibi discovered some rat poison and ate it. Martha called the best veterinarian and then two doctor friends. No one was able to save the poodle. Nelka's "grief," Max wrote later, "was beyond all comprehension and she went into a state of utter despair, verging on the frantic." Susan and Martha tried to help as much as possible but neither was able to console her. Her sense of loss was total.

Just before she left Russia, Princess Wasilchikoff had asked Nelka to reorganize a community of sisters at a hospital near the German border, in the fortress-town of Kovno (today Kaunas, Lithuania). The Princess, whose father had been the Director of the Hermitage in St. Petersburg, had served Tsarina Alexandra as a lady-in-waiting at the Imperial Court. The proposal appealed to Nelka but she had declined. With Tibi's excruciatingly painful death, everything changed. She telegraphed the Princess to say she would accept the offer after all.

When she reached Rotterdam in the Netherlands in October, Nelka was still grieving. "It just seems some times more than I can bear," she wrote to Susan. "I don't know how to get reconciled, – that is the worst." She tried to face the reality in order to "wear it out of my head" but that was no more effective than her effort to stop thinking about Tibi. Even a year later, she continued to feel sharp pangs of despair, as she explained to Susan:

> The approach of this anniversary has been taking me, despite of myself, over every minute of those dreadful, dreadful days a year ago. I don't want to speak of it at all to you or make you feel any more than I have already the weight of a grief that will never leave me, – but I do want to tell you that I shall also never forget how good you were to me and how you helped me through that simply fearful night. I don't know how anything could be any worse but still if you had not been there I don't know what I would have done.

Before Nelka left for Russia, Susan had introduced her to James Putnam for the first time. Putnam was her doctor in Boston. He had diagnosed and relieved Susan's illness when she first moved from St. Louis in 1886. The two had become friends based on their mutual interests in philosophy and psychology. Putnam was particularly attracted to the theoretical work of

Sigmund Freud as well as the notions of Friedrich Hegel. In 1909 he had organized Freud's first and only visit to the United States. Putnam found Susan's skepticism and critique of Freud's ideas useful to his own understanding of psychoanalysis. In particular, she convinced Putnam that even if Freud's analysis could cure a patient of his neurosis, it would be a deficient remedy if there were no set of ideal values to replace the person's neurotic center. According to Putnam's great-grandson and biographer, Susan became his guide and muse. (Prochnik, 71-72.) Susan in turn was relieved by and pleased with Putnam's assessment of Nelka. "I am so glad that you like and admire her," she wrote to him in August, "and it is a great help to me to have you feel sure that the very taxing life she has elected is the best thing for her."

Arriving in Kovno, Nelka took up her new responsibilities with a fury. With fifty beds, forty sisters, eighteen servants, and a separate building with two wards for eye illnesses, the hospital was a little bigger than she expected, but in need of thorough reform. Given *carte blanche* to make the place over, she set about her work with vigor. "Two hours after I arrived," she wrote Susan, "I attacked their hair (the sisters), and now it is as flat as paper on a wall." She also berated a doctor on her first day for skipping the lecture he was supposed to deliver. "I am trying my best to impose terror," she continued. "When I feel the terror getting rooted, I will try for a little affection and good will."

Nelka also demonstrated substantial administrative skills. She devised a new system of keeping patients' charts, opened a new laboratory, weeded out incorrigible sisters, and established a better method for assigning nursing duties. She found that planning was not too difficult; it was simply a matter of "arranging things within given conditions and balancing demands and complaints." She was especially fierce about budgets: "I am now racking my brains how to get 180 dresses and aprons made by Easter and keep within the limit for cost." She wanted to *know* that her "food costs only 15 cents a day."

Nelka enjoyed being the boss. She operated out of large office that she called her "chancellery" where she commanded "an immense big writing table, another table, three chairs, bells and excellent light and telephone." She spent most of her time there "when I am not doing the rounds on a rampage." Next to her office she had "a very nice" bedroom, which was "in the most immaculate order imaginable" because, she said, "I am never in it."

Nelka in her office in Kovno

Through experience, Nelka learned the art and the pitfalls of administration. "I realize tremendously how an institution of this kind depends on the managing head," she wrote Susan. "So much has to be looked after and such constant questions come up that no system or plan suffices by itself." She also recognized a basic contradiction that confronts any manager: "It is very hard to get things done without being somewhat impetuous," while at the same time, "one cannot preserve control over everything without a great deal of calm." The blunt fact was: an institution "cannot be run without a certain amount of injustice." Nelka felt the absurdity of her position – a free spirit bound by rules and policy.

Her managerial routine was temporarily interrupted when early in 1914 Veta telegraphed for help. Nelka left Kovno immediately. "I spent three days in Petersburg – arriving there finding both Veta and Max very ill," she reported to Susan. Both had succumbed to a serious influenza. Max had fever as high as 104 and several complications that led to an abscess in his ear. Nelka nursed him for three days and nights until Veta was well enough to get up and take care of him herself. Fortunately, both recovered in due time.

With the overhaul of her hospital finished by May, Nelka scheduled a trip back to America for the late summer. The political situation in Europe, however, worsened when the heir to the Austrian-Hungarian Empire, the Archduke Franz Ferdinand and his wife were murdered in Sarajevo, the capitol of Serbia, at the end of June. Austria-Hungary threatened Serbia with retaliation. Serbia in turn looked to Russia, which was allied with England and France, for support, while Austria-Hungary expected backing from its military partner, Germany. War in Europe appeared unavoidable.

At the end of July, Susan told James Putnam that Nelka "will be home in September unless she changes her plans on account of wars and rumors of wars." About the same time, Nelka wrote encouragingly to say, "I have written to the Russian Line and got special permission to sail from Copenhagen. If nothing unforeseen happens, I will leave here on the 4th of August for Stockholm." Nelka stopped, and began again with different news:

> I had hardly finished this when the town was put under martial law. Everything is upside down, – the inhabitants are ordered to leave. The bank is packing up, people streaming all day there.

Everyone ordered off the streets at night. The streets are occupied with soldiers and cannons moving to the front, and the aspect seems serious. No one can tell anything. I have already signed a paper not to leave without the permission of the fort. If we have war I am ready to stay to the end. I have the greatest sympathy for Servia and would like to work in the Red Cross there if not here. I shall try to write you again before being shut up for good, if the town is besieged. We are only a few hours from the [German] frontier.

On 4 August German forces crossed into Belgium to attack France in the west. The two great alliances were finally at war. Two weeks later Russia attacked Germany in the east.

Nelka was stuck and excited. The panic of an entire town was something she had not experienced before. "I cannot describe it," she said, but she tried: "Cannons hustling to the front. Cavalry going off." Fearing that communication lines would be cut at any moment, she wrote as much and as fast as she could. Amidst the angst, there was some good news to report: "All the big buildings are to be turned into hospitals. The new bank will be splendid, – tile floors and water." She thought it could "hold at least a thousand." With men and women running madly about, some came her way. "All kinds of specimens are turning up to be enrolled as sisters, but I am relentless and shall take no adventuresses if I can help it."

With a crisis looming the Russian Army decided to merge its large field hospital with Nelka's. Suddenly, she found herself in charge of nearly 300 sisters. When the Princess Wasilchikoff was obliged to return to St. Petersburg, her husband, the Prince, helped Nelka integrate the two operations. When he left to join his own regiment, she gave him letters to Susan and Martha that she thought might be her last.

In one, Nelka told Susan not to worry too much about her. Kovno was fortified and stoutly defended. "This section of the Army will not give in till the last," she said. "The Commander

Grigorieff is splendid and General Rennenkamph is a real fighting man." Nelka's faith was misplaced. By the first of September, the Germans had routed the Russians and were headed in her direction. Commander Grigorieff ordered a hasty retreat, leaving much of his military equipment behind. To add to his disgrace, he and his forces decamped seventeen hours before Nelka. Unflappable, Nelka took her time to gather all her nurses, material and supplies, and made an orderly exit. "Everything in the hospital building which could not be moved was destroyed," Max wrote, "and she went even that far to have all brass knobs removed from the doors and thrown into the river so that the Germans would not get the metal."

As Kovno fell, Nelka followed the Russian forces east to make another stand. She re-established her hospital in a large agricultural building about forty miles to the rear of the new front. She was no sooner set up when she was forced to move once more as the Germans, continuing their advance, pushed through the Russian lines again. Just as the removal got underway, Nelka came down with scarlet fever. The head doctor told her she couldn't move. He arranged a bed for her in a tent and ordered one of her nurses to stay behind. As he left, he slipped a revolver under her pillow so that she could defend herself against the Huns.

Nelka didn't use the gun. She recovered before the Germans reached her position and was able to rejoin her team. As the Russian armies continued to collapse, she moved to Novgorod to set up her hospital. From Novgorod, it was relatively easy to reach St. Petersburg by train. She went often for supplies and to visit the Moukhanoffs. On one of her visits, Max gave her a box of white cream caramels. It was a sweet sign of affection.

Nelka was always in a hurry and frequently late. More than once she nearly missed her return train to Novgorod. Max witnessed two occasions that demonstrated her tardiness and her determination:

> Once she failed to secure the necessary permit to
> board a train going to the front, – there just wasn't

time for it. At the entrance to the platforms armed guards stood and one had to show one's pass to get through. I warned Nelka that she probably would have trouble, but she said there was no time for this now and that she would find a way to get through. Of course we arrived just about the time the train was pulling out and dashed towards the platform. A soldier stood at the entrance with his rifle and when Nelka plunged headlong towards him, he thrust his rifle horizontally in front of her to stop her. Without a moment's hesitation she ducked low and slipped under the extended rifle, and was on the moving train before the sentry knew what it was all about!

The other time, when she did have her pass, they "arrived just a little too late." The train had actually left the station. As they dashed to the platform they could just "see the two receding red lights" of the last car. "To this day," Max wrote, "I do not know what happened, but Nelka raised such fireworks that the train backed into the station. Nelka got on and the train pulled out again!"

Nelka spent the winter of 1914-15 in Novgorod. She then decided to form her own hospital unit to serve the cavalry. She raised money in St. Petersburg and set about selecting the staff she wanted. She chose one of Max's uncles to serve as the head of the unit and one of their friends, Baron Goddert Wrede of Finland, as his assistant. She also chose several doctors and most of the sisters she knew from her time in Kovno. The Red Cross provided the supplies, male orderlies and horses for the enterprise. Attached to the First Guard Cavalry Division, everyone – doctors, nurses, and orderlies – traveled on horseback. Stretchers for the wounded were slung on long poles between two horses. When the hospital unit moved any short distance, it stretched out in a long Indian file.

Unlike a regular field hospital that normally remained stationary, Nelka's unit was highly mobile, moving right along with the cavalry division. If they were to move any great distance, the entire unit was loaded and transported by rail. Nelka remembered one starless night unloading horses from the train while a fierce battle raged nearby. The explosions frightened the horses, just as wounded soldiers started to arrive. Nelka dressed and bandaged the men in "muddy dugouts," and then ran into the woods to soothe her horse, which she had named "Vive la France."

With the war in eastern Europe going badly, Nelka's godmother Mary Beale Bakhmeteff spoke for the Imperial Court about Russia's fight with the Germans, which was poorly understood by many in America. It would be another two years before the United States entered the war on the side of England, France and Russia. In a full-page interview with *The New York Times* (11 April 1915), Mary told how Russian women were helping their country's war effort by working in the Red Cross.

Women were "giving manual service and intelligence," she said, "not merely patronage and money, for the relief of the soldiers and their families." She explained the hierarchical structure of the Russian Red Cross, and pointed out the direct involvement of the imperial family. The Dowager Empress served as Red Cross President, and two of her granddaughters "had passed their examinations as trained nurses, with scores of titled women whose names are famous throughout the world, to daughters of nobles just emerging from the school room. These ladies are working shoulder to shoulder with the daughters of the humblest citizens, and on absolutely the same footing." A soldier, she insisted, never knew whether the nurse changing his bandage was a titled noblewoman or not. The Red Cross in Russia blended, as it were, democratic action and *noblesse oblige*. Mary's many interviews and talks helped persuade a skeptical American public that it was acceptable to align its foreign policy interests with an imperious and autocratic regime.

In the spring of 1916 Nelka left the front for a short break and went to St. Petersburg where she met Max and picked up a letter from Martha. On the train to the Moukhanoff estate, she told Max that she was afraid to open the letter. She had a premonition that something was wrong. "We traveled all the way in silence," Max recalled, "and I could see how very anxious and upset she was." It was painful for him to watch but there was nothing he could do. When they arrived, she went alone to her room to open Martha's letter. "It was what she had expected – the news that her beloved Aunt Susie Blow had died in New York." She was seventy-three years old.

Nelka had no reason to think her aunt was ill. She had sent Susan a Christmas greeting by cablegram that arrived at her Fifth Avenue apartment in New York. In a letter to Dr. Putnam, Susan mentioned receiving it. Six weeks before her death, Susan had written him again and indicated that she felt healthy: "My work here has been very taxing, but I am getting through with it and thus far have kept physically well." Nelka was stunned and blamed herself. She should have stayed in America with her aunt. Instead she had chosen war.

Throughout 1916 and into the following year Nelka was always close to the edge of battle and exposed to the same gunfire as the cavalrymen. Max's uncle was killed by shellfire in July. It could have been Nelka who took the hit.

9

Max received his commission as a second lieutenant in the First Infantry Guard Regiment on the first day of February 1917 and was sent to Galicia. The Tsar had conducted the commissioning ceremony, which turned out to be his last. Before the month was out, a revolution erupted and Nicholas was forced to abdicate. Enraged by military defeat and acute economic distress, the great majority of Russians began to clamor for radical change. Across the Atlantic Ocean, the United States finally declared war on Germany in April, after a series of provocations, most importantly the indiscriminate sinking of American merchant ships by German submarines. Meanwhile Nelka's Red Cross unit had moved across the Romanian border, where the Romanian army, an ally of Russia, was making a last but unsuccessful stand against the Germans. By the end of the summer she found her staff reduced to a handful of nurses, as military discipline disintegrated all over the country. Soldiers began to throw down their guns or, more ominously, join the rapidly forming groups that sought to throw over the government.

When it became apparent that the war with Germany on the Eastern Front was effectively over, Nelka sent what remained of her hospital company back to Russia with Baron Wrede while she stayed in Romania to nurse a dying priest. As she set out to rejoin her unit after the priest's death a few days later, she found a stray kitten. She tied it up in her shawl, hung the shawl around her neck, and mounted Vive la France. Along the way she and the soldier assigned to protect her became separated in the night. She rode alone with the kitten until she caught up with her group. The next day the soldier showed up, chagrined that he had lost his charge in the dark.

Nelka and Max arrived in St. Petersburg about the same time. The situation in the capitol was dire as the economy ground to a halt and the city split into angry factions. With his brief military experience but excellent English language skills, Max was lucky to find a job in the British embassy. The new military attaché Captain Francis Cromie, who had commanded the British submarine fleet in the Baltic, found him useful. Cromie gave Max several clandestine assignments, including one to Murmansk, a northern Russian seaport where British and American troops were gathering to fight the Germans or suppress a Communist revolution, depending on which gained the upper hand in controlling the country. From the perspective of the United States, a Russian triumph that destroyed property rights and threatened capitalism would be as bad, perhaps worse, than a German victory that gave the enemy hegemony over eastern Europe. With the emergence of Vladimir Lenin as the strongest radical revolutionary in late 1917, the Russians accepted defeat in early 1918 and the Germans turned away to concentrate their forces on the Western Front where American troops were now arriving. For the supporters of the Tsar and his imperial regime, life in St. Petersburg became increasingly dangerous.

As long as Russia remained in the war, Max's work with the British government afforded some protection. But, once the war was over for Russia, respect for England diminished. Officers in the Army who came from the aristocracy moreover were suspect. Max recounted what happened:

> One evening about ten, a knock came on the door. I opened. Three men with rifles came in with a commisar. They asked for me by name and said they had an order to search the place. They asked if I had any arms and I said I had a service revolver, which had been given to me by the British. I also had another revolver of mine which lay on the mantelpiece. Nelka, who was there in the room, did at the last moment a most risky thing. Unobtrusively she slipped my revolver into the pocket of her dress. I noticed this, but the men did not. I produced the other gun which they dutifully

> registered and took. They then proceeded to search the place and after examining my papers, announced that I would not be arrested in view of my service with the British. Upon that they left. Nelka had done a most risky thing, for had the pistol been discovered in her pocket, it probably would have been the end of all of us.

After this frightening experience, Max's parents decided to get out of the country if they could. His father went to Moscow to see a Jewish friend who had helped others procure bogus exit permits for a price. It was then that Max told Nelka he loved her. Nelka confessed that she too had fallen in love with him. But, she added, she wouldn't marry him. Their age difference was too great. He was twenty-one; she was thirty-nine.

Max continued to work at the British Embassy until the end of August 1918. The British Ambassador George Buchanan had left the country in January and basically left Captain Cromie in charge. On Friday night, August 30th, an assassin shot Lenin in the neck and nearly killed him. The next morning Max stayed home. It was a prudent decision. In the afternoon the secret police, suspecting, correctly, that the British were plotting against Lenin, invaded the Embassy. Trying to prevent the intrusion, Cromie was shot and bled to death. According to Max, thirteen of the sixteen Russian officers who worked for the British were summarily executed that day. Max was one of three who were absent.

Max was now a marked man. His father was still in Moscow. Nelka went to stay with friends. Veta remained in the family apartment, and Max went to hide in the family's empty house in the country. While they were separated, Nelka decided to marry Max. "Perhaps the Revolution, the circumstances, the constant danger which we were all facing all of the time helped her make her decision," Max wrote. In September they went together to Tsarkoye Selo, the site of the imperial summerhouse, about fifteen miles from St. Petersburg. One of Max's great-aunts lived there. With a few friends attending they were married in the local church. "Nelka wore a white sister's uniform for her wedding dress." Max remembered. "My old aunt who was very fond of Nelka took off a gold bracelet she wore and put it on Nelka's arm. Nelka never took it off throughout her life."

Wedding photograph of Nelka and Max

Max's father returned from Moscow with exit documents for himself and Veta, but none for Max or Nelka. The papers allowed Veta and her husband to take a train to Finland. From there they went to Stockholm. After the Germans ended the war by finally capitulating in the West on 11 November 1918, the senior Moukhanoffs moved to Paris. Max and Nelka needed another way out. With the government hunting them and their money and food running low, their situation became even more precarious. Max finally located a man who knew a peasant who was willing to take people by sleigh across the countryside to within a few miles of the border with Finland. As they had just enough money to pay for a single trip, they decided that Max should go first since he was in greater danger. Nelka stayed behind to gather the extra money for her passage.

Max got safely across the border. But when Nelka failed to appear within a few days, he re-traced his steps, walking thirty miles, to find her. When he did, she was furious. She had collected enough money for her trip and was about to depart, and he had come back, risking his life again and putting them in the same situation that they had been in several days before – two people with only enough money for one passage. Nelka fumed – according to Max – "for about 48 hours."

Now that Max had crossed and re-crossed the border, he knew the way. This time they took a train for Finland and got off two stops before the border, leaving themselves a hike of about seventeen miles. They walked along the road and through the woods. They narrowly escaped capture several times by military patrols. Nelka fell ill along the way. They were forced to sleep in the woods because she couldn't walk any farther. They buried down in the snow; it was Christmas Eve, 1918. In the morning they ran across another couple like themselves – an officer and his wife trying to escape the Revolution. Max, Nelka and their new friends found another peasant who would take them by sleigh to the border for the little money that they had left.

Along the way they experienced another, nearly fatal, encounter. Their driver made a brief stop at a tavern. When he came out, a soldier followed him. Max recounted that the soldier:

> looked at us suspiciously and then asked the peasant where we were coming from. The peasant named a village to the east. The solider then suddenly said: "Why your horse is turned the wrong way, wait a minute," and he stepped back into the tavern. Our driver whipped up his horse and we went down the road as fast as we could. Looking back we saw several soldiers run out on the porch. One of them lifted his rifle and a shot came over us, but we were well on our way. They had no horses available to follow us so did not pursue and we got away.

Eventually, after parking the horse and sleigh and clambering, weak and sick, through deep snow and over fallen trees, they came to a clearing in the woods. The peasant turned around and said simply, "This is Finland."

10

Nelka and Max made their way to the home of their friend Baron Wrede in Helsinki. After resting a few days they went to Oslo where they boarded the *Stavangerfiord* bound for New York in early February 1919. From New York they traveled to Washington and stayed with Martha and Herbert for a while. In the spring they moved to Cazenovia to live in the little house that Susan had bequeathed to Nelka. There they stayed until they recuperated. Having lived several years with little to eat, Nelka gained almost forty pounds in roughly four months.

Nelka and Max in the Adirondacks, 1919

By the summer they felt rested and a bit restless. Civil War between Reds and Whites (supporters of the new Communist government versus the old Imperial one) had broken out, so Max decided to join the White forces in southern Russia under the command of General Denikin. Before going, they visited Lucretia in New Orleans, and from there they sailed to Europe. When they arrived in Paris they learned that Denikin's army was close to defeat. Max joined the French airplane factory of Louis Breguet and escorted a boatload of bombers to the Crimea for the White Forces now under the command of General Wrangel. By the time Max dressed as a Russian lieutenant and Nelka in her Red Cross nurse's uniform arrived in Constantinople the civil war between Reds and Whites was over. Instead of fighting, Max accepted a job with the American embassy in Constantinople as a Russian expert that lasted until the summer of 1921.

From 1921 to 1927 they lived in Menton on the French Riviera. Max worked for a real estate company and gambled at Monte Carlo. By his own assessment, he was "quite proficient" at betting. Nelka liked to claim that it was the only honest and "above board business." It is not clear how much money Max made as a gambler or real estate agent, but it wasn't a lot. He did write a slim handbook on winning at roulette, which didn't sell well. Nelka drew a small income from a trust account in St. Louis, but the fact was that by 1927 they were mired in debt, wanted to leave France and return to America, but didn't have enough money.

When Nelka received news that her uncle Herbert was seriously ill, she turned to Mildred Barnes for help. Mildred had married her step-brother Robert Bliss in 1908 and the couple were living in Stockholm, where Robert served as American minister to Sweden. Nelka asked Baron Wrede in Helsinki to deliver a letter to Mildred in person to obviate the risk that her request for money might be side-tracked by a secretary. She asked Mildred to lend her $5000 against the value of the house in Cazenovia, explaining that she couldn't ask Martha for the funds because of the serious financial losses that Herbert had suffered on his investments in the South (Louisiana and Florida), which she guessed must be worse yet because of the terrible flooding along the lower Mississippi river in the spring of 1927. Nelka felt tremendous relief and gratitude when nine days later Mildred wrote back to say she would help. (Bliss collection.) While they were settling their affairs and preparing to sail away, they learned that Herbert had died during the summer.

They visited Martha at Ashantee, and then returned to Cazenovia, where Max and his friend Count Pushkin started a furniture carving business. Successful for three years, the business collapsed with the onset of the Great Depression. Max and Nelka, frustrated and restless again, decided to go back to France, spending their time between Paris and the Riviera. As the economic situation in Europe was not much better than it was in the States, they continued to struggle to make ends meet.

When Max's father died in Paris in 1934, they decided it was time to return to the United States for good and to bring Veta with them. Martha in the meanwhile had suffered a serious injury in an automobile accident the previous August and was experiencing an excruciatingly slow recovery. Knowing that Nelka and Max would arrive at the port of New York aboard the *Berengaria* on Friday, August 31, Martha was determined to be, not only out of bed and on her feet, but on the back of a horse as well. On Saturday, the first of September, her doctor George Collins made one of his weekly calls. Martha became furious when he refused, yet again, to lift his ban against her riding. "George Collins," she snapped, "I could go out this afternoon and ride any of my horses with reins of number 10 thread." The doctor replied, "I'm sure you could, Martha, but don't try it." After Collins left, she went to the stable and ordered one of the young hands to fashion a set of reins out of heavy thread and saddle one of the horses. Martha rode *Coneflower* out of the barn and promptly fell off. (O'Dea, 37.) Later in the day Nelka and Max arrived to find Martha semiconscious in bed. She died three days later.

In her will Martha left Ashantee, her house in Avon, to Nelka and Lucretia, but it was Nelka and Max who stayed on after

Martha's funeral and lived in the house for nearly thirty years. Max started various businesses, none of which prospered, but the couple now had sufficient resources to live a quiet and comfortable life in the countryside. Nelka became a student of Theosophy, which helped her acquire and maintain a degree of calm and serenity that had been lacking in her life. Accordingly, she jettisoned her combative spirit and reinforced her pacifism. Her love of animals led her to become an active anti-vivisectionist and a committed vegetarian.

In her later years, she became reclusive and was regarded as something of an oddity in the community. She remembered Mildred's anniversary – though a couple of weeks late – and sent her a small gift. It was a picture frame that she had made to give her as a wedding present in 1908, but never sent because the blue she chose for the mounting was all wrong. As "the little thing did not perish in the revolution with everything else…" she wrote, "I decided last year to send it along for your Pearl Wedding simply as a tiny token of my unworthy handiwork and lasting affection." Mildred and Robert Bliss celebrated their thirtieth wedding anniversary in May at their estate Dumbarton Oaks where the orchestra played a concerto by Igor Stravinsky that Mildred commissioned.

Mildred sent a sweet note in reply, saying the picture frame "recalled a hot day in the summer some thirty-six or thirty-eight years ago when you and I sat on the floor at Sharon and discussed Byzantine art." She wondered how many cats Nelka had, and closed by adding, "If you really wanted to be a good Samaritan you would send me a little kodak of yourself which I should put into the frame. That is what I should best like." (Bliss collection.)

Occasionally Nelka had callers at Ashantee. Once or twice Lucretia came to visit, once with her daughter Cri-cri and her grandson Van. Her cousin Henry's youngest son Julien and his mother Dolly stopped in just after Julien graduated from the Naval Academy in 1944. Years later he served as the President of the Navy's War College in Newport, Rhode Island, and retired as

Vice Admiral. Van Adams and Julien Le Bourgeois both vividly remembered the large number of stray animals, mainly dogs and a few cats, which Nelka and Max kept in their yard. Julien also recalled that Nelka wouldn't hurt a fly, adding that, it was true, because there were flies all over the house, particularly at mealtime.

Nelka at Ashantee, ca 1955

A regular visitor at Ashantee was the granddaughter of Austin Wadsworth (Herbert's brother), Martha D. Wadsworth, who lived nearby in Geneseo. Martha was a child when she first met Nelka but never felt put off by the dirt and disorder of Ashantee. She saw instead a husband and wife who adored one another and who adhered to a set of clear principles concerning the sanctity of all life. She remembered the time Max, faced with an infestation of rats, corralled them into a Havahart trap, popped them into the back of his station wagon, and deposited them out of town. When he got back to Ashantee, he saw that the rats had followed him home. He and Nelka lived with the rats as well as the dogs, cats and flies. Either because or despite all of this, young Martha thought Nelka was "magnificent." She also found Max's mother Veta lively and witty, and a fine water-colorist.

For the last twenty years or so of her life, Nelka suffered a chronic degenerative disease. Towards the end, she and Max decided that young Martha and her family should live at Ashantee and offered the house to her at a price she couldn't refuse. Nelka and Max moved into a smaller house on the property, where Nelka died in 1963 at the age of eighty-five. Max, well prepared for her demise, was nonetheless crushed. He had first met her when she arrived in St. Petersburg in 1905. He was seven years old and overwhelmed by her appearance. It was love at first sight:

> Nelka made a tremendous impression on me when I first saw her – an impression which never left me throughout life. From that day on she meant something to me, and that something grew and grew in my feelings for her with time and years.

"Nelka, – a unique name for a unique person," he concluded.

LUCRETIA'S STORY

Lucretia Blow Le Bourgeois Van Horn

1882-1970

(All quotations in Lucretia's Story, except where noted, come from Lucretia Le Bourgeois Van Horn's Letters or Diaries.)

235

1

Artistic, petite, athletic, happy and curious, Lucretia Blow Le Bourgeois moved often in life, but never so far as her aunt Adèle or cousin Nelka.

Her mother, also named Lucretia, was the third of four daughters of Minerva Grimsley and Henry Taylor Blow. All four Blow girls bore apt or silly nicknames within the family: Susan was called Poodie, Ella was Nellie, Lucretia was Lutie, and Martha was Pata. Though very different in their interests and their lives, they were all devoted to one another. As a young teenager, Lutie had fallen in love with her cousin Charless Le Bourgeois, and he with her. She was not quite seventeen years old when they married in October 1878, but quite ready to bear children. Lutie had four within four and a half years – Joseph Charless (called Bush), Elizabeth (called Liz), Lucretia, and Henry.

Lucretia "Lutie" Blow Le Bourgeois   *Joseph Charless Le Bourgeois*

Charless had taken up the practice of law in St. Louis, but decided to return to Louisiana to help his brother Louis revive the family's sugar fortunes after their mother died. So, Lucretia, who was born on 30 June 1882, was barely a year old when she arrived in St. James Parish. Like most good-sized sugar plantations along the Mississippi River, Belmont prospered during the decades before the Civil War. With 1200 acres under cultivation, the plantation produced a lot of sugar and substantial cash. Enough wealth was generated that Charless' parents, Louis and Lizzie Le Bourgeois, had been able to hire the much-sought-after architect Henry Howard to remodel the manor house in the late 1850s. Howard wrapped the residence with a massive Corinthian colonnade and heavy ornate cornice, replacing the columns and decorations of a simpler order and transforming the house into a picture-book vision of an ante-bellum mansion.

Henry Taylor Blow Le Bourgeois at Belmont, 1892
(The dolls belonged to his sister or a cousin who had posed in the spot)

The decade of the 1850s was in fact a bountiful period for Louisiana plantation owners. Between the two Censuses of 1850 and 1860 Belmont's land value more than doubled from $62,000 to $135,000. The later Census also called for a value for personal property, which Louis Le Bourgeois declared as $143,700. A big part of this number reflected the market price for the 132 slaves that Louis owned. The Civil War, of course, abolished slavery and destroyed agrarian prosperity in the South. In the Census of 1870 the value of the land fell back to $62,000 and Louis recorded his personal wealth at $2000 (down seventy-fold in ten years).

By the time Lucretia arrived in St. James Parish, the rich years at Belmont were long gone. Her childhood on the plantation, however, was not much different from the one her father and her aunt Adèle had enjoyed. Like them, she and her siblings learned from private tutors, rode horses on the levee, went hunting, read classics, and pored over the fabulous hand-colored drawings of Audubon and Catlin. From an itinerant acrobat, they even learned tumbling, an activity that Lucretia particularly enjoyed and got quite good at. On the surface, everything at Belmont seemed fine. Two brothers, one single without children and the other happily married with four toddlers, worked hard together to make the old plantation profitable again.

Joseph Charless Le Bourgeois (right) and a friend at Belmont, ca. 1892

Unfortunately, Lutie was unlucky. She had delivered four babies in less than five years and seemed perfectly healthy when she contracted typhoid fever in the spring of 1885. Her sister Susan came to help. Although no one else in the family fell ill, Lutie died on March 31 at the age of twenty-four. With her passing away the senior Le Bourgeois at Belmont once again had no wife, no mother, no woman in charge of the household. It was then that Charlotte, now seventy-five years old, came down from St. Louis to Belmont to help raise her great-grandchildren.

Charlotte Charless with Bush and Liz Le Bourgeois

The *coup de grâce* for Belmont was delivered in the spring of 1892 when the rains came, inundating much of the Mississippi River system. In June, just before Lucretia's tenth birthday, a wall of water crushed the levee in front of the house. The flood uprooted trees, railroad tracks, telegraph poles, and ruined the gardens and fields around the house and across the parish. Rescuers arriving in rowboats plucked the children from the second floor balcony and carried them to safety.

Lucretia Le Bourgeois, ca. 1894

The misfortune was compounded by the fact that two years before Charless and Louis had offered to buy out their siblings' interest in the plantation. They organized a corporation, the Belmont Planting and Manufacturing Company Limited, and agreed to pay their brothers and sisters $45,000 in notes and capital stock in the new company. The papers were signed just five weeks before the flood. A year later a New York financier, William L. Scott, bought most of the notes at a steep discount and then foreclosed on the Belmont Planting Company. At a sheriff's sale in April 1894, Mr. Scott became the owner of the plantation. Charless packed up his unhappy family and moved to New Orleans. His brother Louis stayed in the area, and soon after was elected – ironically – sheriff of St. James Parish, an office he held for many years.

With four children to support, Charless struggled to make ends meet and keep his family together. Adèle offered important help. She called on her friend Grover Cleveland, who was back in office as President again. Cleveland appointed Charless a special agent of the United States Treasury to inspect imports from China at the port of New Orleans. The position was definitely a sinecure, for the Custom House in New Orleans had long operated as a great source of patronage. A year earlier, Theodore Roosevelt, appointed one of three Civil Service Commissioners by President Benjamin Harrison, had gone to New Orleans with his fellow commissioner Colonel Lyman to investigate allegations of widespread corruption. The Collector of Customs for the Port of New Orleans was Henry Clay Warmoth, the first governor of Louisiana in the immediate postbellum period and a master of patronage. He took serious umbrage at the charges young Roosevelt brought in his brief case. Rightly proud of his efforts to weed out incompetent appointees across the country, Roosevelt met with a rude rebuff from the seasoned Warmoth, who, like Roosevelt, had been appointed to his post by President Harrison. Warmoth wrote in his memoir:

> I opened the paper and looked over the charges, and the further I went the madder I got; so finally turning upon Colonel Roosevelt, with a great deal of spirit, I said: "Mr. Roosevelt, President Harrison has put me here to run this Custom House and I'll be damned if I don't intend to do it in my own way, and you fellows can go to hell!"

Confronted by an unexpected and voluble assault, Roosevelt and Lyman backpedalled quickly. Roosevelt went off to shoot hogs in Texas and Lyman accepted Warmoth's invitation to spend the weekend at his stately home, Magnolia plantation, on the Mississippi River. (Warmoth, 262-3.) When Cleveland returned to the presidency in 1893, he kept Roosevelt as a commissioner, relieved Warmoth as collector, and appointed Charless Le Bourgeois a special agent.

Charless soon found a comfortable house at 1215 Napoleon Avenue, a short streetcar ride from his office at the Custom House. His son Bush went to work as soon as he could, taking a job as a clerk with the Illinois Central Rail Road. Daughter Liz began taking classes in the college preparatory program at Newcomb College, now a part of Tulane University. Lucretia enrolled at Newcomb the following year while Henry went to grammar school in the neighborhood. Charlotte (whom the great grandchildren called Grand or Grandzie) continued her role as a mother-figure.

When Charless began to think of getting married again, Susan and Martha took the opportunity to make their cousin/brother-in-law an offer that was too appealing to ignore. They would educate and look after his two youngest children, Lucretia and Henry, just as they would take their niece Nelka under their wings after their sister Nellie died the following year. In the summer of 1897, Lucretia and Henry (fifteen and thirteen years old) bid Louisiana farewell and moved east. Susan enrolled Henry at the Chestnut Hill Academy in Philadelphia and Lucretia went to live with Martha and Herbert in New York. Charless married Alys Duer Relf in the summer of 1899 and moved to the west bank of the Mississippi River to live at Louisa, a sugar and rice plantation that Charless had bought in 1885.

2

Lucretia showed artistic talent at an early age. Her first extant work is a book of watercolors entitled *A Basket of Flowers*, which she made shortly after moving from Belmont to New Orleans. For some of the flowers she wrote poems, such as this one for clovers:

Down by the sugar house
Where the clovers grow
Down by the old sugar house
Make me think of long ago
Down by the old sugar-house
Where the clovers grow
Makes me think of Belmont
and the things of long ago

In her clover drawing there are five distinct stems, three with leaves and two with flowers, perhaps representing her motherless family – father and two boys, and two girls.

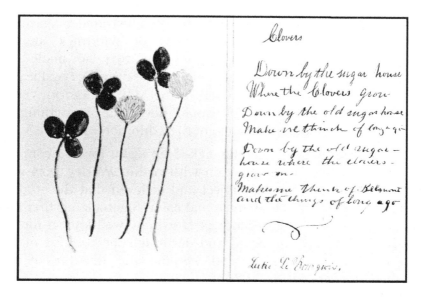

Arriving in New York, Lucretia experienced immediate stimulus and encouragement. Martha and Herbert were in the midst of drawing up plans to build a marvelous Beaux-Arts style house in Washington. Herbert, an accomplished amateur painter, quickly recognized Lucretia's talent and spurred her interest. In the fall of 1899 Lucretia registered at the Art Students League in Manhattan, but took no courses until the following October when she signed up for two: Antique painting with Bryson Burroughs and Kenyon Cox, and Illustration with Benjamin West Clinedinst. Any illusion she had about her artistic ability was corrected even before she began classes. In her diary in September 1900, she confessed, "Last year when I came to New York about this time, I felt consumed with the feeling of genius .... I imagined myself already a recognized artist .... What a mirage!"

She made some other important discoveries in her first year. She found that she preferred the rigor and strong lines of Cox and Clinedinst to the more fluid and vague style of Burroughs. Burroughs had studied in Paris with Puvis de Chavannes, whose soft and thin oil paintings often looked as if they were watercolors. Cox, who produced a set of murals at the Library of Congress, relied more heavily on clear structure and precise drawing as did Clinedinst whose work often appeared in illustrated magazines. Burroughs later became the curator of paintings at the Metropolitan Museum of Art, where in 1911 he made the memorable decision not to accept eighty-one drawings by Picasso that Alfred Stieglitz offered to sell to the Met for $2000. "Such mad pictures," he explained, "would never mean anything in America." (Metropolitan Museum of Art exhibition catalogue.)

In the fall of 1901 Lucretia signed up again for two courses. She chose a class in Composition with Arthur Wesley Dow who had written a book on the subject and believed that the student needed a firm grasp of line, mass and color. She took her first Life drawing class with Henry Siddons Mowbray, well known for his skill in drawing. He designed and decorated the rotunda of the Pierpont Morgan Library, and became the director of the American Academy of Art in Rome.

When Dow's Composition class finished in January, Lucretia added another Life drawing class, with Kenyon Cox, and squeezed in two short courses: Illustration with Clinedinst and a sketching class with Charles Courtney Curran. When the two short courses ended, she signed up for Perspective with Frederick Dielman, a German, who, like Cox, produced a set of murals at the Library of Congress. In May Lucretia was awarded an honorable mention for her work in Clinedinst's illustration class.

It was as if Lucretia had spent her first year discovering which artists would quicken her appetite and her second year devouring as much as they would feed her. All seven of her instructors had trained in the classical tradition in Europe and most had spent considerable time in Paris. Bryson Burroughs, who had studied at *l'Académie Julian* in Paris (as did Dow and Curran), recommended that she go there to continue her education. The school had an excellent reputation, catered to Americans and welcomed women. Lucretia embraced his advice and made arrangements to go to France in the fall of 1902. Her departure, however, was delayed when her sister became engaged and planned an October wedding.

Lucretia, Bush, Nelka, Liz, and Henry in Washington, DC, 1902

3

When Lucretia left New Orleans, her sister Liz had continued her studies at Newcomb College. Even though her father's house on Napoleon Avenue was close to the school, Liz chose to live in the college dormitory. Friendly and bright, she was very popular. Her classmates – about a dozen or so – elected her president of their class. After she graduated with highest honors, she continued to take courses in the arts and remained closely connected with the life of the college.

Martha and Herbert invited Liz to Washington to admire their creation and to enjoy the social season when they opened their new mansion on Dupont Circle in January 1902. Liz gladly accepted the invitation, for she had rarely seen her sister in the past five years or her cousin Nelka in ten. Their reunion was tender and sweet, but attenuated by the fact that Lucretia was mostly in New York taking art classes. At first Liz found the Washington experience overwhelming and exhausting. "Every afternoon, we go out calling, calling! Oh! And dress and undress! Truly it is weary, stale, flat and unprofitable," she lamented to her Aunt Nannie, who in fact was her fiancé's mother. Although unaccustomed to such a heavy and frenetic social regimen, she told Nannie, "I will not 'give way to the bastard emotion of self pity' as my dear Aunt Susie [Susan Blow] would say." (Richardson Papers.) And, indeed she didn't, for when she returned to New Orleans in April, she told everyone what a grand and wonderful time she had had in Washington.

In September Liz traveled east again to shop for her trousseau in New York and was able to spend more time with her sister. In her diary Lucretia reflected on their reconnection during the year: "It seemed as though I had just found her to lose her again. To be separated for a long time and then for a while to have seemingly lost touch – then all of a sudden to have the glow of mutual understanding flame up between you is to meet newly and keenly all over."

Lucretia was also excited because she was coming in contact with important artists who recognized her as an emerging talent. During Liz's visit, Lucretia lent her aunt Adèle an illustrated book that she had recently made. In her diary (17 September 1902) she noted:

> [Adèle] says in her letter that Maxfield Parrish (who I admire more than any American illustrator) said about the little Booka B that she showed him that: "any girl that can do work like that ought to give up everything for art, such composition and technique combined with such painstaking neat work in the printing and binding etc was most unusual." I am so encouraged and happy! Oh how I long to get back to work! To think of Maxfield Parrish saying that about my poor work.

Parrish had recently illustrated L. Frank Baum's *Mother Goose in Prose*, published in 1897, and Baum's big book *The Wonderful Wizard of Oz* had just appeared in 1900. Buoyed by Parrish's praise, she was now even more charged up about going to Paris, despite some countervailing advice:

> I do think that going abroad will be the best thing for me – although Cecilia Beaux doesn't think it best.

Beaux, raised and educated in Philadelphia, had spent two years in Paris when she was in her early thirties studying at *l'Académie Julian* and taking classes with the grand master of classical 19th century French art William-Adolphe Bougureau. After her return to Philadelphia in 1889, she decided to move to New York in 1900 where she befriended Richard Gilder, the well-connected editor of *The Century Magazine*, and met Adèle Chapin and thus Lucretia. Despite Ms. Beaux's caution, Lucretia couldn't wait to go abroad:

I am just aching for Paris, and one can get life work there as in no other place. I learn much more from watching the advanced pupils about me than from the criticism of the instructors. And there is no place where such wonderful life drawings are made than in Paris. Then the influence, the atmosphere! I must go and get the fever out of my blood! I am never so happy as when I am just hard at work. It is a real stable thing that stays by us. I could be more happy with a few of my dear books and a life of hard, tolerably good work. There is nothing like the artistic life! I have played with fire it burns ones fingers!

But first she had to go to New Orleans for Liz's wedding. Lucretia left upstate New York on "a crashy train" that "bumped all night," met Nelka in Manhattan, and arrived in New Orleans just as a local transportation strike broke out. Instead of streetcars, "Broken down wagons ply up and down St. Charles Avenue with loads of shoppers and businessmen." Lucretia found Liz's fiancé John Francis Richardson nicer and more charming than she had expected, and she was delighted that her brother Bush and John were such good friends. As for Liz, she positively beamed. Neither Lucretia nor Nelka could understand why she showed no sign of nervousness, especially when, on short notice, Martha insisted that the wedding be pushed back a day to accommodate her busy schedule. Charlotte, now ninety-two years old, however, did cause a flap when she told Liz that she should not "make her self conspicuous" by going out to Church the day before her wedding. It took all of Nelka's diplomatic skills to convince Grandzie to let her go.

On the wedding day Lucretia and Nelka kept Liz company. The ceremony was scheduled for eight in the evening, so they had their supper sent up to their room. Liz, Lucretia wrote in her diary, "was the most composed little bride in the world. Nelka and I were so excited that we couldn't eat any dinner, but little Lizzie sat on the floor with the tray before her and ate for three."

The ceremony in Newcomb chapel was small and intimate. Lucretia served as maid of honor, and Nelka and John's sister Mary were bridesmaids. John chose Bush as best man. Liz's brother Henry, aunt Martha and uncle Herbert stood nearby, while her uncle Louis accompanied Charlotte – who entered the church on crutches – to her seat. Her step-mother Alys also attended.

Charless walked his daughter to the altar. "The bride looked as if she had stepped from an old picture," the local newspaper reported. Liz wore the wedding dress that her grandmother Lizzie had worn fifty years before. The dress was "a rich, white, lustrous satin brocade, made with very full skirt, just touching the floor, the low-necked and short-sleeved, tight-fitting corsage trimmed with bertha of rare old lace and filled in about the neck and arms with guimpe and sleeves of filmy tulle." She also wore "the old-fashioned pearl necklace of her great-grandmother" – the same necklace that Joseph had given Charlotte for their wedding seventy years before.

"Nelka and I were crying so that we couldn't see very much," Lucretia confessed, "but Liz was beaming and smiling all the way down the aisle." At the reception John and Liz mingled easily with their friends and family as if nothing out of the ordinary had happened. In contrast, "Nelka and I disgraced ourselves – we wept at intervals throughout the evening." Afterwards Liz and John left for a brief honeymoon to Pass Christian on the Mississippi Gulf Coast. The next day Lucretia suffered a letdown. "Grandzie is tired out with the effort of going to the wedding," she wrote in her diary, "and is in a very fault finding and scolding humor – so I am quite blue."

After the wedding, Lucretia returned to the Genesee Valley, made ready for her voyage to Paris and enjoyed a few farewell parties. Mrs. Buckley gave a dinner for her that included Nelka and several pleasant young men. "I sat next to J. G. Averell," Lucretia recorded. An accomplished golfer and graduate of Harvard, "he seemed amused and quite stuck with me all evening. I like Harry Colt better every time I meet him; he is I think a very interesting little person." A few days later Harold Barclay arrived. Martha, Lucretia, and Nelka took Harold horseback riding in the morning. "He is one of Nelka's young men. He is rather good looking and has some charm," she noted. That evening the young men gave a small dinner dance at the Big Tree Inn in Geneseo. Lucretia was also delighted to see that one of her classmates from art school, Florence Wyman, had three illustrations in the December issue of *Scribner's Magazine*. "She studied with me in Mowbray's class last winter – I thought that she was one of the two most talented girls at the League – Ida Dougherty and she." In her diary, she confided further:

> I shall be glad to get back to work again. Oh how I love something to happen I don't care what but just anything to make one forget. I shall do something – oh how unhappy one is to feel the power of doing and yet not to have mastered technique enough to make it possible to express it. Oh to be doing something really good and meritritious [sic].

Martha assigned one of her maids to go with Lucretia to France. "I shall have a fine deck cabin, so shall be very comfy with Octavia to take care of me," Lucretia wrote, "as she is a splendid sailor and will be sea-worthy. She is a satisfying little person and is, what she calls herself, an encourager of genius." Lucretia and Octavia departed New York harbor on December 11th on the Hamburg-American line bound for Liverpool. From there they proceeded to Paris. Before they left, Liz wrote the first of a series of letters to Lucretia.

"Dearest ickle one," she wrote, "This is just to tell you that your Lios [within the family "Liz" was pronounced as two syllables; Lucretia spelled it "Lioz"] is thinking of you and that she is making you a Xmas present which will be done some time after New Years." The promised gift was a scarf.

When she wrote again just before Christmas, Lucretia had arrived in France. Liz wanted to know how she liked Madame Beck, who ran the boarding house at 7 rue du Docteur Blanche where Lucretia was staying. She had heard that Madame was "a woman whom you either love or hate," and wanted to know from Lucretia, "Which [is she]?" As for herself, she had succumbed to a terrible cold, which meant that she had made little progress with the scarf. She and John had gotten a puppy named Colette to keep her company. "Our little pup is too sweet for words," she cooed. "She has learned to carry a pencil from one to another, bring back a ball when thrown, lie down, give paw and roll over. Don't you think that's wonderful?"

In early January 1903 Liz reported that she was well again and would start embroidering Lucretia's scarf that afternoon. "I hope you will like it," she wrote. "I think it is going to be very nifty." She also reported that Grandzie had been very sick but was now quite well again. Charlotte's indisposition, however, had been a trying experience for her: "Such a cross convalescence and illness it was!" Liz was "worn to a frazzle" by the time Grandzie had recovered.

When Lucretia arrived in Paris she began drawing right away. In her sketchbook her first picture is a street scene dated "New Years 1903." Other pictures of everyday life quickly followed. In an open competition in early February, she won first prize for one of her drawings. She was quick to convey the news. In response, Liz sent a congratulatory note: "We were so pleased to hear of your grand success. Do write again soon; Grand says she is so happy to hear of your success." Another passage in the letter seems to identify the winning work. "Please send me some pictures. Can't you send me the Bois de Boulogne one?" She then added, "I suppose that would be asking too much." In her sketchbook there is a drawing that Lucretia titled and dated "Dans le bois Jan. 21 03" which depicts a grandfather walking hand-in-hand with his grandson. It is a finely executed picture and most likely the drawing that won the prize.

Liz wrote Lucretia again a few weeks later that a dear friend in St. Louis had died unexpectedly. "I can't tell you how sad I felt when I heard the news. I just cried and cried." Then she said, in words that suggest she was thinking of the time their mother had died when they were small children, "I must not dwell on this painful subject; it only arouses long trains of sad thoughts of old times, so I will stop."

"Dans le bois Jan. 21 03"

In the same letter, she chided Lucretia for being a poor correspondent. "I am eager for news from you! Why don't you write?" In the next sentence, she confessed to her own remissiveness: "I was working on your scarf this evening. It is going to be really lovely when it is finished but I am afraid that won't be for quite a while." She closed by saying that "Grandma and Bush and John are well."

Lucretia continued to attract favorable attention in Paris. In a letter written in April, Liz again sent her congratulations. "I am overjoyed," she wrote, "at your great success and knew all along that my Baba [her nickname for Lucretia] was going to beat them all." She told Lucretia that Poodie [their aunt Susan] had just visited New Orleans, perhaps to see for the last time her aunt Charlotte whose health was failing. "She was only here three days but we got lots in in that short while." Among various topics, they discussed Lucretia's negligence. Poodie, she wrote, "is very much hurt that you never answered her letter and so is Grand whose present and letter you have never acknowledged."

Liz wrote once more in April to say that she and John had taken Charlotte to a nursing home in Covington, Louisiana and that Grand had "stood the trip very well." She also begged for communication: "I wish my ickle one would write often and tell me all about herself!" She closed by saying that "Bush sends his love" and then "How I wish I could hug my little one in my arms!" It was her last letter.

Lucretia received a telegram from Henry Baldwin, a family friend, with a message four words long: "Lizzie died this morning." Before the day was over she opened another telegram from Adèle: "Won't you come to us. Twenty-one Sloane Gardens, London tomorrow." The next day Bush telegraphed from St. Louis to say, "sister passed suddenly painlessly away Thursday. Funeral here tomorrow." With no sign of serious illness, Liz had died on May 7th in New Orleans. At the funeral, John Richardson told Martha what had happened, which she conveyed in a letter to her friend Mildred Barnes:

> ... the doctor found she had dislocated her neck, the vertebrae near the neck being all affected by necrosis, a condition which must have been coming on for some time without any symptoms. It appears that had she lived she would probably have had

paralysis and I am glad she herself knew nothing of the nearness of death. She was eating her breakfast upstairs as she hadn't been well for a few days, nothing serious according to the doctor but just a run down condition from having done too much which culminated in a fainting spell, after which she stayed in bed for, as I said, a few days. The doctor had told her to go out and get fresh air and she was going to dress immediately feeling perfectly well, when suddenly she had an attack of nausea and in the midst cried out, "oh my neck" and fell back. The doctor who happily was in the next house tried everything but she died in half an hour without regaining consciousness. I hope she was spared suffering, it is the only comfort to think of. Her life was so happy and full that it seems incredible that she could die so young. (Bliss Papers.)

Liz was buried in the Blow family plot in Bellefontaine Cemetery in St. Louis three days later.

Susan, who had just seen Liz in New Orleans in April, also attended the funeral. Remembering her niece's motherless childhood, Susan took comfort in knowing that, "My dear little Lizzie used to love Cazenovia and saw it gave her her best sense of a home." (Blow, Susan, Papers, St. Louis.) A notice in a New Orleans newspaper described Liz as "one of the brightest and most popular girls who ever passed through Newcomb College. Even after graduating, she continued her deep interest in all the classes till each and every girl seemed dear to the merry, sparkling maid whose sweet, fascinating ways so charmed and inspired. The news of her death ... cast down every heart from the Faculty to the High School."

Lucretia, who never talked about her sister, must have been more stunned than anyone. Liz died at nearly the same age as their mother had.

4

Lucretia had enrolled in the atelier of the august Bouguereau at *l'Académie Julian* in January 1903. Although seventy-seven years old and near the end of his career, Bouguereau was the premier master of high academic art. Lucretia, however, was not intimidated. Though young, female and new to the master's studio, "she immediately assumed her place in the highest ranks, competing in the month of February and taking home a prize! From then on, she continued to win awards," wrote the editor of *l'Académie Julian's* monthly publication.

As a result of her triumph, Lucretia switched courses. She abandoned Bouguereau to join the evening program that offered classes in drawing and illustration. Rather than shading, modeling and coloring, Lucretia realized that her strength lay in lines and figures. A year after her initial success, she competed for the prestigious Julian-Smith medal, awarded annually. From seventy works submitted in February 1904, the jury selected Lucretia's entry for first prize. She was the first woman to win the honor, which conferred cash and a medal. Lucretia, happy to have the honor and the medal, graciously deferred the money part of the prize to the runner-up who needed it much more than she.

Concours Julian-Smith medal awarded to Lucretia in 1904

The March edition of *l'Académie Julian's* monthly publication gave Lucretia considerable coverage. The cover featured a head-and-shoulder drawing in profile of Lucretia by Mlle. M. Parisot. Inside the reader found a full-page reproduction of Lucretia's drawing. In Japanesque style, it showed a young woman standing in a garden of long-stemmed chrysanthemums. The drawing was a design for *une carte d'invitation pour une exposition de chrysanthêmes*. At the International Exhibition in Paris in 1900 the Japanese participants had provided a huge display of long-stemmed chrysanthemums that created a sensation. For several years, they were the flower à la mode in Paris.

In the accompanying story, the editor was effusive. "Brunette, rather petite in stature, Mlle. Le Bourgeois has a disposition that is cheerful, prepossessing, and fun-loving," he wrote. He spoke about her remarkable imagination and spontaneity and the way "original details seemed to just spurt out of her spirited pen." The story continued: "The splendid ranking that she has suddenly received in the Julian-Smith competition, shows her that she can expect similar success in sketching and painting. She couldn't believe it when she found herself awarded the highest distinction out of the 70 art works submitted; how charming it was for the visitors to the February exposition to witness her joy, so well-deserved!" The writer predicted that Lucretia was "destined to become one of the most interesting of American artists." (Translation by B. and C. King.)

After the news reached America, she received separate telegrams from Washington. Her uncle Herbert was ecstatic; her aunt Martha was too. "Congratulations," she wrote, with tongue-in-cheek, "on your tolerable success."

Martha Wadsworth took a keen interest in her two nieces, Nelka and Lucretia. Four years apart in age, each cousin had lost her mother. Without children of her own, Martha wanted her girls to find their proper place in life. She took seriously her self-appointed task of keeping both young women in the forefront of society, whether in the horse-country of upstate New York or the diplomatic and military circles of Washington. Before going abroad, Lucretia had attended some of the events of the social season in Washington when she could break away from her art classes in New York. When she returned from Paris in July 1904, she became a regular winter resident at Martha and Herbert's fashionable house on Dupont Circle.

Herbert knew that Lucretia was exceptionally bright. At some point he introduced her to his friend Henry Adams, who loved Paris and most things French. Adams agreed that Lucretia was special and was happy to tell her so. They also shared a connection with President Lincoln. Adams' father and Lucretia's grandfather both supported and served the President as emissaries abroad:

Charles Adams as Minister to England and Henry Blow as Minister to Venezuela. Invited to Henry Adams' house on Lafayette Square, Lucretia read chapters with him from his *Mont-Saint-Michel and Chartres* before it was published. In the preface to the book, Adams wrote disparagingly about the lack of interest among young men in books about culture and aesthetics; they were the kind of books his nephews would never read. *Mont-Saint-Michel and Chartres* was written for his "Nieces and Nieces-in-Wish," one of whom was Lucretia. (Hunt, *Recollections*.)

Like Nelka before she joined the Russian Red Cross, Lucretia oscillated between finding a husband and pursuing a career in art. Though somewhat competitive, Lucretia and Nelka were devoted to each other. She was very sorry to see Nelka leave Washington in the fall. She grew even more despondent the following spring, 1905. Twice she traveled to Bellefontaine Cemetery in St. Louis to bury first her great-grandmother Charlotte in March and then her father Charless in May. From her new friend, the Japanese artist Yokoyama Taikan, she received a long, consoling letter in September for her double loss.

Lucretia had met Taikan the year before when he and his colleague Shunso Hishida accompanied their mentor Kazuko Okakura on his return to America. Okakura's friend John La Farge – who was also a close friend of Henry Adams and William Sturgis Bigelow (who appointed Okakura advisor on Chinese and Japanese art at the Museum of Fine Arts in Boston) – offered Taikan and Hishida an exhibition of their work at the Century Club in New York. An exchange of paintings between Lucretia and Taikan sealed their friendship. It was an apt connection since Lucretia's recent prize-winning drawing in Paris featured the Chrysanthemum, the symbol of the Japanese emperor.

In his letter – written with ink and brush on a scroll three feet long featuring a decorative floral design – Taikan told her that after he left the States he had exhibited in London and Paris. "My exhibition in London," he wrote, "was very successful notwithstanding of its out of the season and I am quite thanked for the honorable visiting of our exhibition by Her Majesty of Great

Britain and Princess Victoria, Duke and Duchess of Sparta." He was especially pleased that he had sold three of his pictures to buyers from Paris before his London show opened.

Shortly after receiving the letter from Japan, Lucretia wrote in October to Nelka (who had made a brief visit back to the States before going to Russia again): "Your poor Jah [their private nickname for Lucretia] is in the very saddest condition imaginable – so blue as nearly dead – wants its Nell – and is broken-hearted she is going away, so far away." Jah wished she were going abroad too:

> It seems sometime that I would give ten good years of my life only to be able to be back there working. I just die to get to work. I don't know why but I am absolutely atrophied here. If I could only get to work - - paint like mad and get all these horrid kinks out of my mind.

Part of her despair also centered on Martha. Although, she told Nelka, at the moment "we were never in a more affectionate and positively intimate mood," she felt oppressed. "Goodness knows I hate to have to watch every move. I am only glad you are out of it dear little Nelly." Closing a second note, she said, "I hope you will have a most truly successful time [and] come home married to a grand young man."

In a more cheerful and chatty vein the following May 1906, Lucretia talked at length about marriage and art: "Zaidee Cobb was married to Cornelius Bliss of New York last Thursday; he is not very attractive but is very opulent," and "Hyacinthe Bell is engaged to Lord Kelburn, the Earl of Glasgow's oldest son; she seems radiantly happy; she wrote me such an ecstatic letter," and, then, "What do you think of Harold Barclay's marriage?" Three years earlier, a match between Nelka and Harold seemed possible, but didn't take fire. In April Barclay married his cousin Helen Potter. "As the wedding day was not set until less than a week prior to the ceremony," wrote *The New York Times*, "it came as a surprise to the many friends of the bride and bridegroom." As to her art, Lucretia reported a busy and productive winter. She had just finished two decorations for the *Metropolitan Magazine* and several illustrations for Helen Hay Whitney's poems, received a commission to create five drawings for an edition of Browning's poem "A Toccata of Gallupi's," and was busy illustrating a book of poems entitled *Chinatown Ballads* by Wallace Irwin.

Returning to her first theme, Lucretia wanted to know about Nelka's love life. "Has anything sentimental transpired in Russia," she asked? "I shall consider the trip a failure if you don't come back with a handsome young Russian checked with all your trunks." Concerning herself, she confessed, "Nothing has happened that way this winter but no matter; [I've been] very prolific notwithstanding though it is rather a blow to think one is sentimentally a failure!"

Lucretia Le Bourgeois, ca. 1906
(Courtesy of the Martha Blow Wadsworth Photographs Collection, Milne Library, SUNY Geneseo)

All that changed in the fall of 1906 when Lucretia met Douglas MacArthur. MacArthur, who became the supreme commander of U.S. Armed forces in the Pacific during World War II, was two years older than Lucretia. Academically, militarily and athletically distinguished, MacArthur not only graduated first in his class at West Point but received the honor of First Captain of the Corps of Cadets. On graduation he became a second lieutenant in the Corps of Engineers. Assigned to eastern Asia, he went to the Philippines and visited Japan at the end of the Russo-Japanese War. The War Department then assigned him to a graduate engineering course at Washington Barracks and appointed him as an aide-de-camp to President Roosevelt. Handsome, gallant, sociable and well connected (his father was a lieutenant general in the Army and his mother came from an aristocratic Virginia family), MacArthur negotiated an easy entry into Washington society. Lucretia and Douglas were introduced to one another soon after his arrival in the Capital. Before the year was over they had fallen in love.

At the end of April 1907 Lucretia went south to stay with her brother Bush at his summer house on the Gulf Coast of Mississippi. In the ten years since she had lived in New Orleans, Bush had started his own business. Making the most of his family's long connection with the sugar industry, he had established himself as a broker connecting raw sugar producers to refiners. He and his wife Kitty Powell had two sons and one on the way. Around the time of Lucretia's visit, Herbert joined Bush's firm as a silent partner, providing ample funds to eventually transform the brokerage company into a sugar landowning business as well. When Bush and Kitty's third child was born in August, they named him Herbert Wadsworth.

Abandoned in Washington, Douglas wrote Lucretia the first in a series of romantic letters just before her departure. Postmarked 30 April, the letter began, "Lucretia – Dear Child, This is just a little line to press your sweet hand and wish you Sayonara." He confessed that he spent a miserable evening without her, found consolation in the fact that each minute that drags by brings him closer to seeing her again, and felt confident that his dreams will carry him to "a little drawing room, and to an open grate – and to thy side – sweet lady." A week later he wrote again:

My Sweet Child –

There is little to write of from these gloomy old Barracks save to tell you the old, old story – I love you. I love you – love you – love you. How many countless millions in every land, in every age have used the same phrases! And yet as I whisper it to you now how poignant with meaning, how heavy with memories, the words seem!

I am desperately tired and sick of everything about me tonight. Even my ride today has failed to drive away the little "blue devils." On my way back I lingered by the river until sunset. There were just enough clouds to make it beautiful and I sat on the bluff above and waited for it. Purple and gold and azure and crimson changed to opal and grey – and at last in a wondrous glow to blind my eyes, the sun went down in a flood of molten glory – the river trembled into shadow, then into twilight and finally dark. And thus it has been with me. My sun is down. Shadows are all about, and the dark stark night is really out for me. But through my window Avon ways to the north I can see upraised on a slender pillar of purple cloud, the faint exquisite lamp of a star.

Douglas

From Pass Christian, Lucretia went to the Wadsworth's summer home in Avon, New York. She wrote Douglas to say she had arrived safely after a disagreeable and beastly trip. In his reply he wrote, "You are haunting me. Not a bird sings under my window but carols your name – not a breeze stirs the leaves but whispers of you – not a wind in the storm last night but moaned out 'Lucretia – Lucretia.'" He told her that she made it impossible to work or even read a book. Every light in the house seemed to reflect the sparkle of her dark eyes. "I even fear to let people look into mine," he added, "lest they see you there."

While Lucretia was in Avon with Martha, Nelka, who had returned from Russia, visited Susan in Cazenovia. In a letter to Nelka written in June, Lucretia made no mention of Douglas. Instead she described a harrowing day canoeing in the woods with Martha and friends. After shooting several rapids, the canoes capsized attempting to go over a dam. Cold and drenched, the boaters trudged some distance to where they were met by a wagon to take them back to Avon. Along the way, Lucretia wrote, "Pata stopped to pick a flower and almost stepped upon a rattlesnake – Fitzhugh yelled just in time and she jumped back just as he was going to strike. There he was a great big 4 ft. snake rattling like mad coiled in the grass." One of the men killed it. "It was a perfect beauty," she continued, "dark velvety brown and eight rattles and a button." Martha planned to have the skin made into a belt.

Douglas and Lucretia often sent one another flowers. In June he thanked her for the violets she had sent him. "Their faint, delicate fragrance reminds me of you as what beautiful thing does not," he wrote. "I close my eyes and put my face down to them and – lo – your sweet lips are smiling gently back at me, your soft hand groping for mine." He told her that he was in High Point, Virginia leading a group of twenty-one soldiers on a surveying mission. Most were recent college graduates getting their first practical experience in engineering. At the age of twenty-seven, Douglas was the venerable old man of the party with deep mysteries to impart: "And at night they come to my tent, and build their little camp fire, and they gather round me and I tell them of the old days on the plains, when I was a little boy, of life as a vaquero, of cadet days, of the Philippines, of China, India, Siam, of hunts and camps and fights – but never do I tell them of what is ever in my mind – the memory of your sweet, serious eyes."

Ten days later he wrote again. Spring was in full bloom in Washington, and, although the weather was mild, he built a fire in his grate because it reminded him of her. "How like, too, it is to you – a fire!" he told her. "The sparkle of it, your nimble wit – the warmth, your sweet tenderness enveloping softly everything within its radius – the flow, the light that lies at the bottom of your eyes. And the gold of it, which is like unto nothing in this wide, wide world but your loyal true heart." (MacArthur Letters.)

Nelka teased her cousin about Douglas. She thought him pompous and insufferable. Observing that his little finger stuck out when he drank tea, Nelka called his way of holding a cup "pretentious." "Why does he do that?" she asked Lucretia, so Lucretia asked Douglas. His answer: He couldn't bend his little finger; he had broken it playing baseball. Lucretia was relieved by the explanation, but she didn't need it. She loved Douglas, could overlook his stuffiness, found him endearing, sweet, thoughtful and intelligent. She wanted to marry him, but something was amiss.

When Douglas's father and mother, General and Mrs. MacArthur, returned to the States after their tour of duty in eastern Asia, they moved to Washington. The General took up his former position as commander of the Pacific Division of the Army and his wife resumed her role as society matron. Mrs. MacArthur embraced Lucretia and asked her to assist at her weekly salons. Lucretia accepted the invitation to pour tea and help entertain her guests. At the end of each visit, Mrs. MacArthur would direct her guests to a prominent table. On the table lay a huge album of photographs. All, except one, were pictures of Douglas, from childhood to the present. Mrs. MacArthur slowly turned each page and provided glowing comments. The next to last picture was a photograph of the Taj Mahal. Mrs. MacArthur called it the most magnificent building in the world. Turning to the last page, which displayed a current photograph of Douglas in full uniform, she said, "And, this is the most magnificent man in the world." (Hunt, *Recollections*.)

Sometime during the year, Lucretia experienced a change of heart. She realized she just couldn't marry a man whose mother was so wedded to him. When the Army re-assigned Douglas from the Capital to Milwaukee, his heart was still in Lucretia's hands.

On 23 December he sent his calling card with a simple inscription: "I am pledging you this Christmas tide with a full glass and the glass is no fuller than is my heart." By 1908 the romance was over.

Douglas MacArthur
(Courtesy of the Library of Congress)

5

After Lieutenant MacArthur left Washington in August, Captain Robert Van Horn arrived in December to become an aide-de-camp to the President. Four years older than MacArthur, Van Horn had enlisted in the Army in 1897. Shortly after the outbreak of war with Spain, he went to fight in Cuba. Distinguishing himself in battle, he rose through the ranks from private to second lieutenant in twelve months. After Cuba he served in the Philippines before returning to his appointment in Washington.

Robert met Lucretia soon after his arrival. Their attraction to one another was immediate. Whatever lingering attachment Lucretia might have felt for Douglas vanished. A notice in the *Washington Post* on 17 May 1908 broke the news:

> Among the most interesting of the engagements announced this spring is that of Miss Lucretia Blow Le Bourgeois to Capt. R. O. Van Horn, Seventeenth Infantry, U.S.A., at present on duty at the White House as aid to the President. Miss Le Bourgeois, who is a niece of Mrs. Herbert Wadsworth, spends much of her time at Washington. She accompanied Mr. and Mrs. Wadsworth to the White House reception on Friday afternoon, when Mrs. Wadsworth made the interesting announcement to the President and Mrs. Roosevelt.

Years later, Lucretia told a friend that Douglas had sent her beautiful bouquets of cut flowers nearly every day, but Robert, knowing he couldn't compete on that level, brought her a single potted palm. Lucretia found the contrast both amusing and endearing.

They fell deeply in love and set a date to marry for the fall. During much of the summer Robert was on military assignment in Indiana and Tennessee, while Lucretia stayed with Martha in Avon and paid short visits to Susan in Cazenovia. The two wrote one another nearly every day. In one of her letters to Robert, Lucretia enclosed one she had just received from their friend Gutzon Borglum, who, having suffered an unhappy first marriage, offered heartfelt encouragement. "Your letter," he wrote, "was a bully letter. All the splendid big woman I always saw in you expressed itself and Van has done it. I don't know what your plans are, or just where on the map you plan to pitch tent. But I'm sure of this, if you are both going with all your natures have to give to the other and don't ever stop giving, you'll walk straight in paradise October 19th."

Wedding Party at Ashantee after Robert and Lucretia changed into their travel attire. Henry Le Bourgeois (usher), Capt. Frank Ross McCoy (best man), Nelka de Smirnoff (maid of honor), Robert Van Horn, Frances Hayden (flower girl), Herbert Wadsworth, Lucretia Le Bourgeois Van Horn, and Capt. Irving J. Carr (usher).

The wedding took place at the Wadsworth's home in Avon in October as scheduled. It was a major social event. Martha engaged the Dossenbach Orchestra, which four years later became the

Rochester Symphony, to play for the assemblage. Lucretia was given away in marriage by her uncle Herbert. Nelka served as maid of honor, and Bush and Henry (who had graduated from the Naval Academy in June) attended as did their aunt Susan and sixty other friends and relatives. After the wedding, the couple took off for Cuba, where Robert had his next military assignment.

When they arrived in Havana, they were received like visiting royalty. The Governor sent his "machine" to the port to convey them to their hotel where Lucretia found a beautiful bunch of Cuban roses waiting for her. Once settled, they were taken to the Palace where they were served "hot or warmish champagne and cakes." The senior Army officers and their wives also gave them warm welcomes and tours of the city. Major Slocum took them to the Punta, the oldest fortress in Cuba, where they saw the sea beating against the walls and the prisons within. Lucretia confessed to Susan, "I simply couldn't look at the garroting chair." They had lunch at Major Slocum's apartment "in the same rooms where de Soto [the early 16th c. Spanish explorer, Hernando de Soto] lived with his wife" and where the major's Chinese cook made "the most wonderful corn pones."

"After luncheon," she continued, "you would have thought Major Slocum would have had enough of us, but no, off we went in his big touring car, he, Major Kean, Van and myself and went about thirty miles in the country – passing the insane asylum and the home of the eccentric Cuban millionairess who has her great apes that travel with her to Paris every spring and sit at table." That night they dined at the celebrated Dos Hermanos restaurant where they ate the local specialty, fish cooked in paper, and where years later Ernest Hemingway would dine. Another day they went shopping in the morning; then Mrs. Kean, Mrs. Stark, Mrs. Grebble, Majors Slocum and Kean stopped by and whisked them off to Major Slocum's to eat a scrumptious dish of crabs prepared by the Chinese cook. "I have never had such a delicious time," she told Susan.

One evening, Robert, standing with the other officers and their wives, waited as Lucretia descended the grand staircase of their hotel to join them. Halfway down, she caught the toe of her shoe on her long evening gown. Tripping, she tucked in her chin and executed a perfect somersault. Landing on her feet, she continued down the remaining steps without a hitch. While their astonished friends remained speechless, Robert cooed in her ear, "That's the most remarkable thing I've ever seen." (Hunt, *Recollections*.) There were definite advantages to learning acrobatics at Belmont and jiu-jitsu on Dupont Circle.

Lucretia was ecstatic. Marriage was the perfect antidote to the blues of single life. At the end of November she told Nelka that Robert was "the sweetest and most considerate man" she had ever met. "I am more and more in love with him every day." She encouraged Nelka to find such a man : "Dear Nello, when I think how much beauty and joy being happily married gives to life, I wish you could find a thoroughly congenial soul and get married – there is nothing like it – it is the best life has to offer."

A month later, on New Year's Eve, she wrote Nelka again about her good news – "about my sweet little baby – that is coming some time in August: Isn't it adorable Nell? Rob and I are so happy about it that we don't know whether we are standing on heads or feet!" She was happy too that she hadn't suffered any morning sickness yet. Moreover, Robert had given her "the most beautiful embroidered bedspread for Christmas – simply grando."

Their stint in Cuba was exciting but lasted only three months. At the end of January 1909 the Army transferred Lucretia and Van, as she sometimes called him, to Fort McPherson near Atlanta, Georgia. Lucretia was not disappointed. "It is simply ideal here," she wrote to Nelka in February. The plum and peach trees were already in bloom. A magnificent pine forest that invited "delightful walks" surrounded the military base. She very much wanted her to come and visit. Nelka would be able to get away from the frantic pace of Washington and New York. "I know you would love the peace of our quiet life – the simplest and quietest you can imagine," she cajoled.

Most importantly, Lucretia was still very much in love.
Referring to their aunt Martha's unhappy marriage, she wrote:

> Poor Pata – I feel so deeply all she has missed in life
> – when I think of the richness and beauty of the
> real married life Van and I are living. Every day
> brings us new blessings of joy and peace. I did not
> realize by half the depths and sweetness of Van's
> nature when I married him. I don't believe there
> could exist a simpler, stronger nature than his – we
> can hardly believe that such great happiness is
> really ours – and are in a continual state of
> wondering delight.

Part of her delight came from her husband's sense of humor.
The soldiers in Van's company had brought a small deer to the
base from Cuba. It became F Company's pet and mascot. Lucretia
told Nelka that one morning, "I woke up and found Van pulling it
in bed with me. He had brought it over from the company's
quarters and carried it upstairs in his arms. You would have loved
seeing it nibbling toast off my breakfast tray." Writing a week
later, Lucretia continued to speak of her happiness:

> Every one in the regiment has been more than nice
> to me and I already have a few real friends among
> them. Rob and I walk in the beautiful wood about
> the post nearly every day. My little sitting room is a
> perfect bower of peach and plum blossoms that we
> have found in bud and persuaded to bloom in
> doors. This afternoon after luncheon we went out
> with a brass bowl and trowel and dug up little
> blooming wood violets and starry quaker ladies.

Mindful of the contrast between herself, now happily rooted
in her marriage, and Nelka, leading an agitated, rootless life, she
tried to encourage her cousin:

> Nell darling – I do hope you will very soon find in
> your way the peace and quiet that I have found in

mine. Every one must find it, without seeking and naturally, if it is of the best and for life – how I wish I could help you but that is impossible – but I think it would make you happy to see the current of life flow smoothly – for I think our family has been singularly unfortunate in this regard.

The baby arrived on schedule in August 1909. Lucretia and Robert named her Margaret, and she kept everyone very busy. Visiting Bush and his family in Pass Christian, Lucretia wrote Nelka in October to apologize for being so out of touch. She had been without a cook for a month, she hadn't been able to sleep for weeks because she suffered from an exposed nerve that had been "killed" only a few days before, and the nursemaid had come down with ptomaine poisoning. But the baby and everyone else were fine. Her brother, "sun burnt a beautiful bronze," was the epitome of health, his wife Kitty looked "so young and tiny with her three lusty boys." Herbert, the youngest boy and nicknamed Pat, was "a little dream." But Margaret was the center of the universe. Thriving on the sea air and perfect weather, she was growing like "the proverbial green bay tree." Not two months old, she had already outgrown her clothes, "and the little cap that looked so large on her even pleated in the back, let out all the way, can barely stretch over her little pate." Lucretia described her as "a big chunk of a girl" with fair skin, red gold hair and enormous black eyes. "Nell darling!," she wrote, "I am simply happy beyond all words!!"

In the spring of 1910 Lucretia told Nelka that they would soon be moving to Fort Leavenworth, Kansas for Van's next assignment, and that Margaret now had six teeth and more on the way, weighed 19.5 pounds stripped and could stand up on her own. She also mentioned that she was finishing up the illustrations that she had been commissioned to do four years earlier for Helen Whitney's book of poems, *Herbs and Apples.*

Lucretia also wrote to Susan to ask if she, Van and the baby could visit between their leaving McPherson and arriving in Leavenworth. The timing was not too good. Susan wanted her good friend, the psychoanalyst James Putnam to come at the same time. Writing to Putnam in June, Susan explained:

> My niece with her husband, baby and nurse arrived this week. I do not know how long she may stay but I want you to promise me to come to Cazenovia whether my little house is overflowing or not. I can always get you a room near by and you won't mind walking a square twice a day. You will come for breakfast in the morning and depart late in the evening. We will banish the family to one porch and we will take the other. And we will talk about the greatest issues.

Foremost among the great issues to discuss were the repercussions of Sigmund Freud's first and only visit to the United States, which Putnam had orchestrated in 1909. In particular Susan wanted to help Putnam reconcile Freud's psychoanalytical constructs with the philosophy of Hegel.

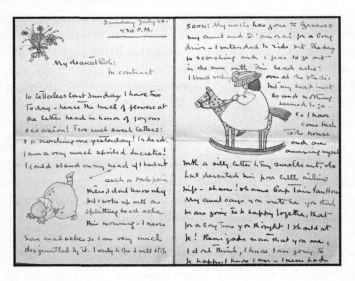

Letter from Lucretia to Robert with drawings

6

The Van Horns lived two years at Fort Leavenworth where Robert attended the School of the Line and graduated with distinction. He then enrolled at the Staff College. When he completed the course in June 1912, he was ordered back to Fort McPherson where he rejoined the 17th Infantry.

Before returning to Georgia, Lucretia visited Susan in Cazenovia for the third summer in a row. There Lucretia found a letter that Nelka had sent from Russia. "Your postal reached me the morning of my birthday," Lucretia wrote in reply. "I was so touched dear sweet little Nell – to think that you had remembered and planned so far away." Lucretia told her how proud she felt when Susan conveyed the news that the Russian Empress and the Queen of Greece had witnessed and approved her Red Cross work.

Much of her letter was taken up with news of the baby. Nearly three years old, Margaret, Lucretia wrote, "looks like a real little girl." In the bathtub, "she swims like a fish ... also floats on her back." Out-of-doors, "She runs like a little deer and is the most strenuous little person you can imagine – one continual jump to keep up." She talks a lot "and says many original things, recites little verses and does a thousand and one entertaining things." Seeing a picture of a lovely girl, Margaret "exclaimed 'aunt Nell.'"

While she and the baby were at Cazenovia, Martha and Herbert drove over from Avon "in a brand-new 40 horse power 1912 Packard" that Herbert had bought. Martha had just come back from Alaska and was about to go off to England. In a postscript, Lucretia indicated that their aunt and uncle had lost vitality. Martha was "fat and more bland," Herbert "older and not very well."

Back in Georgia, Lucretia reciprocated with a birthday letter to Nelka a month later. Her memory was aided by the fact that Margaret and Robert also had August birthdays. "Margaret celebrated her third birthday very simply," she told Nelka, "one little girl, a sponge cake and frozen custard made for the grandest of parties. The dear little things looked lovely in wreaths of wild flowers at a tiny table with candles lighted and dainty little white flowers." Unfortunately, Robert was away and missed Margaret's birthday as well as his own. Separated for nearly the entire summer, Lucretia looked forward to his return. "I shall be more than glad to have him back and be able to enjoy him again. My dear Van grows dearer every day."

For Nelka's birthday, Lucretia was embroidering a shawl, "a real Jacobs' coat of many colors." Not unlike the scarf that her sister Liz had promised Lucretia ten years earlier, Lucretia's shawl was a bit behind schedule: "I hope to have it finished before too long. I intended it to be a birthday present. Maybe you will have it by Christmas." She invited Nelka to visit them in Georgia and wanted very much to hear in person about her adventures in Russia. "I never cease wondering and admiring from the depths of my heart the wonderful courage and unselfishness you have to carry on such a work as you have done." As for herself, she had been riding horses all summer and playing some tennis to good effect. She felt healthy and energetic. She weighed "only 120 in my clothes" and intended to keep it that way.

Robert received orders to join the War Department General Staff in Washington in January 1913, which proved to be good timing. For, in June, her brother Henry, now an Ensign in the Navy, married Beall Daingerfield, from a wealthy and well-connected family, in Alexandria, Virginia. *The Washington Post* proclaimed the wedding "one of the most brilliant in this city in recent years, the uniforms of the bridegroom and his attendants adding to the picturesque scene made by the gowns of the bride and her maids." Lucretia and Robert, Martha and Herbert, Susan and Nelka, and Bush and Kitty all witnessed the event, which featured the orchestra of the *USS Dolphin* playing the wedding march. Afterwards Henry and Beall spent their honeymoon at Susan's house in Cazenovia.

Not quite two years after moving to Washington, Robert and his family were transferred to Plattsburgh Barracks in the northeast corner of New York. War in Europe had erupted in 1914, and the world appeared darker. While they were stationed at Plattsburgh, Susan died in New York City. Though her health had been deteriorating for several years, her spirit had remained strong, up to a point. But the outbreak of war put a serious dent in her Hegelian optimism. In a letter to her friend Putnam, she described how she had recently suffered a physical collapse and lost her sense of self-control:

> I suppose these breakings up of equilibrium will beset some of us always. When they come they must be faced. That many others are facing them as well as myself I know. How can it be otherwise when everything we thought is challenged by the great world tragedy and when the depths of sin revealed by that tragedy find so much like themselves in our hearts. "If thou gaze into an abyss, the abyss also will gaze into thee."

Six weeks before her death in March 1916, she wrote her friend again: "I shall not say anything about the war. I realize I am not in a state to form calm and equable judgments. I wish some one with clear and piercing vision might arise to show us what we ought to do."

In fact, no one knew what to do – either how to prevent the war from happening in the first place or how to put an end to the mindless slaughter of millions of young European men after it began. In 1916, Martha decided to sail to Europe to help her cousin Adèle at the American Hospital for British Soldiers in London. Distraught by the horrific injuries suffered by the fighting men, Martha became captivated by the miracles of reconstructive surgery. She travelled to the continent to observe French medical procedures and to help Mildred Bliss in Paris at the American Distributing Service, which Mildred and her husband had established to provide medical supplies to French hospitals.

Returning to Washington, Martha transformed her home on Dupont Circle into a nursing school. The "house which had once been the scene of brilliant entertaining became the headquarters of Mrs. Wadsworth's reconstruction classes, whose pupils went out to Walter Reed Hospital, as they progressed, for demonstration and practical work under the surgeons there." (*The New York Sun*, 28 July 1918.)

In the meantime, Lucretia had given birth to her second daughter in June 1916 in Boston, just a few months after Susan's death. She and Robert named her Lucretia, but always called her Cri-cri. About the same time, the Army transferred Robert back to Washington to join the Office of the Adjutant General at the War Department. Having stood aside for three years, the United States decided to join the fray. Too many provocations, especially the sinking of unarmed American ships at sea by German submarines, forced President Woodrow Wilson and the U.S. Congress to declare war against Germany and its allies on 6 April 1917.

In the autumn Robert went to France with the U.S. 2nd Division, as commander of the 9th Infantry Regiment, just about the time Lenin was nearly assassinated in St. Petersburg. In early November 1918, his division stood in reserve just outside the town of Bayonville-et-Chennery. Located on line between Sedan and Verdun, about two hundred kilometers northeast of Paris and thirty from the French-German border, the town was just a few kilometers from the Front Line. In early November, headquarters approved Robert's request to advance his regiment against the German position with the intention of cutting across the front to get behind the enemy. After getting its bearings from the 4th Army brigade and the 5th Marines holding the front, the regiment knifed across the line at night. It encountered but overcame several pockets of resistance. When the soldiers reached the Bois de Belval, a large forest just south of the Meuse River, they met a stiff defense and had to call in artillery fire, which proved effective. The 9th Infantry pressed forward and forced the Germans to retreat. It was a bold plan successfully executed.

The U.S. Army's Combined Army Center still cites the maneuver as an excellent example of strong leadership:

> Discussion: Here is a remarkable action. During a single night a regiment, in column and on roads, marched five miles through the enemy position! This feat becomes still more remarkable when we consider the fact that it was preceded by four years of stabilized warfare during which such an operation would have been classed as the height of insanity.

> The plan was revolutionary. It was contrary to all the tedious rules that had been evolved while the war stagnated in the trenches. Perhaps that is the very reason it succeeded. Of course, some praise this operation and others damn it as poor tactics and a dangerous gamble. But no matter what the rule books say, one unassailable fact remains – the American commander's estimate of the extent of German demoralization and confusion was thoroughly upheld by the success obtained. And we judge by results. (Rules, *Infantry in Battle*.)

For his leadership, Robert was awarded the Distinguished Service Medal, with the citation:

> For exceptionally meritorious and distinguished services. On the night of November 3, 1918, he led his regiment, the 9th Infantry, against the enemy position in the edge of the Bois de Belval. The regiment passed through the woods and the enemy lines and took up a position six kilometers in the rear of the enemy, capturing many prisoners and much war material. At daylight November 4 his regiment was heavily counter-attacked but not dislodged. The effect of night penetration of the enemy lines caused the enemy on the right and left of the 2d Division sector to fall back to the east

bank of the Meuse River. (Van Horn, *War Department.*)

A week later the war was over. Germany signed a ceasefire agreement on 11 November 1918; the day became known as Armistice Day.

Margaret, Cri-cri, Lucretia and Robert Van Horn, 1917

7

It was just after the war that the Van Horns strengthened their friendship with the Borglum family. Lucretia had first met Gutzon when he returned after several years of travel and study in Europe in 1901. An avid and able horseman, Borglum had made friends with Herbert and Martha and soon came to know and admire Lucretia. The year after Lucretia and Robert married, Gutzon married Mary Williams Montgomery. They soon had two children of their own, Lincoln and Mary Ellis. After the war Lucretia and her girls spent several summers at the Borglum's home in Stamford, Connecticut, where the Van Horn and Borglum children became friends. Margaret was three years older than Lincoln but Cri-cri and Mary Ellis were born the same year.

Gutzon Borglum (left) with Cri-cri and Mary Ellis, Margaret (sitting, center), Mary Borglum, and others
(Courtesy of Robin Borglum Carter)

After returning from Europe in July 1919, Van was assigned to Fort Leavenworth, Kansas. From there, the two families kept up a steady correspondence. Margaret wrote to Mrs. Borglum, whom she called Aunt Mary: "We have a nice house here looking over the Missouri river. Your river could make a little stream compared." She also told Mary that she and her Dad had gone duck shooting and had caught three ducks. After inquiring about Lincoln, who apparently had fallen ill, she asked Mary to "please tell Mary Ellis Cri-cri misses her very much, Lovingly, Margaret." In 1920 Lucretia returned with her children to Stamford again for the summer. One afternoon Gutzon took her and all the children for an hour long ride in "a silver plane" over Long Island Sound toward Manhattan and back. From on high, Lucretia thought the Brooklyn Bridge looked like "a beautiful spider web." She told Robert the view was thrilling but none of the children (ages eleven down to four) were frightened. Two years later the Borglums spent the summer in Colorado, where Lucretia and the girls joined them. On one of these family holidays, Borglum created a beautiful bronze statue of Margaret seated on a rock. He also executed a head of Lucretia in clay, which was later reproduced in marble. (The original and reproduction are part of the collection of the library of Brenau University at Gainesville, Georgia.)

Lucretia by Gutzon Borglum
(Courtesy of Robin Borglum Carter)

Margaret by Gutzon Borglum
(Courtesy of Robin Borglum Carter)

Before Lucretia and her troop left Fort Leavenworth, Martha paid them a visit. As much as she loved her niece, Martha adored her husband. "I'm really devoted to her 'Van' who is one of the solidest and most delightful standbys I ever had," she wrote to her friend Mildred Bliss, "and as I haven't seen any of them since the spring of 1919 and haven't seen Van since 1917, it is high time for me to 'connect up' with them again." In the same letter she reported that Nelka and Max were back in Constantinople after the White Russian forces under General Wrangel collapsed. "I'm trying my best to get them to come back to America but have as yet had no answers to either cable or letters." (Bliss Papers.)

When Robert was transferred to Fort Sam Houston near San Antonio in 1922, new vistas opened for the family. Writing to Nelka, Lucretia explained that Robert, who had "looked dreadful the first year or two after getting back from France," now looked better than ever. It helped that he was in charge again of the same regiment that he had led through the Bois de Belval, and that his troops loved him. Cri-cri at the age of six, according to Lucretia, was the cleverest member of the family. With a very fair complexion and long, thick blonde hair, she possessed "such a charm of manner that all fall victims." Margaret, thirteen years old and taller than Lucretia, was dark, strong and vigorous – "a truly beautiful girl." She was "the idol of Van's heart. They are great companions and Margaret looks adorable in her riding habit, riding off with her old dad." The family also acquired a sweet pet – a de-natured skunk that came and went through a small swinging door in the kitchen.

Content with the state of her immediate family, Lucretia worried about Nelka. Except for Nelka's brief visit to America after her harrowing escape from Russia, Lucretia had not seen her cousin for nearly ten years. Writing to her before Christmas 1922, Lucretia lamented that, with Susan dead, Martha rarely writing, Herbert chronically ill and Nelka stuck in Europe with few resources, "I feel at times the world a very lonely place full of memories that wring my heart." It seemed "as if the whole structure of the past had suddenly broken and the family ties broken even more than it. The life I live now seems in a new world without tradition and roots."

She wanted very much for Nelka and Max to come to Texas. "We have a large old barrack for a house most rambly and artistic with lots of room – a lovely view. It would be most cozy if you were here." Now that Robert was a colonel, they possessed a big "Buick six touring" car with driver that allowed them to motor out into the countryside to visit old missions. The missions, some dating from the early 16th century, were outposts founded by Spanish religious orders, such as the Jesuits, Franciscans and Dominicans, seeking to bring Catholic Christianity to Native Americans. There was also excellent hunting and fishing, which Lucretia believed would appeal to Max. They could stay for as long as they liked. But Nelka was not yet inclined to move. Instead, Lucretia found a new world of tradition and roots in Texas and Mexico when one day she received an unexpected invitation to have tea at the Maverick Ranch.

Lying in the flood plain of its river, the city of San Antonio had been inundated in the summer of 1921. A huge wall of water had ravaged the downtown district, destroyed property, uprooted trees and taken several lives. To prevent future disasters, city fathers planned to sell bonds to divert the river and knock down a number of old buildings that stood in the path of progress.

On a sunny morning in late February 1924 Rena Maverick Green, a woman of high energy and important connections, was downtown when the newspapers announced that the Old Market House was to be torn down. There by chance she met Emily Edwards admiring the hand-carved facade of the handsome neo-classic building designated for removal. The two women were appalled by the news, and decided to take immediate action. "As individuals we will not be listened to, but if we should organize, we would," Rena said to Emily. They went straight to the office of a prominent lawyer friend to ask him how to form an organization to combat the proposed desecration. Since Rena was already over-committed to many causes and charities, she insisted that Emily be the president. "She knew it needed someone's undivided attention. She made me take it," Emily later recalled. Rena also insisted that the organization should be run by women who, like themselves, were artists and who would be drawn from all sectors of the city. Hearing that "there was an artist who was enthusiastic about San Antonio at the [Army] post," Emily continued, "she invited her and some others out to tea at the Ranch" to get their new society off the ground. "And, so we did, and Lucretia and I made friends." (Odom, 42-43.)

The San Antonio Conservation Society held its inaugural meeting in March at a charming little stone house, newly restored by Lucy Maverick (also an artist and Rena's sister) at 220 Belvin Street. Emily accepted the post of President; Lucretia was elected First Vice President and Rena Second Vice President. There were four other Vice Presidents (numbers three through six), and a

Treasurer and a Secretary, for a total of nine officers. The purpose of the Society was ambitious and far-reaching. It aimed "to promote restoration of the Missions, to preserve old buildings, documents, pictures, objects, names, customs, and to protect all natural beauty and everything that is admirably distinctive of San Antonio." Although the women failed to prevent the destruction of the Old Market House, they moved quickly to mobilize public opinion. They began calling on city officials and local business leaders to elucidate the Society's goals. A major breakthrough came when Emily conceived the idea of putting on a puppet show to appeal for community support.

With much verve and vigor, Emily and Lucretia created a version of "The Goose That Lays the Golden Eggs" to dramatize the river's contribution to the City. The play centered on the dispute between Mr. and Mrs. San Antonio about their Goose, a metaphor for the San Antonio River. Mr. San Antonio was determined to chop off her head and get all her Golden Eggs at once. Mrs. San Antonio defended the Goose as a lovable and productive asset. Unable to come to an agreement, husband and wife decide to take the Goose to City Hall to let the City Fathers determine her fate. Five puppets represented the mayor and four commissioners. Each puppet looked like his real counterpart with faces drawn by Emily and Lucretia. Mrs. San Antonio appeared with the Goose and a basket of her Golden Eggs; the eggs were labeled the Alamo, the four Missions, old buildings, groves of native trees, and parks. After both husband and wife had their say, the mayor put the question to the commissioners: "Shall the old Goose die?" The answer was a resounding, "NO!" The play was performed for Mayor Tobin and the four commissioners after their regular board meeting in September 1924. Emily was the voice and puppeteer for Mrs. San Antonio, Lucretia played Mr. San Antonio and the parts of mayor and commissioners; Lucretia's daughter Margaret jiggled the puppet-officials in reaction to the proceedings. The audience was delighted. Rowena Green, Rena's daughter who witnessed the performance, remembered that, "The

women enjoyed it more than the men, but the men had to laugh....
And it was very successful."

Two months after the puppet show, the Conservation Society
invited the mayor, the commissioners, and the city's new flood
control engineer to embark on a two-hour boat ride down the river
and through the city to impress them with the natural beauty of
the surrounding landscape. In each of four rowboats a city official
(male) was paired with a conservation member (female). Emily
Edwards rode in the first with the city engineer, while Van,
substituting for one of the commissioners, sat in the third boat
with Fourth Vice President Amanda Taylor. Lucretia was picked to
ride in the final boat with Mayor Tobin, because, it was thought,
she was "very attractive and very enthusiastic." (L. Fisher, 183.)

Treating the event as a festival as well as an opportunity, the
Society leaders planted supporters on the bridges along the way to
cheer the rowboats as they passed below. The one-two punch of
puppet show and river trip convinced the reluctant to join the
movement. When the Conservation Society received a state
charter as a historical society the following year, many important
business leaders signed the charter along with their wives and the
original members. The concept of preservation took immediate
and deep root in San Antonio soil in a short two-year period.

Aside from community activism, the Society also identified
particular buildings and public spaces for renovation and raised
money to carry out the work. In this connection, they invited
prominent architects and artists to speak about related issues. One
of the first speakers invited by the Society was Lucretia's friend
Gutzon. For several years Borglum had been working on a massive
project to carve a monument memorializing the heroes of the
Confederacy on the face of Stone Mountain in Georgia. In the
spring of 1924 the project finally fell apart for lack of funds and
clashes of personality. Borglum received an invitation from the
Texas Trail Drivers Association to consider a monument to
commemorate the cowboys, horses and cattle of the Lone Star
State. Disgusted with Georgia, he accepted the project. It was a

happy reunion for both families when the Borglums decided to live in San Antonio.

Whether Lucretia was the one who extended the invitation, the Conservation Society asked Borglum to be one of their first speakers. The event, which was co-sponsored with the Alamo Mission Chapter of the Daughters of the Republic of Texas, took place in October 1925 at the Menger Hotel. Borglum spoke about a proper setting for the Alamo as a way of opening a general discussion about raising money to buy additional land south of the Mission. He proclaimed that, "Where the Alamo stands is probably the most precious spot in the United States. Weigh the amount of martyrdom represented by the Alamo and you cannot equal it anywhere in history." Lucretia, vice chairman of the event, showed lantern slides of plans for improvements to the historic site. Altogether it was a festive evening that brought out "virtually every civic organization in San Antonio," and launched a major fund raising drive. (L. Fisher, 104.)

Through their work together in forming the Conservation Society, Lucretia and Emily Edwards became fast friends. Like Lucretia, Emily led a peripatetic life. She had grown up on a ranch on the outskirts of San Antonio, and moved to Chicago in 1906 at the age of seventeen to enroll as a student at the Art Institute. After graduating, she taught art classes in schools in Chicago and Charleston, West Virginia, and did theater design in New York and staged puppet shows in Provincetown, Massachusetts. When she returned to San Antonio for vacation in the summer of 1923, the city looked so beautiful that she couldn't think of leaving again. It had been easy for Rena Green to persuade her to become the president of the Conservation Society.

Still, Emily continued to travel. In the summer of 1925 she and a friend went down to Mexico City for a holiday and to sketch street scenes. They began attending classes that Diego Rivera was giving at home on Sundays on art analysis and the history of Mexican art. Emily recalled that, "The classes cost nothing, as we couldn't have afforded to pay, and it would have been beneath his dignity to have accepted what we could have paid." As she spoke no Spanish and Diego spoke little English, she began teaching him English "out of a book by William Blake." The following summer when Emily returned to Mexico, Lucretia went with her.

Four years younger than Lucretia, Rivera had lived and worked in France for fourteen years before returning to Mexico in 1921 at the behest of the Mexican ambassador to France. He was fully engaged on a massive mural project at the Secretariat of Public Education building in Mexico City when Emily introduced him to Lucretia. The two artists hit it off right away, perhaps in part because they had lived in Paris, could communicate in French and were full of enthusiasm. They read and howled over the Katzenjammer Kids comic strip, which Lucretia translated for him. More importantly, Diego saw that Lucretia was talented and dedicated. The scope of her visit to Mexico consequently expanded. She begged for more time. In a telegram to Robert dated October 18, she wrote:

> Tenderest love on our anniversary all my thoughts are with my dear ones my ticket expires the 31st please send me 100 dollars am learning so much could I possibly stay longer? could get refund on ticket wire me what you think best love from Lucretia.

Robert must have thought it was alright, for in November she went with Diego to Chapingo, just outside of Mexico City, where he was painting the chapel at the Universidad Autonoma. She was thrilled that he allowed her to work on her own. "Last week Diego let me paint a whole big tree and some corn and some ivy plants and the ground forms on one of the big fresco, and seemed greatly pleased at the way I did mine [and] didn't retouch anything," she told Robert. She felt it was "a great privilege to paint along side of him" and see the way he handled color and form. The experience bouyed her self-confidence. "I have advanced incredibly in these few months," she added, "I shall paint the rest of my life."

On their return to San Antonio in December, Emily and Lucretia both felt rejuvenated. Emily stepped down as president of the San Antonio Conservation Society and, acting on Diego's suggestion, embarked on a monumental history of Mexican murals, eventually published as *Painted Walls of Mexico*. Lucretia re-dedicated herself to a life of art. From 1926 when she went to Mexico City to 1931 when he painted a series of murals in San Francisco, Lucretia and Diego maintained a close friendship that was important to her artistic success.

8

In the spring of 1927 the Van Horn household was astir. Robert expected a transfer to California, Martha invited Margaret to spend the summer in Avon, and Lucretia packed for Mexico.

Margaret Van Horn

Margaret, now seventeen years old, drove east with Mary Borglum and her children in May. When she reached Avon, she learned that her father had been appointed Professor of Military Science and Tactics at Berkeley. "Dad's orders to the U of California are really out now!" she wrote in her diary in June.

"Cheers! This is going to mean more to me than almost anything I could think of! You see I think it has the best archaeological dept. of any school in the U.S. Whoops Whoops!" A week later she took the train to Ipswich, Massachusetts to visit her great-aunt Elizabeth Le Bourgeois Crockett. She was bowled over to learn that her cousin Kitty, who was eight years older than she, also had a deep interest in archaeology:

> Kitty is just what I would like to be at her age – tho she is a little lawless – by that I mean she is a law unto herself. She told me some of the most fascinating stories of her wild expedition after Neanderthal bones in the south of France. Kitty is just too wonderful. We are going to the Peabody Museum next week sometime and I know it's going to mean a lot to me. (Margaret Van Horn diary.)

When she returned to Avon, Margaret was put to bed with a high temperature and a persistent cough. While she was recuperating, her great uncle Herbert, who was in declining health, died. Martha waited several days before she broke the news to Margaret; she didn't want to upset her. Forced to postpone her departure several times, Margaret finally left Avon to head home.

Lucretia had rejoined Diego in Mexico City where he was painting the murals of the Secretariat. She was delighted that everyone was glad to see her. "I had a wonderful welcome," she wrote to Robert. Looking over forty drawings that she had done, Diego was greatly impressed. "I am very proud of his approbation," she added. She was also very happy that he was glad to have her paint with him again. Best of all, he wanted to include her in one of the murals. In a letter to Robert dated 9 July, she wrote:

> Poor Diego is very suffering with his sinus. Has to go to the doctor every other day for very painful treatment. Lupe [Diego's wife] is very ill seriously affected nervously and we are most anxious.

However Diego keeps working steadily he is going to paint my portrait in the panel he is working on now – at the Secretaria. I am one of the women sweeping out the rubbish of Catholicism. I am delighted to be the model, having decidedly the inclination to sweep things out.

She closed by asking him to send some more money as her costs running "about six or seven dollars a day makes my two hundred vanish." She added, "I should feel very depressed if it were not my money earned by ye glorious sweat of brow."

Portrait of Diego and Lupe by Lucretia

291

While Lucretia was away, Robert and the girls had to manage the move alone. In the same July letter, Lucretia began, "No letter has come for a long time but I imagine my poor dear up to the ears with packing and in much dolor. I hope my darlings all survive the ordeal. I feel very conscious stricken when I think of being away from all the flurry of crating." Her absence during the "ordeal" perhaps accounts for Cri-cri's complaint years later that, when she was a child (she was eleven when they left Texas), her mother "disappeared."

The move to California was nonetheless successful. The family found a pleasant house at 1825 Highland Place in Berkeley, which Margaret described in her diary:

> A good (?) description of our house –
>
> It clings tenaciously to the side of a hill, with the bay and all it sycophantic cities below. An old clingely garden around it, and a beautiful eucalyptus grove on the left side.
>
> The house itself is three story that is, cellar, studio, library on one floor; kitchen, dining room, living room, sun room, and Dad's abode; then the third floor is the "hen coop." Cri-cri, Mother and I exist there – Mother has a room "Estilo Proliteriat" with all her Mex. things around – Mine is decidedly refined – a sort of unrefined refinement, if you see the point – a turquoise blue dresser and desk, – in the walls are many cupboards where collections may be hidden from the eye.

Margaret was happy to be in Berkeley, but in fact was unwell. A thorough medical examination in early October disclosed that she had tuberculosis. A week later, she entered the Alum Rock Sanatorium in San Jose – "my home for the next six months, I guess." Faced with an uncertain outcome, she was stoic, angry and funny: "Life is <u>highly unjust</u> – here I am – a perfectly useless and thrill-less human – as I said to Mother, 'please bring me some French novels – wild ones that will supply the romance and thrill I used to supply *moi meme.*'"

In her diary, on 16 October 1927, Margaret also wrote, "Mother says Diego may come up to do a mural – I am so glad we were ordered here, because she has a great chance here." The news was now out that the California School of the Fine Arts had commissioned Diego to create a mural in one of its halls and that he would also deliver a series of lectures in December. Two weeks after Margaret's diary entry, the Oakland Tribune reproduced a section of Diego's Secretariat of Public Education Building mural depicting Lucretia's head and shoulders. At the same moment, the East-West Gallery of Fine Arts in San Francisco held an exhibition of Rivera's work from October through the first week of November, which included one or two of his works that Lucretia owned. Mildred Taylor, the director of the East-West Gallery, and Jehanne Bietry Salinger, editor of *The Argus* art magazine, arranged a series of Saturday afternoon lectures on "Art Criticism" over the radio. They invited Lucretia to give the first radio talk in early February 1928. She spoke about the art life of Mexico City based on the two summers that she had spent working there.

Inspired by her friendship with Diego and finding herself, finally, in a highly active artistic community, Lucretia threw herself into her art. She joined the Oakland Art League and other Bay area associations. The *Tribune* noted on Christmas day that Lucretia, among others, had sold works at the East-West Gallery. She showed again, at the Oakland Art League's first no-jury exhibition, in June 1928. Reviewing the event for the newspaper, Florence Wieben Lehre, the assistant director of the Oakland Art Gallery, found Lucretia's painting "Fruit of the Earth" the best in the show. Reflecting the strong influence of Diego Rivera, Ms. Lehre said that Lucretia's work "possesses clarity and sureness of treatment" and described the piece, in keeping with its title, as "organic and earthy." "There are those," she concluded, "who declare that had prizes been awarded, Lucretia Van Horn should have won first."

Lucretia's self-portrait

Arriving in the Bay Area virtually unknown, Lucretia became connected with the art community mainly because of her friendship with Diego but also because she met and became friends with W. H. Clapp, the director of the Oakland Art Gallery. Clapp, who painted in an impressionist style, was one of a group of landscape artists who for several years during the late 1920s showed their paintings under the name the Society of Six. Like

294

Lucretia, Clapp had gone to France and studied at the *l'Académie Julian*, but their paths didn't cross in Paris for he arrived in the summer of 1904 just after Lucretia returned to Washington. When they met in late 1927, Clapp immediately recognized her as a fine and serious artist.

She also began to make other valuable friends. For the most part, they were all younger than she. John Emmett Gerrity was among the first. A well-known Bay Area painter, Gerrity ran a studio in Berkeley a short distance from the Van Horn's house and became a frequent visitor. She soon met Worth Ryder who taught art at University of California at Berkeley and Marian Simpson another noted Bay Area painter who was chosen as one of five jurors, which included Diego Rivera, for the 53rd annual San Francisco Art Association exhibition in 1931.

Lucretia became friends with David Park and Galka Scheyer. Lucretia probably first met her when Scheyer showed pictures from her collection at Berkeley in December 1928. Scheyer had begun her career as a painter, but decided to represent a group of central European artists known as the Blue Four – Lyonel Feininger, Alexei Jawlensky, Wassily Kandinsky and Paul Klee. Lucretia drew a striking black and white portrait of Galka that resides in the Norton Simon Museum. And, Albert Bender, who was a good deal older than Lucretia and one of the leading patrons of the arts in the Bay Area in the 1920s and 30s, became her friend.

Lucretia knew Bernard Zakheim. Impressed with his work, she introduced him to Diego in San Francisco. Zakheim, who was one of thirty-two artists who created the stunning Work Progress Administration murals in the Coit Tower on Telegraph Hill in San Francisco, painted a dramatic portrait of Lucretia, now in a private collection. When she first visited Mexico in 1926, she had met and befriended Paul Higgins, a young artist from Utah assisting Rivera on the Ministry of Education murals. Higgins fell in love with Mexico, embraced Marxism, and soon changed his name to Pablo O'Higgins. In 1930 when he decided to travel to Russia, he asked Lucretia to vouch for him on his passport application.

Lucretia felt uplifted by her immersion in the local art world. Her enthusiasm affected the whole family. Released from the Alum Rock Sanatorium with her health much improved after less than a year, Margaret started drawing and painting in what she called her Persian style. Mildred Taylor invited all four Van Horns to exhibit at the East-West Gallery in August 1928. Jehanne Salinger wrote a lengthy review of the family's work for *The San Francisco Examiner* (26 August 1928), beginning with an incisive analysis of Lucretia's art.

> It would be vain to try to blind oneself to the fact that Lucretia Van Horn, a personal friend and fervent admirer of Diego Rivera, has been strongly influenced by the spirit of the Mexican master, but it would be impossible to uphold the opinion that her work is in any way imitative of that of Rivera, either in intention or in result. Her technique has undoubtedly become almost as strong as the technique of "Diego" (as we have become accustomed to speak of Mexico's great artist). There is not the faintest trace of a stroke in her oil paintings. It is all as smooth and as warm as flesh itself. Her design is decorative and much sophisticated, despite an attempt at primitiveness. Its mannerism, though, is always elegant and bears the stamp of culture and intelligence. Her forms are solid and dynamic, and her colors, especially her blues and reds, show a refined restraint.

Robert had exhibited several woodcarvings, a craft that he had taken up years before when he had been stationed in the Philippines and for which he had won an honorable mention at an exhibition in Kansas in 1922. Borglum saw several in 1920 and thought they would sell in a gallery, and Diego saw photographs and praised them too. Mrs. Salinger declared the Colonel's work was "as great and as naïve in character as any of the African or New Guinea wood carvings," and that his "Salambo, with its repeated design of snake in the hair motive and around the ears, is a gem of art and will leave many an art lover craving for its ownership." She thought Margaret's flower sketches and fanciful landscapes were delightful and full of whimsy. Cri-cri's work, she thought, reflected the "unconscious art" of childhood and the "sheer love of pattern and color." Of the four artists, Robert was evidently the most self-conscious. When they showed again as a family in Berkeley six months later, Margaret wrote in her diary that, "Dad was called up by the reporter on *The Examiner* who wanted to know if he would let them take a photo of him and his carving for the paper – he said <u>no</u>!"

In February 1929, just before the Berkeley show opened, Lucretia's brother Henry arrived in San Francisco from Samoa. He and his second wife Dolly and son Julien visited for several days before heading to New Orleans where the Navy had transferred him. The Van Horns were thrilled, especially Margaret. "Dolly is a perfect dear and little Julien is a darling," and "Uncle Henry is my <u>bestest</u> uncle. I'm crazy about him. I think he likes me too," she wrote in her diary. All three sang and danced and told great stories. "When Uncle H twangs his guitar and starts to sing I just sit enthralled – heavens how that man can play!!" He could sing all kinds of songs "– old sea chanties Whiskey Johnny – Blow the man down and minstrels – divine old ones." One evening the entire gang went out to dinner to a friend's house. Henry dressed in Samoan costume and performed his sword dance. Margaret was taken home early because of her health, but, she confided in her diary, "on the way home dad drove the rest of the family in the ditch – had to come home in a taxi."

Lucretia was always adventurous and interested in anything new. One day in April she went to a military drill where she met Lieutenant Greenlaw and Commander Nimitz, who as Fleet Admiral would lead the United States Navy against the Japanese in the Second World War. Chester Nimitz had been appointed Professor of Naval Science and Tactics at the University of California at Berkeley in 1926, the counterpoint to Robert's position as Professor of Military Science and Tactics at the university. A week later Greenlaw took Lucretia flying in a small fighter plane. They flew over Sausalito and Alcatraz and around the Bay. The lieutenant treated Lucretia to a roll and dive, and she thoroughly enjoyed the entire experience, except the outfit she had to put on. "She says," Margaret wrote in her diary, "she looked a choice sight in the flying teddies and parachute she had to wear. (I think all those D—N aviators take a fiendish glee in dressing women up in those horrible things.)"

Diego Rivera mural, Ministry of Education, Mexico City.
Lucretia is the woman on the right wearing the necklace.

9

Lucretia entered the larger and older San Francisco Art Association fifty-second annual show in May 1930. Held at the California Palace of the Legion of Honor, the exhibition featured over four hundred works of art. Lucretia won the $100 prize for the most interesting drawing in the show. Out of the nine moneyed awards, including the top prize of $500, Lucretia's work was the only one reproduced on the Art page of the *Oakland Tribune*, under the banner "Lucretia Van Horn Wins." In November the California Palace also held a major exhibition of Diego Rivera's art. Three of the works in the show belonged to Lucretia – Diego's paintings "Portrait of Lucretia" and "The Pink Dress," and a drawing "The Bridge."

Portrait of Lucretia by Diego Rivera

A year later, she again received prominent notice in the Oakland press. An exhibition at Mills College showed a wide array of American, European and Mexican works, which the reviewer, H. L. Dungan, wrote at the end of December 1931 "trace the line of modern endeavor" from impressionism to Cezanne to Matisse and Picasso. "Lucretia Van Horn of Berkeley," Dungan continued, "shows two drawings and a work in color. If these are recent works, then Mrs. Van Horn is getting more and more modern." In the next paragraph, perhaps in contrast or as a joke, Dungan briefly noted that, "Diego Rivera's oil and drawing are primitives which arouse a mild interest."

Just after the show at Mills College, Lucretia received a letter from Martha, thanking her for sending holiday greetings and the good news about Margaret. Your note, she said, "made a very very different Christmas for me than I would otherwise have had" as things were "getting gloomier and gloomier" in New York. She had ceased living at the great house on Dupont Circle after she and Herbert had turned the use of it over to the Red Cross during the First World War. The house had remained largely unused ever since the end of the war. They tried selling it in the mid-1920s but found no buyer. The mansion was considered as a possible temporary residence for President Coolidge and his family while the White House was renovated in 1927. The Patterson House, across P Street from the Wadsworth's house, was chosen instead to serve as the "temporary White House." Now with the onset of the Great Depression, Martha sold the mansion to a women's group who made it into the Sulgrave Club.

Living exclusively at her country place in Avon, she had to let staff go and cut the wages of the few she retained. "I want of course to make every effort to keep Ashantee," she explained, "even reduced as it is to its utmost as it is the only home I have had since I left St. Louis." In order to do that, "I am planning to close the house like last year and get off in the motor for some six weeks as that is literally the cheapest thing I can do, but I won't be able to get out to California. I really don't know just where I'll go."

She closed by saying that she had recently received a letter from Nelka, who was planning to return to the States in May to live in Susan's little house in Cazenovia.

The good news about Margaret, however, was premature. Within a few months her tuberculosis flared up. Lucretia and Van decided to take her to the Fitzsimons General Hospital in Denver, Colorado. The Army had built the medical facility in 1918 to treat soldiers injured by chemical warfare. The hospital also admitted patients with tuberculosis. On their return to Berkeley, Lucretia, Van and Cri-cri drove through New Mexico and Arizona. Once home, Lucretia wrote Margaret a series of letters in October 1932.

Daily life in Berkeley, she reported, was pretty routine. Van was enjoying golf now that his game had improved and was looking well. Cri-cri was elated; she had a date to the Scabbard and Blade dance at the Phi Betas and was going to wear "a lovely little canary yellow dress and will look charming." Their friend Jack Gerrity stopped in and asked Lucretia to send Margaret his best wishes. They were all excited about the outcome of the big football game between Cal, Berkeley and St. Mary's. The game ended in a 6 - 6 tie, even though the odds favored St. Mary's by 4 to 1. One day she went with a friend to San Francisco to look at the work Bernard Zakheim had done while abroad. "Some of it is very interesting and along his original lines. Paris affected him not at all. He hated it there, though he met a number of Jewish painters, [Marc] Chagall and [Moise] Kisling and a number of others." Within ten years both Chagall and Kisling would emigrate to America to escape the spread of Nazi persecution of Jews in Europe. In Chinatown she bought Margaret a red-lacquered leather trunk "to keep your eiderdown and extra blankets in." On another day, Lucretia invited a few of her artist friends, including Worth Ryder and Marian Simpson, to look over her recent paintings. She was both a bit relieved and a little miffed that Van's strong mint juleps diverted their attention.

After the first letters arrived, Margaret wrote back to say that she very much enjoyed her mother's account of their drive through the Southwest. Lucretia responded by providing a reconstructed diary of their trip, including their stops at Taos, Santa Fe, Keams Canyon, Hubbell's trading post, and various Navajo and Hopi villages along the way. In Taos she visited her friend Marjorie Eaton who lived with and painted her handsome Indian lover and artist, Juan Mirabal. She was not sorry to get away, though, for she found Taos "too picturesque, too arty, utterly ruined as regards the Indians." She much preferred the smaller indigenous towns, and provided Margaret detailed descriptions of the textures and colors – beautiful earth tones, reds and blues – of blankets, shawls and rugs. In the village of Wolpi, they entered a house to see a stunning set of kachina dolls hung against a white-washed wall. They also witnessed several tribal dances: the "rhythmic stomping like some primitive force" and "chanting low almost like thunder." Lucretia felt a strong kinship with Indian culture. "Something in my heart cries out to the wild untamed Navajos, but I can't help loving the Hopis – very gentle people." She told Margaret, "I love the simplicity of the Indians – their dignified acceptance of life and their tender love of their children."

Lucretia wrote again near the end of the month, "Your letter came telling us that you are feeling better. Such happiness it brought to my heart my darling – and to hear you have been drawing – don't tear up the opuses." She cautioned Margaret that we never "know whether our things are good or not" and that she was not a good judge of her own work. Yes, she conceded, we can easily assess "the superficial plastics" in a piece of work but not the deep. "I am more interested in inner content than all the plastic pyrotechnics in the world." She also told Margaret that she had been invited to show at a major exhibition of international art to be held in San Francisco:

> There are to be many European works and works from all parts of the United States. Thirty-five Americans were asked to show by invitation jury free and I am one of the numbers. I shall probably send a large abstract nude I have done recently. For the first time I feel perfectly freed from everything but my own stuff – and independent of what others

think – a great step for the feeble tottering of the past. But I put a more searching analysis in my work.

The show took place at the Legion of Honor in San Francisco in May 1933 with forty paintings from Europe, including work by Picasso, and other parts of the world, including pieces by Diego Rivera and José Orozco. Of the thirty-five artists from the States, Lucretia was one of ten from the western part of the country.

Toward the end of her letter, Lucretia confessed to Margaret how important to her their correspondence had become. "Darling," she wrote, "since I started writing to you I love it more than anything in the day and look forward to the peace of talking with you. My sweet love you are always held close in my heart and everything I do seems connected in some way with you." She signed all the letters, "Madrecita," little mother in Spanish.

Soon after she sent the last letter, the hospital notified the family that Margaret's condition had suddenly grown worse. Margaret died a few days later, before her parents could get to Colorado. She was ten months shy of her twenty-fourth birthday, dying at about the same age as her grandmother, Lutie, and aunt, Liz. Van and Lucretia buried her at the San Francisco National Cemetery in October 1932.

Family and friends were shocked and crushed. Early in the next year, Lucretia told Albert Bender, who had sent her a scarf and note of consolation at Christmas, that she would "have answered sooner but I have not been well and have greatly disturbed in mind." She had delayed writing because she wanted to be able "to express in my letter the deep love and high appreciation I feel for you, for all you have done for me and my dear Margaret. Your devotion to her was of so beautiful a quality I can only think of it with tears in my eyes." (Bender Papers, Mills College.)

10

Lucretia's inclusion in the major and select international exhibition at San Francisco in May 1933 marked the high point of her artistic career, but was little consolation following the unexpected horror of Margaret's death. She felt overwhelmed by a sense of guilt for not being with her daughter when she died. She also experienced a wave of *déjà vu* as the awful memories of her mother and sister's sudden disappearances flooded over her. It was a terrible blow too when in August she learned that Martha had been seriously injured in an automobile accident that had killed her business manager Colonel Shiverick. And still the cascade of tragedy continued. In November Lucretia heard that her brother Henry, the executive officer of the battleship *USS Utah*, had suffered a sudden, fatal heart attack aboard his ship. It was all too much to bear. When the Army promoted Van to the rank of brigadier general and re-assigned him from Berkeley to Fort McPherson at the end of the year, Lucretia decided to visit Martha before it was too late. Van and Cri-cri consequently sailed from California in December 1933 without her.

Lucretia spent several months at Ashantee with Martha, whose recovery was exceedingly slow. When it became apparent that she was out of danger and needed only time to recover, Lucretia rejoined Van and Cri-cri in Georgia. Just as Nelka and Max arrived in Avon in September, Martha – determined to assert control over her broken body and defying her doctor's advice – mounted one of her horses, rode out of the barn, fell to the ground, and died three days later. Lucretia returned to Avon for the funeral and again in July 1935 to meet Nelka to sort out the possessions Martha had bequeathed them. Her estate, valued at $51,000, was divided equally between her two nieces. Lucretia wrote to Mary Borglum for advice on how best to dispose of her aunt's collection of fine China and various antiques, but Mary was in South Dakota where Gutzon had begun his most ambitious and famous sculpting project. He was now totally occupied carving on the granite face of Mount Rushmore four giant heads of his favorite American presidents – George Washington, Thomas Jefferson, Abraham Lincoln and Theodore Roosevelt. Mary was out of reach and unavailable to assist Nelka and Lucretia at Avon. Combing through the house left the cousins feeling exhausted and valuing the virtues of simplicity.

Lucretia's oldest brother Bush, and last remaining sibling, died from heart failure in March 1938 at the age of fifty-nine. The Great Depression had crushed his businesses and damaged his health. For nearly twenty years he and Herbert had owned and operated three sugar plantations in southern Louisiana, but the combination of terrible weather, plummeting sugar prices and too much debt had driven the firm into bankruptcy in 1930. A month after Bush's death, Cri-cri married James Adams, a young military officer whom she had met at Fort McPherson. Cri-cri had preferred an heir to the Coca-Cola fortune, but for some reason Lucretia and Van had prevailed against him.

Cri-Cri Van Horn Adams

In 1940 Van retired from the United States Army after forty-three years of distinguished service. Before leaving Fort McPherson for good, Lucretia travelled to Avon to visit Nelka. The two were asked to honor Martha by presenting the Mrs. Herbert Wadsworth Memorial Cup at the Genesee Valley Breeders' Association's 26th annual meeting. The trophy was given to the brood mare judged the best of the breed. Martha had started the annual meeting of horse breeders in 1914. After the event, Lucretia and Van moved to Monterey, California, where there was a large community of retired military officers. There they expected to live modestly but comfortably, and devote themselves to a quiet life of painting and carving. The happy plan, however, collapsed in less than a year when Van, who was always a heavy cigarette smoker, fell ill and died of lung cancer in June 1941. He was sixty-five years old.

Lucretia was bereft. All of her support systems had vanished. In October 1941, she wrote to Mary Borglum whose husband had died in March just before Van's death. "The last year," she said, "was one of long anguish – fighting against despair. Seeing my dear Van slowly dying before my eyes. Afterwards I seemed frozen and paralyzed – now I am feeling the great down sweep of loneliness." She asked Mary about her plans for the future. "Perhaps," she suggested, "we could meet somewhere. I need you so much – a dark terror of soul comes over me that is almost beyond endurance."

At first she thought that she had enough courage and money to live by herself, but now she was unsure about either. Since the Army had recently transferred Cri-cri and her husband Jim to Monterey, she planned to move with them into their house. But she knew it would be difficult, not just for herself but for Cri-cri as well. "These are terrible times for a young captain's wife," she told Mary Borglum, "and Cri-cri suffered great grief over Van's passing." Unlike Van, Jim was a hard-boiled military man who demanded control and obedience. Lucretia sensed that the living arrangement would not work out, and said so, if perhaps unintentionally. "If I did not know I was an iron dog, I would think

I was on the verge of a crack up." The crack up came quickly. After an ugly argument, Jim ordered his mother-in-law out of his house.

Literally homeless and at a loss where to go, Lucretia telephoned her friend Marjorie Eaton. Like Lucretia, Marjorie was an artist, knew Diego Rivera, and loved Mexico and the Indian culture of the Southwest. From the mid 1940s she also began taking small supporting roles in Hollywood movies, including "Anna and the King of Siam," "Mary Poppins," and "Snake Pit." Marjorie's mother Edith Eaton had bought a historic adobe house and property known as the Briones Estate in Palo Alto near the Stanford University campus in 1925. Marjorie and her mother lived there, although Marjorie spent most of her time on the road. With Edith's approval, Marjorie drove down in her Lincoln Zephyr to bring Lucretia up to the Hill Top, as the place was also known, for a few nights. Although not intended or expected by Lucretia, Marjorie or Edith, a few nights turned into nearly thirty years.

Edith, who was a few years older than Lucretia, had been the leading couturier in San Francisco at the turn of the century and was happy to have Lucretia's company. She was also a fabulous cook and enjoyed making anything and everything. She produced a wide variety of dishes: popovers, Yorkshire pudding, cafe mousse, and homemade mustard. She charged Lucretia no rent, but asked her to contribute $100 a month for meals. Every evening at dinner Edith wore her best clothes and diamond brooch, while Lucretia with a less elaborate wardrobe always looked elegant in her mandarin jacket. Edith, a rock-ribbed Republican, and Lucretia, a southern Democrat with a socialist twist, agreed not to talk politics, but were quite willing to discuss anything else heartily and with good humor. And, only once did Marjorie – who took no interest in politics – get seriously angry with Lucretia for telling a particular story and forbade her from ever telling it again. Lucretia had recounted that, as a child at Belmont on cold winter nights, several small Negro children (she called them "pickaninnies") were brought into the house to get under the covers to warm the beds for the family members.

During the Second World War, Lucretia's life, like that of everyone else, was severely restricted. As a result she developed the pattern of staying at the Hill Top as she had no car and never learned to drive. With little money to spend, her activities were simple. Aside from lively conversation and Edith's delicious cuisine, she liked to smoke and drink a glass or two of whiskey in the evening. She continued to draw and paint but no longer with any intention to exhibit. As a military officer's wife, she was very much affected by the war. Several of her paintings from the 1940s portray the horrors of the battlefield. One in particular that she called "Jungle Death" is especially striking, done in the style of Paul Klee.

She sent her old friend Douglas MacArthur Christmas greetings along with a present for his five-year old son Arthur. At the time MacArthur was fighting in New Guinea and planning to attack the Philippines as prelude to an ultimate invasion of Japan. Lucretia received a cordial response in January 1944. Douglas had not heard until her letter arrived that Van had died. "I am so cut off from the United States that I had no previous news of it," he wrote. "He was one of God's best." The two communicated at least once again. After President Truman dismissed him in 1951 as supreme military commander during the Korean War, MacArthur arrived in San Francisco, hailed by many as a national hero, and telephoned Lucretia at the Hill Top. They talked for about five minutes. MacArthur and his family then flew to Washington where he was invited to address both houses of Congress. In an eloquent and emotional speech that received wave after wave of applause, he ended with a sad and evocative phrase drawn from an old Army ballad – "old soldiers never die; they just fade away."

With her health declining, Lucretia's hostess Edith placed a classified ad for a gardener cum handyman/painter in the local paper in the summer of 1956. A pair of brothers, graduate students at Stanford in need of funds, responded. Charmed by the apparently capable young men, Edith hired them. Jerry worked for a year or so, but Tom Hunt was hooked and decided to forsake his Asian History program for a life at the Hill Top. He confessed his interest in art and especially stained glass. Seeing the impracticality of doing stained glass with inadequate studio facilities, Lucretia encouraged him to make mosaics. Tom not only became a well-known artist, he also soon assumed the roles of chef, chauffeur and bookkeeper in addition to his gardening and house repair assignments. He even persuaded Lucretia to spend a little money on herself. He drove her into San Francisco to Saks where, with Tom's encouragement, she bought two fine, knitted suits, one blue and one brown, which she wore on alternate days for the rest of her life.

Tom also brought to Hill Top his mother's friend, the artist Morris Graves. Twenty years younger than Lucretia, Graves moved to Loleta in northern California in 1964. He had by then a well established reputation as a painter of birds, often wounded, blind and mysterious. Lucretia and Morris liked one another immediately. Returning from a trip to Santa Cruz on one occasion, he introduced Lucretia to marijuana, which, she decided, made a quite good cigarette. She in turn, understanding his love of winged creatures and untamed nature, sent him a pair of books, *Butterflies and Moths* and *Wild Flowers of America*. Chagrined at his failure to thank her sooner (she had sent the books in August), Morris wrote in January 1967 to say he would be in San Francisco in February and would like to stop by and see her for a few hours on his way back home to Loleta. Fearing he would not be able to see her because she had developed a severe pain in her knee from gout, he offered to "paint her a letter" if he couldn't thank her in person for her kind gift of books.

Lucretia sent Morris the following year a card with a picture of an ibis, inscribed a "Bird of the Timeless World." She knew that he was going through a difficult period with his art, and told him that the bird might happily dwell on one of the islands in the lake near his house and "perhaps lay an egg for a new conception of a projected image or rather a total essence." Several months later for his birthday in August, Lucretia sent him a papyrus plant. He wrote back to say that the papyrus "is well planted in a favored spot on the edge of the lake." Responding to Lucretia's overture of encouragement, he continued, saying, "I hope the papyrus plant will so thrive that it will induce the arrival of the bird and the magical event of the magical egg. I hope too to be clarified [sic] enough – and selfless enough – to qualify for fulfilling at least some of your continuing hopes for me as a painter." He went on to add that, "We drank a toast to you the night of the beautiful birthday dinner here. We missed you."

Lucretia Le Bourgeois Van Horn

Lucretia was particularly pleased when her grandson Van Adams came to stay with her at the Hill Top for a few years. He was eighteen years old in 1963 when he arrived after having a serious falling out with his father. He had left home in Virginia where Cri-cri and Jim lived and driven cross-country to visit his grandmother, whom he had seen off and on as a child. He and Tom Hunt became close friends. Tom invited Van to research and write a book with him entitled *Ghost Trails to California*. Lucretia took an active interest in her grandson's romantic life. When, on one occasion, she heard that Van was dating a particular beautiful girl with a fast reputation, she cried out teasingly, "the queen of the prostitutes." Her sense of fun extended to the movies as well. When the Beatles' "Yellow Submarine" came out in 1968, Tom took her to see it. Lucretia laughed and roared and called it brilliant.

The little community swelled further in the 1960's when Marjorie wound down her acting career and brought her friend Consuelo Cloos to the Hill Top. Consuelo had helped her husband Maxim Panteleieff form the Russian Grand Opera Company, which began touring in the United States in the 1920s. Maxim (who died in 1958) had taught Consuelo to sing (she had a dramatic mezzo-soprano voice) and also encouraged her to paint. Referring to her paintings as her children, she refused to sell them. Once, to settle a bill, she gave a set of her paintings to her dentist. On a return visit, she slipped the small items into her handbag as she left his office. She was happy to show off her "children," who she said were "inspired through the psychic ethers," but sell them she would not. "Would you sell your children?" she would ask whenever someone offered to buy one. Nonetheless she was unpretentious and maintained a wholesome sense of humor. "It is no fun being a genius," she would say. "I much prefer being the idiot." (Hunt, *Recollections*.)

By the late 1960s Lucretia's health and energy began to deteriorate. She was greatly saddened when she learned of Nelka's death in 1963. The two cousins had been very dear and close to one another since childhood and that closeness had diminished only partially during the last years of their lives, even as they lived far apart and communicated infrequently. Some of her remaining friends continued to stay in touch. Hyacinthe Bell, her childhood friend from school, now the dowager countess of Glasgow, wrote to her from abroad. Emily Edwards, writing from San Antonio, tracked her down in May 1970, sending her a note along with a copy of the just published "A Review by the San Antonio Conservation Society, Of Its Aims and Accomplishments, Awards, Tributes and Citations." Emily wanted Lucretia to know that the organization that she, Lucretia, Mrs. Green and Mrs. Taylor and all the others had started nearly fifty years earlier was still strong and active. "This week," Emily wrote, "the society succeeded in buying the old Navarro home and store on Laredo Street, and we think we can save them from demolition."

After she read Emily's letter and looked over the Review, Lucretia told Tom Hunt that her involvement with the Conservation Society might have been her most important contribution to the arts. Tom disagreed. He told her that her work as an artist was greater. Though largely unknown today, Lucretia Van Horn enjoyed an ascendancy in the artistic circles of California between 1928 and 1933 that still resonates among the few of her friends and admirers who are alive today.

Two months after receiving Emily's letter, on 27 July 1970, Lucretia died, the last of the Blows of Yesteryear.

SOURCES

Acts of the State of Alabama, 1827.

Adams, Henry, *The Letters of Henry Adams,* ed. J.C. Levenson, *et al.* Cambridge, MA: Belknap Press of Harvard University Press, 1982.

Alexandria (VA) Gazette.

Art Students League, Registration Record of Lucretia Le Bourgeois.

Bainton, Roy, *Honoured by Strangers, The Life of Captain Francis Cromie CBDSORN – 1882 – 1918.* Shrewsbury, UK: Airlife Publishing Ltd, 2002.

Bender, Albert, Papers, F. W. Olin Library, Mills College.

Bliss, Mildred Barnes, Papers, Harvard University.

Blow Family Papers, Missouri History Museum Research Center.

Blow, Peter, Will and Estate Papers, St. Louis, Mo. Court Records.

Blow, Susan, Letters to James Putnam, Harvard University Medical Library.

Bryan, John A., *The Blow Family of St. Louis.* St. Louis: Self-published, 1948.

Carter, Robin Borglum, *Gutzon Borglum, His Life and Work.* Austin: Eakins Press, 1998.

Cassini, Marguerite, *Never a Dull Moment, The Memoir of Countess Marguerite Cassini.* New York: Harper & Brothers Publishers, 1956.

Chapin, Adèle, *"Their Trackless Way": A Book of Memories.* London: Constable & Co, Ltd., 1931.

Charless, Charlotte Taylor Blow, *A Biographical Sketch of the Life and Character of Joseph Charless In a Series of Letters to His Grandchildren*. Saint Louis: A. F. Cox, Printer, Office of the Missouri Presbyterian, 1869.

Charless, Charlotte Taylor Blow, *Jesus*. Toronto: S. R. Briggs, 1886.

Charless, Charlotte Taylor Blow, Journal. Private Collection.

Cincinnati Commercial Tribune.

The Critic: A Weekly Review of Literature, Fine Arts, and the Drama.

"Death of Brigadier General Robert G. Van Horn, U.S. Army, Retired," *War Department, Bureau of Public Relations*. Washington, DC: 27 June 1941.

Duncan, Isadora, *My Life*. New York: Boni and Liveright, 1927.

Edwards, Emily, *Painted Walls of Mexico, From Prehistoric Times Until Today*. Austin: University of Texas Press, 1966.

Fisher, Lewis F., *Saving San Antonio, the Precarious Preservation of a Heritage*. Lubbock: Texas Tech University Press, 1996.

Fisher, M. M. and Rice, John J., *History of Westminster College, 1851-1903*. Columbia, Mo.: Press of E. W. Stephens, 1903.

Fulton, John Farquhar, Collection, Yale University.

Hager, Ruth Ann, Dred & Harriet Scott: Their Family Story. St. Louis, Mo.: The Dred Scott Foundation, 2010.

Hale, Edward Everett Jr., *The Life and Letters of Edward Everett Hale*. 2 vols. Boston: Little Brown, 1917.

Hatch, Alden, *The Wadsworths of the Genesee*. New York: Coward-McCann, 1959.

Holt, L. Emmett, *The Care and Feeding of Children – a catechism for the use of mothers and children's nurses.* New York: Appleton, 1894.

Hunt, Thomas, *Recollections.* Private Collection.

Kaser, David, *Joseph Charless, Printer in the Western Country.* Philadelphia: University of Pennsylvania Press, 1963.

Keckley, Elizabeth, *Behind the Scenes, or Thirty Years a Slave and Four Years in the White House.* New York: Oxford University Press, 1998. [Originally published: New York: G. W. Carlton, 1868.]

Lanius, Judith H. and Park, Sharon, "Martha Wadsworth's Mansion, The Gilded Age Comes to Dupont Circle," *Washington History, Magazine of the Historical Society of Washington, DC* (Summer 1995), vol. 7, no. 1, pp. 24-46.

Le Bourgeois, John Y. and Evans, Jonathan, "Mark Twain's Secret Mission to the London Hospital," *The New England Quarterly* (June 2008), vol. 81, no. 2, pp. 344-347.

Le Bourgeois, John Y., "Isadora Duncan: Stockbridge to Stardom," *The Berkshire Eagle* (8 March 2007), p. D3.

Le Bourgeois, Lucretia, Diaries. Private Collection.

Liszt, Franz, *The Letters of Franz Liszt to Olga von Meyendorff, 1871—1886,* tr. Tyler, William R. Washington, DC: Dumbarton Oaks, Trustees for Harvard University, 1979.

Livingston County, New York, Public Records.

MacArthur, Douglas, Letters to Lucretia Le Bourgeois. Private Collection.

Missouri Republican.

"Mlle Le Bourgeois," *L'Académie Julian, Publication Mensuelle donnant des Renseignements utiles aux Artistes* (Mars 1904), Troisième Année, Le Numéro 10, pp. 1-3.

Moore, Bob and Zapalac, Kris, "Emancipations [in St. Louis, 1817-1864]." ww.nps.gov/jeff/historyculture/upload/EMANCIPATIONS.pdf

Moukhanoff, Michael, *Nelka: Mrs. Helen de Smirnoff Moukhanoff. 1878 – 1963, A Biographical Sketch*. Privately Printed, 1964.

The New York Times.

Oakland Tribune.

O'Dea, Joseph C., *Genesee Valley: Land of the Blue Grass Sod. Volume Two*. Geneseo, NY: O'Dea, 2004.

Odom, Marianne and Young, Gaylon Finklea, *Early Days of the San Antonio Conservation Society, An Oral History Project*. San Antonio: San Antonio Conservation Society, 1984.

Prochnik, George, *Putnam Camp, Sigmund Freud, James Jackson Putnam and the Purpose of American Psychology*. New York: Other Press, 2006.

Pulszky, [Ferencz Aurelius] and Theresa, *White, red, black: sketches of American Society in the United States during the visit of their guests [Louis Kossuth], Volume 2, 1853.*

Raleigh Register.

Ramsdell, Charles, *San Antonio, A Historical and Pictorial Guide*. Austin: University of Texas Press, 1959.

Richardson, Henry Brown, Papers, Louisiana State University.

Rochester Democrat and Chronicle.

Roosevelt, Franklin Delano, *F.D.R.,His Personal Letters – Early Years*. Duell, Sloan and Pearce, 1947.

"Rules," *Infantry in Battle*. Washington, D.C.: The Infantry Journal, Inc., 1939.

The San Francisco Examiner.

Sluyter, Gary V., *St. Louis' Hidden Treasure: A History of the Charless Home, 1853 – 2003*. St. Louis: The Senior Circuit, 2003.

Saint James Parish, Louisiana, Public Records.

St. Louis Democrat.

Southampton County, Virginia, Public Records.

The Springfield (MA) *Daily Republican.*

Twain, Mark, Papers, University of California, Berkeley.

United States Census.

VanderVelde, Lee, *Mrs. Dred Scott, A Life on Slavery's Frontier.* New York: Oxford University Press, 2009.

Van Horn, Lucretia, Letters. Private Collection.

Van Horn, Lucretia, Sketchbooks. Private Collection.

Van Horn, Margaret, Diaries. Private Collection.

Vogel, Susan, *Becoming Pablo O'Higgins.* San Francisco: Pince-Nez Press, 2010.

Warmoth, Henry Clay, *War, Politics and Reconstruction, Storm Days in Louisiana.* New York: Macmillan, 1930.

The Washington Post.

Weekly Herald (NY).

ACKNOWLEDGEMENTS

We would like to thank Charlotte Charless for writing her letters to her grandchildren; Adèle Chapin for writing her memoir; Nelka Moukhanoff for sending letters to her aunt Susan Blow, and her husband Max for collecting and publishing them; and Lucretia Van Horn for sending and keeping letters, writing diaries and painting wonderful pictures.

We also want to acknowledge the groundwork of Charless Le Bourgeois and Julien Le Bourgeois whose deep interest in family history paved the way for our research, and give a very special thanks to Mimi Le Bourgeois and Penny Le Bourgeois for their enthusiastic support and help.

We wish to thank Robert Alsop for sharing his memories of his grandmother and grandfather Adèle and Robert Chapin, Martha D. Wadsworth for recalling her friendship with Nelka and Max, and Julien Le Bourgeois for his memories of his cousin Nelka and aunt Lucretia. We also wish to thank Van Adams, Lucretia's grandson; Tom Hunt, her good friend and colleague; and Mary Von Saltza, who loved her but never knew her, for preserving Lucretia's correspondence, diaries, and paintings, and providing us their recollections. Without their help, there would be hardly a story to tell.

To the many other individuals who provided us other valuable information and encouragement, we thank them too: Barbara Allen, Liz Argentieri, Beth Batlle, Briana Benesh, Julia Bergman, John Blow, Nancy Boas, Robin Borglum Carter, Stephanie Cassidy, Pamela Dempsky, DeeDee DiBenedetto, Bernard Drew, Jonathan Evans, David Foglesong, Sharon Ford, Elaine Grublin, Joanne Fox, Mauro Garcia, Laurie Jasinski, Ben King, Celeste King, Maureen Kingston, Molly Kodner, Ellen Lamb, Tara Laver, Bush Le Bourgeois, Joe and Susan Le Bourgeois, Louise Le Bourgeois, Woodie Le Bourgeois, Carol Mackin, Pat Mahan, Peter

Nestor, Greg Newby, Dennis Northcott, Elizabeth Novara, Sherry Owens, David Parish, Tom Pearson, Jessy Randall, DeeDee Reynolds, Linda Rhoads, Farrar Richardson, Neda Salem, Maddie Silber, Gary Sluyter, Beth Standifird, Umberto Tosi, Susan Vogel, Ben Whisenhunt, David Widger, Ann Woodhouse, and Lynda Updike.

Many libraries and institutions helped us in our research, and we wish to acknowledge them: The Art Students League, Bethesda Health Group, Brenau College, Harvard University Archives, Harvard University Medical School's Francis A. Countway Library of Medicine, Hopkins School, Library of Congress, Livingston County New York Court House, Louisiana State University's Hill Memorial Library, Madison County Alabama Records Center, Mills College's F. W. Olin Library, Miss Porter's School, Missouri History Museum Library and Research Center, National Archives, National Museum of Women in the Arts, Norton Simon Museum, Saint James Parish Louisiana Court House, St. Louis Library, San Antonio Conservation Society, Southampton County Virginia Court House, SUNY Geneseo's Milne Library, Swarthmore Public Library, Tulane University's Howard-Tilton Memorial Library, the University of California, Berkeley's Mark Twain Project and Papers, University of Maryland's Hornbake Library, and Yale University's Harvey Cushing/John Hay Whitney Medical Library.

Finally, we acknowledge our reliance on those wonderful inventions and services of the Internet age: Google and Wikipedia.

CONCISE INDEX

Made in the USA
Monee, IL
17 December 2022

22148332R00194